the birth of satan

the birth of satan

TRACING THE DEVIL'S BIBLICAL ROOTS

T. J. WRAY

GREGORY MOBLEY

First published 2005 by
PALGRAVE MACMILLAN™
175 Fifth Avenue, New York, N.Y. 10010 and
Houndmills, Basingstoke, Hampshire, England RG21 6XS.
Companies and representatives throughout the world.

PALGRAVE MACMILLAN is the global academic imprint of the
Palgrave Macmillan division of St. Martin's Press, LLC and of Palgrave
Macmillan Ltd. Macmillan® is a registered trademark in the United
States, United Kingdom and other countries. Palgrave is a registered
trademark in the European Union and other countries.

ISBN 1–4039–6933–7 hardback

Library of Congress Cataloging-in-Publication Data
The birth of Satan: tracing the devil's biblical roots / T.J. Wray, Gregory
Mobley.
    p.   cm.
  Includes bibliographical references and index.
  ISBN 1–4039–6933–7
  1. Devil—Biblical teaching.   2. Devil—History of doctrines.
I. Mobley, Gregory, 1957-   II. Title.

BS680.D56W73   2005
235'.47—dc22

                                                              2005043046

A catalogue record for this book is available from the British Library.

Design by Letra Libre, Inc..

First edition: Ocotber 2005
10 9 8 7 6 5 4

Printed in the United States of America

For Rob and Page
and
our six little devils

contents

list of tables

acknowledgments

Together, we would like to thank our family, friends, and colleagues for their encouragement and support in this project. Special thanks to the absolute best literary agent on the planet, Rob McQuilkin, of Lippincott Massie McQuilkin. We would like to also say thanks to our editor, Amanda Johnson, for her enthusiasm, dedication, and editorial expertise. Finally, we would like to express our heartfelt gratitude to the faculty, staff, and, especially, the wonderful students at Salve Regina University and Andover Newton Theological School for their continued affirmation and prayerful support.

preface

beginnings

Speak of the Devil and he appears.
—Italian proverb

Satan, also known as the Devil, Lucifer, Mephistopheles, and by a legion of discarded names and epithets drawn from the Index of Dead Gods, is the archvillain of world culture. All incarnations of this Devil, the supreme opponent of God in the monotheistic religions (Judaism, Christianity, and Islam), can be traced to a character in the Bible and to stories and lore in early Jewish and Christian writings not found in the Bible. The purpose of this book is to explore the biblical roots beneath the tangled jungle of Satanic lore and demonic conspiracy theories that cover vast acres of our imaginative, narrative, artistic, and cinematic landscape.

Most references to Satan or satanic characters and symbols in popular music, movies, fiction, occult and orthodox religions have evolved from this biblical matrix and virtually all modern conspiracy theories, whether they speak of the Devil or not, can be traced to the primal story of Satan in the Bible (and other Jewish and Christian writings from the biblical period).

The "cosmic conspiracy theory" first composed by Jewish writers in the final centuries before the Common Era (ca. 200 B.C.E.—zero C.E) is the template for thousands of stories. These ancient Jewish thinkers told the story about an invisible, universal plot dedicated to world conquest in the name of Death, led by an arch criminal mastermind, Satan, and his network of demons. This dramatic story has been retold countless times ever since, though the cast changes in every generation and place.

Most recently, in Dan Brown's *The Da Vinci Code,* the conspirators are not Satan and his underworld demons but certain subterranean cells of Roman Catholic clerics dedicated to suppression of the Divine Feminine. Members of white supremacist groups imagine a confederation of the Elders of Zion controlling the fortunes of the world behind, in one era, European banking houses, and in another, the Jewish magnates of Hollywood and Manhattan media empires. Right-wing survivalists and left-wing paranoiacs substitute cabals hidden within the legitimate governments of the world, whether they are Communists, atheists, or military-industrialists, for the demonic villains of ancient versions. In a surprising but predictable development, given the scientific cast of modern culture, aliens have replaced demons in many stories, without affecting the plot: the demons possessed souls, the aliens invade and snatch bodies; demonic *incubi* and *succubae* sexually assaulted medieval Europeans in their sleep, the "gray men" take humans aboard their flying saucers to violate them. The legitimate fears of terrorist attacks in light of the attacks on the World Trade Center and Pentagon show every sign of mutating into a narrative of a worldwide network presided by a satanic Bin Laden who controls a demonic army of Muslim terrorists.

So Satan, by many names, remains alive and well on the Planet Earth, and this book sketches the process by which the Devil first emerged in the Bible. As we trace this character through the books of the Bible, we will also observe the ways in which virtually every contemporary idea and image of Satan has evolved from ideas and images of the ancient Jews and Christians who first told Satan's story. But first, we will begin by exercising (or exorcising?) our authorial prerogative, telling our own stories about childhood encounters with the Devil.

T. J. Wray's Encounter with Satan

The incarnation of evil who terrorized me as a child returns now for a rematch. Banished for many years and relegated to the ranks of superstitious mythology, Satan is back and demanding his say. I have spent the better part of three years thinking about him and carefully tracing his complex origins. But, despite all my scholarly detective work, vestiges of my childhood fears still linger and, truth be told, I still will not sleep with my back facing the door.

As I grew up Catholic in the 1960s, Satan was as much a part of my childhood as God. But, unlike the wispy image of God I held only in my mind's eye, I had actually *seen* the Devil a few times. Once, just moments after teasing my little sister until she cried, I saw his shadow pass from behind the laundry room door in our basement into the family room. I remember bolting up the stairs and slamming the cellar door, terrified and breathless. "What on earth is wrong with you?" my mother asked. "I saw a spider," I lied, adding yet another bead to the necklace of naughtiness I had been fashioning for myself for years.

On more than one occasion I had seen Satan scurrying through the thin trees beyond our back fence. I was convinced he was spying on me as I sloppily raked leaves or deposited the trash in the rubbish bin, leaving the lid off out of pure laziness. Indeed, there were days when I was too terrified to venture into my own backyard for fear that the Devil and his minions were lying in wait for me, eager to include yet another bad little girl to their fold.

But perhaps my scariest "Satan sighting" of all happened at one of the most unlikely places of all—church. One Friday afternoon during Lent, as I exited St. Frances de Chantel Holy Roman Catholic Church after my weekly confession, I was sure I saw him lurking just outside the heavy glass doors of our church. Father Anthony had prodded me to search my ten-year-old conscience for graver sins than swearing and punching my sisters. "Honest, Father," I had stonewalled, "I haven't done anything else that I can think of." I neglected to tell him, of course, that I often skipped Mass, regularly ate meat on Fridays (even during Lent), frequently took the Lord's name in vain, and, oh yes, lied to priests.

As I rushed down the church steps that afternoon, skipping out halfway through my ponderous penance, I was certain the Devil was hot on my heels. Hunched in the back of my parents' old Plymouth station wagon, I fended off terrifying images of Satan's bony red fingers clutching my ankles and dragging me into his fiery pit. At the ripe old age of ten I was convinced that, as in Dante's famous inscription, I should abandon all hope. "I'm going to hell," I thought miserably.

Satan also appeared in my dreams occasionally—his face red, his teeth pointy and yellowed, sneering and breathing long streams of gray smoke through hideously engorged nostrils. He had a twisted horn on either side of his head and a scruffy-looking black goatee. Most frightening of all, he carried a pitchfork, his personal instrument of terror, used to spear bad children like shrimp on a cocktail fork. Petrified for weeks after one of these Satan sightings, I learned to never, *ever* sleep with my back to the bedroom door for fear that the Devil might catch me unawares.

Gregory Mobley's Encounter with Satan

In my nightmare, the most vivid dream of my life, I was watching television with my feet dangling over the edge of the living room couch. The Devil grabbed my feet and began pulling me into the chasm between the department store sofa and the bare wood floor. I could not get any purchase on the slick vinyl and was descending, kicking and screaming, into hell. I could see my savior, my paternal grandmother, in the adjacent kitchen, but even she, the adult in my world most powerful in love, seemed blind and dumb to my plight. I must have been about seven or eight. For the rest of my childhood, I crouched on top of that couch, legs bent at the knees, a clenched-up ball of vigilance against the Adversary, who as a roaring lion prowled about suburban domestic crawl spaces, seeking whom he may devour.

I now know that I carried the same mental map in my head that the ancients did: of a three-part cosmos, our world sandwiched between an angelic overworld and demonic underworld. The ancients imagined that ruptures in the earth's surface—pits, chasms, and wells, caves and aquatic beds—were Death Valleys and Hellholes, the portals to the underworld. As children, we did not require learned analyses about conceptions of sacred space, the liminal, and rites of passage. Already, somehow, we understood all this and had translated these ideas into features of our housescapes. The thresholds we feared were the marginal, undomesticated places in our homes: dark closets and damp basements, the linty, dusty wildernesses under beds, and, worst of all, the eddying chaotic waters of toilet bowls that threatened to pull us in and from which, in our urban legends, chaos monsters—sewer rats and transmogrified pet alligators—sought to enter our world.

Why Were We So Terrified?

Like most people, our early understanding of Satan was shaped by an amalgamation of (mostly) distorted Christian doctrine, inept Sunday school teachers, superstitious relatives, and popular mythology as portrayed in books, film, and television. We grew up on the terrifying tales of the Brothers Grimm, rife with evil stepmothers and frightening chaos monsters. And, we believed in a literal evil being who stood in direct opposition to the goodness of God. That being was Satan, and he was not alone in his malicious meanderings. Indeed, Satan commanded a legion of malevolent spirits who were only too happy to work in concert with him. And these spirits, quite literally, lurked everywhere.

We were taught (and believed) in a world of opposites: If there is a God, then there is a Devil; if there are angels, then there are also demons; if there is a heaven, then surely there is a hell. We also believed that Satan, God's archenemy, was responsible for all the evil and suffering in the world. How else could we explain terrible things like wars, babies dying, or the existence of an evil empire that threatened to annihilate our country with atom bombs? Anyway, this was the worldview shared by most of those in our families and immediate social circles. It gave life a certain order: Evil and suffering entered the world through the Devil, who continues to wreak havoc in the lives of good and decent people. God, on the other hand, is all knowing, all loving, all powerful, and all good. God is on *our* side; he is our only chance against the powers of Satan.

The weighty, reflective questions concerning this arrangement—including the fairness of God, the power of God, and the meaning of life—would surface occasionally, but they were generally brushed aside by our parents or termed "a mystery" by clergymen. The world, though seemingly random and chaotic to some, in a strange way made perfect sense to us.

An essential component of this worldview is "the Doctrine of Terror" that was (and still is, in many places) used by churches to quite literally scare the laity into obedience. It was a strategy used by parents, clergy, and parochial school teachers to regulate our behavior when we were not under their ever-so-watchful eyes. Even today, the use of the ever-present threat of eternal damnation—by which even the formerly faithful may be remanded to the custody of Satan and the torments of hell for all eternity—

perpetuates this doctrine. Incredibly, no one ever questioned the validity of this teaching.

We have long been fascinated with the origin of the Satan. We are intrigued with the role that villains, monsters, and demons play in literature, film, and especially in religion. But this intrigue and attraction to the terrifying things that go bump in the night leads us to an important question: Why do we humans intentionally seek out ways to feel fear? Is life not frightening enough? One need only watch the evening news on a regular basis to know that simply living in this precarious and uncertain world is a scary prospect, even on the most ordinary of days. So why are we drawn to roller coasters, stories of serial killers, and reality television shows like *Fear Factor*?

The truth is, there is something appealing about being afraid. We flock to horror movies and devour the frightening tales of Stephen King and Anne Rice faster than they can write them. Even outside the world of fiction, we are a nation that feeds on things fearful. We read about the horrors of war over our morning coffee, and for many of us, the last evening ritual before retiring at night is a final glimpse at the news in all its sensational gore. The material we subject ourselves to every day is enough to terrify even the stalwart.

Could this addiction to fear be responsible for—or at least help explain— our sustained and literal belief in the most feared monster of all, Satan? A recent Gallup poll found that the majority of Americans—across every demographic group—express a belief in Satan.[1] Why do perfectly rational people who would eschew any belief in Bigfoot, the Loch Ness monster, Frankenstein, werewolves, vampires, or flying monkeys still cling to this belief? And just who—or what—is this Devil, this Satan, this Lucifer whom we all seem to know and fear? What does the Bible *really* say about the Prince of Demons? Moreover, what do we lose when we attempt to edit Satan out of our belief system? In the pages that follow, an exploration into the origin, form, and function of the biblical Satan will shed some much-needed light on these and other questions.

Satan. As children, we feared him; as adolescents, we were intrigued by him; as young adults, we merely dismissed him—but as scholars, we understand him. For anyone who has ever felt a shiver of fear at the mention of his name, spent a sleepless night after viewing one of the many films about him, or just plain wondered about the Devil's role in the Bible, this book is for you.

Authors' Notes

There are three issues worthy of mention at the outset of this book. The first has to do with the use of inclusive language. Thus far, the references to both Satan and God reflect our childhood understanding of both as male. As Christian children (both Protestant and Catholic) during the 1960s, it was largely an unchallenged assumption that both God and the Devil were indeed masculine characters. Throughout the rest of this work we will use inclusive language for both God and Satan when possible and appropriate. There are times, however, when literarily, inclusive language makes reading difficult and confusing. Often the practice appears contrived and artificial, to the point of making a mockery of the convention. To avoid both confusion and the appearance of political correctness for political correctness' sake, at times we reluctantly resort to the archaic practice of assigning the male pronoun to God and Satan.

The second issue has to do with the way in which we refer to the two main sections of the Bible, commonly called the "Old Testament" and the "New Testament." Although we will refer to the second main section of the Bible by its common designation, the "New Testament," we prefer the term "Hebrew Bible" rather than "Old Testament" when referring to the first main section. The terms "Old Testament" and "Hebrew Bible" are often used interchangeably, but we feel the latter designation is not only more accurate, but also more respectful of Judaism. (The Christian designation of "Old Testament" carries a somewhat negative connotation for many because the adjective "old" implies something outdated and in need of replacement.)

Finally, in keeping with the conventions of modern historical (and biblical) scholarship, we will use B.C.E. ("before the common era") instead of B.C. ("before Christ") and C.E. ("common era") rather than A.D. (*anno Domini*, Latin for in "the year of our Lord") when indicating specific dates.

the birth of satan

introduction

One of the most startling facts about Satan is the lack of direct biblical references to this character that occupies so large a place in our religious imaginations. Indeed, most people are surprised to learn that the popular image of Satan as a pitchfork-toting demon is completely absent from the Bible. Satan makes less than a dozen appearances in the Hebrew Bible, and the fullest exposition of the Devil's dastardly deeds does not occur until the final book of the New Testament, the book of Revelation.

Although the biblical stories of Satan may vary, his role is always an adversarial one. The word "satan" has been variously translated to mean *adversary*, *obstacle*, *opponent*, *stumbling block*, *accuser*, or *slanderer*. In the Hebrew Bible, the name usually appears with an article—the satan—which describes a *function*, rather than being a proper name.[1]

It is also important to note that Satan's adversarial role in the Bible changes over time. In the Hebrew Bible, Satan can best be described as a rather low-level heavenly functionary. The real change in Satan's character comes only in the New Testament, where he appears as *tempter provocateur*, demon extraordinaire, and Jesus' personal adversary in the ultimate battle between good and evil. So how—and why—did this relatively innocuous character in the Hebrew Bible morph into the Titan of Evil? There seems to be no single event that propelled Satan on his cosmic collision course with God, but one can cite a series of historical and social events that seem to have contributed to Satan's metamorphosis. For example, the religious traditions and practices of Israel's neighbors, most notably the Canaanites, the Egyptians, and especially the Persians, are often cited as influencing Satan's rise to evil prominence. Each of these cultures had evil beings of their own whose fingerprints smudge the pages of Satan's script: the Canaanite god Mot who dwells in a terrifying subterranean abode; the evil Egyptian god Set, often depicted in Egyptian art as red in color; and the fiendish Persian demon Ahriman, who is pitted in an eternal battle with the god of light, Ahura Mazda.

The Greeks and Romans, with their pantheon of gods, goddesses, and spirits, not to mention certain Jewish and later Christian beliefs in angels, divine messengers, and demons, also figure into Satan's development.[2] Likewise, the growing popularity of apocalyptic literature (a body of literature dealing with the "end time") in early Judaism at the beginning of the third century B.C.E. certainly added fuel to Satan's fire.[3] As early as the first century C.E., certain Jewish groups, such as the Essenes (the purported writers of the Dead Sea Scrolls) and the followers of Jesus, emerged and began to speak of Satan in concrete terms.[4]

The Satan of the early common era had a growth spurt under the influence of Hellenistic Judaism and emerged in the New Testament fully grown, as the opponent of Christ in the battle for the Kingdom.[5] The biblical Satan of the New Testament morphed further under the influence of a host of medieval superstitions. Portrayals of Satan in Dante's epic poem *The Divine Comedy* and Milton's *Paradise Lost*, literary works revered as sacred by the faith-filled but biblically ignorant masses, added definition to Satan's character and popularity. The 300-year period of witch-hunting from the fifteenth to the eighteenth centuries did much to remind the faithful that Satan was alive and well and apparently infiltrating God-fearing communities and calling (mostly) women into service. All of this, and more, laid the groundwork for the modern Satan, who still commands a significant amount of attention both in the human imagination and, for a small number of people, in religious practice.[6]

But, in addition to these often-cited social and literary influences, there is another, subtler, development occurring in Satan's infancy. Perhaps the seeds of Satan were sown not by later Christian imagination, but in the beginning, with God, the self-proclaimed author of both good and evil:

I form the light and create darkness,
I make weal and create woe;
I the LORD do all these things. (Isa 45:7)

And it seems reasonable to assume that God's people eventually find it difficult to synthesize a God who claims to love them while, at the same time, inflicts suffering and death upon them.

> Is the trumpet blown in a city,
> And the people are not afraid?
> Does not disaster befall a city,
> Unless the LORD has done it? (Amos 3:6)

The eventual emergence of the "theodicy question" (the theological problem of reconciling a good and loving God with a world riddled with evil) seems unavoidable in such an arrangement. We can surely resonate with the ancient worshippers of the One—for they, like some of us, question how it could be that a loving God could also be the harbinger of pain and suffering. The theodicy question, as we shall see, plays a prominent part in the story of Satan.

As we explore the various factors that contributed to Satan's development, it is the theodicy question that leads us to a rather startling possibility: Could it be that along with the development of monotheism is a growing existential frustration that makes it difficult for God's people to accept a deity who is responsible both for good and evil? This basic question leads to another: Is it possible that at some point, God's negative attributes (or, as the Bible often calls it, God's wrath) are excised—in a sort of divine personality split—and appropriated to an inferior being (Satan)? In the pages that follow, we will investigate these and other provocative questions surrounding Satan's birth.

Summary of Chapters

Together we have worked to make this book a readable resource for both scholar and novice. To briefly summarize, this book begins with a general overview of the Bible that will serve as both a starting point for our discussion of Satan and as a guide for understanding the Bible as a whole. Chapter 2 explores the nature of God in the Hebrew Bible and how God's various *aspects* or *manifestations* may have contributed to the evolution of

Satan. This initial exploration is followed by a more in-depth discussion in chapter 3 of the passages in the Hebrew Bible that specifically refer to Satan, as either a celestial being (Num 22:22–35; Zech 3:1–7; Job 1:6–2:10; and 1 Chr 21:1–22:1) or a terrestrial being (1 Sam 29:4; 2 Sam 19:17–24; 1 Kgs 5:4; 11:14, 23, 25; Ps 109:1–6).

Chapter 4 delves into the influence from Israel's neighboring cultures and the ways in which their evil beings helped to transform Satan. Chapter 5 explores selected intertestamental and rabbinic writings and their connection(s) to the biblical Satan, particularly the Dead Sea Scrolls, Enoch, and Jubilees. Many of these texts contain stories of a demonic leader—known by various names, such as Azazel, Semihazah, Mastema, Beliar, and, of course, Satan—who commands a legion of cosmic trouble-makers. This leader appears to be the prototype for the New Testament Satan. Chapter 6 examines Satan's remarkable metamorphosis in the New Testament, especially his appearances in the Gospels, Pauline Epistles, and the book of Revelation. Having thus explored Satan's dramatic transformation, chapter 7 focuses on Satan's subterranean abode, hell. Chapter 8 concludes with a discussion of what we lose when we edit Satan out of our belief system. It is our attempt to explain why Satan's story matters.

chapter 1

the bible and
other preliminaries

An apology for the Devil—it must be remembered that we have only heard one side of the case. God has written all the books.
—Samuel Butler

In the beginning (Gen 1:1; John 1:1), there was God: the creator of all things. For a brief moment in time (or before time) the world was utterly good, and evil was a concept that does not seem to have been part of the original divine plan. But by the third chapter of Genesis, temptation, sin, and punishment pollute the paradise created by God. A chapter later, the first murder, a fratricide (Gen 4:8), makes it clear that another force is at work in a world that is suddenly unpredictable, uncertain, and precarious. So begins the story of God, humans, and the ever-present struggle of good versus evil. And it is in the existential struggle of good versus evil that the embodiment of evil, a character named Satan, emerges.

Satan fell to earth from the pages of the Bible. Or, more precisely, Satan fell to earth from the religious imagination of the Jewish people in antiquity. Our best knowledge about ancient Jewish religious thought comes from the Bible, a collection of books that includes history, prophecies, poetry, legends, myths, letters, gospels, and other types of writings. Although the Bible is not our only source (we sometimes refer to literature from antiquity outside the Bible), the story of Satan, as written, begins with the Bible, first with its earliest Jewish edition and then its subsequent Christian editions. For that reason, we must begin our study with a brief introduction to the Bible, the single book most of us own but have likely never read.

We begin our investigation with a brief exploration of the world of the ancient Near East, the cradle of civilization that gave birth to the Bible—and to Satan.

The World of the Ancient Near East

The geographical, historical, cultural, economic, and political world of the ancient Near East serves as the backdrop for the Bible. Although this world is explored in greater detail as Satan's story begins to unfold in later chapters, it is important to have some basic understanding of the "setting" of the Bible. The geographical setting of the ancient Near East begins in Egypt and includes Israel, Syria, Arabia, modern-day Iraq, Iran, Turkey, and the fringe areas beyond these borders.

Various ethnic groups were scattered throughout this region, largely along the arc of the Fertile Crescent. The largest of these ethnic groups, of which the people of Israel were a part, was the Semites. The geographical location of Israel was both a blessing and a curse. Its location was part of a larger trade route, which facilitated the transmission of stories and ideas from other lands (the Bible contains numerous references to other cultures and foreign religious practices), but this location also made Israel vulnerable to attacks—not only from the powerful northern empires of Assyria and later, Babylonia, but also from the south (Egypt) and even from beyond Israel's shores (the so-called Sea Peoples, such as the Philistines, from whom we get the geographic term "Palestine") from the eastern Mediterranean.

When we discuss "biblical history," we usually are referring to the historical setting according to the biblical authors, which may not reflect our modern understanding of history. For example, the creation stories in Genesis assume that the world and the various forms of life (including humans) were created by God in a single week. Modern science, on the other hand, presents a gradual evolution of life, beginning with the creation of the earth roughly 4.5 billion years ago. Another difference between the view of history assumed in the Bible and our contemporary view is that, often, a biblical story may have begun as an oral tradition. Because the account was not written down until hundreds of years after the purported events, it is nearly impossible to be confident about the exact details of the story. Of course, the biblical writers were not interested in relating the sort of history found in modern textbooks. Theirs was a religious history that looked at life through the lens of their own particular religious community and place in time.

Certainly, the subject of "biblical history" versus "secular history" is part of an ongoing debate that will not be settled here. Scholars on all sides of the fence continue to argue fiercely and persuasively for one date or another regarding the composition of the books of the Bible, and it is hardly our intention to become the authoritative source when it comes to dating ancient manuscripts. Despite scientific advances in fields such as archeology, the truth is, that there is still a great deal we simply do not know about the world of the ancient Near East and the Bible.

What we do know for certain is that the Bible relates several pivotal events that seem to have shaped the consciousness and religious perspectives of the people of Israel. Very briefly, these events begin with the creation of the world and of humankind, as narrated in the first three chapters of Genesis. As part of the so-called primeval history that spans the first eleven chapters of Genesis, the creation stories are expressions of Israel's particular worldview. This worldview holds that God is the author of life, creator of everything, both human and nonhuman, and that the world and all of creation is good.

The call of Abraham, from his home in southern Mesopotamia to the land of Canaan, where he would enter into a covenant with God with the divine promises of descendants and the land is the second major event in the Bible (Genesis 12). Although Abraham receives the promise of a long-awaited son, it is not until the book of Joshua that the people of Israel gain a relatively secure dwelling place in the Promised Land. A mere two generations after Abraham, his grandson Jacob (also known as Israel) will leave his famine-stricken Promised Land for Egypt, along with his twelve sons and their families.

The early portion of the book of Exodus details this period when Jacob/Israel's descendants lived in Egypt. Moses liberates the Israelites from slavery and leads them on a forty-year trek back to Canaan. Along the way, at the pilgrimage site of Mount Sinai, Moses receives the *Torah*, the "Teaching," the religious-legal code that binds the people of Israel to its God. So now we have the creation of the world and of a community ethic, and the Israelites living in the Promised Land. This seems like the end of the story—but the tale is only just beginning.

Little Israel grows up and becomes a nation in its own right. Israel demands from God a king, the greatest of whom is David, proclaimed in the Bible as God's unrivaled favorite against whom all other future kings are measured. The rise and fall of the monarchy (1–2 Samuel and 1–2 Kings) and the parade of mostly ineffectual kings is followed by the eventual loss of the land, first to the Assyrians, who attack the northern kingdom of Samaria in 721 B.C.E., and then to the Babylonians, who invade Judah to the south and capture Jerusalem in 587 B.C.E.

Both of these events are narrated in some detail in the Bible, but it is the Babylonian invasion under King Nebuchadnezzar (and the subsequent exile of the Jewish people to Babylon) that is considered perhaps the turning point in the growth of the Hebrew Bible. In fact, when we speak of the two general time periods in the Hebrew Bible, we usually refer to them as either "pre-exilic" or "postexilic." Although the Jewish exiles, under an edict of liberation from the Persian king, Cyrus, eventually return to the Promised Land, their problems are far from over.

The roughly two hundred years of rather benign Persian rule was followed by the Greek period (332–63 B.C.E.). Hellenistic culture was introduced and flourished in many parts of the Near East, including much of Palestine. Following the death of Alexander the Great, Judah was ruled by the despised Antiochus IV, a Syrian, whose violent persecutions of pious Jews is described in grisly detail in the books of 1–2 Maccabees, found in the Apocrypha. This persecution resulted in a revolt and a brief period of Jewish self-rule (142–63 B.C. E.).

In 63 B.C.E. Pompey and his Roman soldiers conquered Judea, absorbing the land as part of the Roman Empire for the next 130 years. Jesus of Nazareth would live and die under Roman rule, and eventually the Jews would rebel against the Romans. Sadly, this rebellion would result in the devastation of the Promised Land in 70 C.E.

The tumultuous world of the Bible is the world into which Satan is born. Let us now turn to the Bible and explore the pages that gave Satan life.

The Authorship of the Bible

The word "Bible" is an English spelling of the Greek word *biblia*, which means "little books." The name itself reminds us that what moderns know as the Bible, a single document contained between two covers, began as a collection of individual books, or scrolls, written over a long period of time by different authors. The original texts (of which there are no surviving copies) were usually written on a paper-like material called papyrus (made from the papyrus plant). The pages were wrapped around a short wooden pole to form a scroll. Unfortunately, papyrus is not a very durable material, so most ancient manuscripts have been lost in the sands of time.

The Bible is divided into two main sections. The first section (the larger of the two) is the Hebrew Bible (commonly called the "Old Testament" by Christians), and the second section (much smaller) is called the "New Testament" or the "Christian Testament." There are twenty-seven books in the New Testament and either thirty-nine (in the Jewish and Protestant Bible) or forty-six (Catholic editions) in the Hebrew Bible. Many translations of the Bible are currently in use, including the New Revised Standard Version (NRSV—the version used when citing biblical passages in this book), the King James Version (KJV), the New International Version (NIV), the Jerusalem Bible (JB) and the New American Bible (NAB), plus scores of others.[1]

Several books of the Bible announce their primary author in their opening lines—Micah: "the word of the LORD that came to Micah," Galatians: "Paul . . . to the churches of Galatia." Others do not—Genesis: "In the beginning, God created the heaven and the earth" (KJV); John: "In the beginning was the Word." The titles given to biblical books, such as 1 Samuel and the Gospel According to St. Mark, often suggest authors. But these titles were appended to the books after their composition. In fact, in the books of Samuel and Mark, there is no indication that they were written by the prophet or saint with whom the book has come to be associated.

The pious have always considered the contents of the Bible to have been inspired by God, but the cross-section of the inner workings of this divine-human collaboration between Author and secretary has been drawn in various ways. Among the pious and impious over the centuries, inquiring minds have demanded and produced a set of traditions about the authorship of every book of the Bible. According to tradition, Moses wrote "the Five Scrolls" (in Latin,

Pentateuch; i.e., the *Torah*), David wrote most of the Psalms, Solomon wrote Proverbs and Ecclesiastes, and Paul wrote the Epistles. Historians, however, are not satisfied with these answers, and a vast scholarly enterprise, producing tomes of competing theories, has been devoted to naming "the real authors" of scripture. As the books themselves do not directly name their authors, and an unbiased reading tends to make the traditional answer suspicious (did Moses *really* write the account of his own death in Dt 34:5?), scholars have developed an alphabet soup-roster of hypothetical authors such as J, E, D, P, Dtr, and Q to refer to the actual authors of biblical books.

But we should keep in mind that ancient ascriptions of authorship were not designed to protect the intellectual property rights of poets and priests. They were designed to give the writing an air of antiquity and authority. And the older and more revered the author, the better. Thus the impulse to firmly associate texts with respected elders, as a way of expressing their significance, has guided the traditions that link the biblical books with the greatest names of biblical history.

Jewish and Christian traditions and scholarship provide varying answers, and sometimes the traditionalists in the choir and the scholars on the back pews harmonize: Paul *did* write Romans; Amos *did* speak many of the oracles contained in the book that bears his name. As much of the material now found in written form in the Bible was first recited and narrated in oral form, and passed on from generation to generation in a great chain of anonymous saints, we refer most often to "the Jewish community" or "the Christian community" that produced the various books of the Bible. And although the term "Bible" is commonly used to refer to the Jewish and Christian scriptures, the truth is that there is more than one Bible.

The Bibles

The Jewish Bible is quite different in many ways from the Christian Bible. And even among Christians, different versions of the Bible are read by Protestants, Catholics, and Orthodox Christians. We are not talking here about the differences among translations of the Bible. The Bible continues to be translated and revised, and is available in hardcover or paperback, with or without pictures, maps, and marginal notes from televangelists who will send you one for free. We are talking about substantial differences in content and sequence of books between the Bibles treasured by Jews and Christians and among the various families within Christendom. Most of us know the Bible of our tribe. Regardless of whether we are Jewish or Christian, the fact remains that all Bibles derive from the Jewish Bible, which came into existence over the course of roughly a thousand years and grew incrementally over time. We cannot say with any certainty when the earliest Hebrew religious teachings, songs, prayers, ritual protocols, and stories were written, but by around 500 B.C.E., it is safe to say that there existed a set of scrolls known as the *Torah* ("the Law," or "Instruction"). Within another couple of centuries, the Prophets section (in Hebrew, *Nevi'im*) had coalesced into something approximating the prophetic books we know today. A final section, the Writings (or *Ketuvim*), anchored by the Psalms, emerged in the final centuries before the common era.

So by that odd measure of year 1 of the common era, with our fingers crossed, we can say that the Jewish scriptures existed in three sections: Law, Prophets, and Writings. In Hebrew, these terms are, respectively *Torah, Nevi'im,* and *Ketuvim,* and Jews often use the resulting acronym *TaNaK* (*Tanach* or *Tanakh*) to refer to their scriptures.

The Bible, at this point around the turn of the common era, was not a book but a filing cabinet of the various scrolls on which each individual book was scripted. Virtually every line of these scrolls was written in the Hebrew language, but portions of two scrolls, Daniel and Ezra, were written in Aramaic, the language that served as the lingua franca of the Persian Empire (540–330 B.C.E.), which encompassed Jewish communities in Persia, Babylon, and Judah. Aramaic was also the spoken language of Jesus. Thus, here is another complicating fact: This Jewish Bible, which we will refer to as the "Hebrew" Bible, was not written solely in Hebrew, but in Aramaic as well.

The most important intellectual centers of Jewish life in the final centuries before the common era were in Babylon and Israel (known under Roman occupation as Palestine). The manuscripts of the Hebrew Bible we now possess—handed down, copied, lost, decayed, recopied, and transmitted over the centuries—stem from ancient Jewish scribes in Babylon and Israel. The version of the Jewish Bible written in Hebrew and Aramaic is called the Masoretic Text (MT), in honor of the Masoretes ("transmitters"), the class of scribes who, over centuries, preserved the Hebrew Bible and ensured its safe passage from the ancient world into our own.

The Egyptian city of Alexandria was another important center of Jewish learning in the ancient world. Between 300 and 100 B.C.E., the Jewish community in Alexandria translated its collection of scriptural scrolls into Greek. This edition of the Bible, Jewish in origin but later adopted by Greek-speaking Christians, was called the Septuagint ("The Seventy," often abbreviated in Roman numerals as LXX), after a tradition that *seventy-two* Jewish scribes, working in isolation for seventy-two days, providentially emerged from their labors with identical versions of the scrolls on which they were working.

The most germane feature of this Greek version of the Jewish Bible is that it is *not* identical to the Masoretic Text, which came to be the standard among Jews. The Septuagint contains extra portions of some biblical books—Daniel, Esther, the Psalms—and another set of Jewish religious texts, whether translated from lost Hebrew originals or originally composed in Greek. These books include 1 and 2 Maccabees, Judith, Tobit, and Wisdom (not *Song*) of Solomon, among others.

As we move now from an overview of the Jewish Bible to the various Christian Bibles, the status of these additional writings—the books in the Jewish Bible produced in Alexandria (the Septuagint) but missing in the Palestinian and Babylonian canons—will become crucial. The differences among the canons of each respective family within Christendom—Roman Catholic, Protestant, and Orthodox churches—all stem from their acceptance or rejection of these writings that were part of the Septuagint but not part of the Masoretic canon.

Differences between the Jewish and Christian Bibles

The chief difference between the Jewish and Christian Bibles stems from the fact that the early Christians (a breakaway sect of renegade Jews who were convinced that the life and work of a certain first-century C.E. rabbi, Jesus of Nazareth, marked a new era in Jewish life) produced a sequel. We know this sequel as the New Testament (also referred to as the New

Covenant), and its creators were convinced that it represented a new chapter in the epic story of God's covenant with the people Israel and all humanity. Once the sequel—the Gospels, Acts of the Apostles, various Epistles, and the Apocalypse of John—was in distribution, the church retitled the original. What for Jews was the Bible, Christians now referred to as the Old Testament and considered it part of a two-part Bible.

The Protestant Christian Old Testament, or "Gideon's Bible" (the edition of the Bible we often find in Holiday Inns), is identical in content to the Jewish Bible, the *Tanakh*, although the sequence of books in the Christian Bible is different from the Jewish sequence. (We discuss this in more detail later in this chapter; see Table 1.1.) Protestants and Jews refer to the extra material from the Septuagint as the Apocrypha, literally "hidden" or "esoteric," although these writings are thoroughly biblical in style and substance. These writings include additions to the biblical books of Esther, Daniel, and Psalms, as well as the extra books, such as 1–2 Maccabees, Judith, and Tobit. The Roman Catholic and various Orthodox churches include the thirty-nine books of the Hebrew Bible in their Old Testaments but also accept greater or lesser endowments from the disputed Septuagintal material.

So, the term "Apocrypha" refers to a certain set of ancient Jewish religious documents that first emerged in the final centuries before the common era, in the Greek translation of the Jewish Bible produced in Alexandria (the Septuagint). (See Table 1.1.)

"The Apocrypha" should not be confused with "apocryphal," which refers to any document of an esoteric nature. The Apocrypha has a stable set of contents, and some editions of Christian Bibles include it between the Old and New Testaments. Catholics call these books Deuterocanonical, or "secondarily canonical." These books include such texts as Tobit, 1–2 Maccabees, Wisdom of Solomon, Ecclesiastes, Sirach, Baruch, Judith, and the additions to the book of Daniel: the Prayer of Azariah and the Song of the Three Young Men, Susanna, and Bel and the Dragon.

The tone of the Apocrypha varies from the patriotic machismo of the account of the Maccabean revolt against their Syrian overlords in the second century B.C.E., to the august reflections of Ben Sira ("Let us now praise famous men"), to the entertaining story about Susanna, the virtuous Jewess saved from a capital sentence for adultery by the shrewd courtroom tactics of Daniel.

The library of documents that have been labeled "apocryphal" at one time or another, in contrast, is legion. Scholars sometimes use the term "apocryphal" in a specific way to refer to the religious documents of early Jews and Christians, an ever-expanding list, that did not make the cut and are not among the books of anyone's official Bible. These include some books that have been known for centuries, such as the Infancy Gospel of Thomas with its tales about Jesus' childhood miracles; the Gospel of James with its account of Mary's miraculous conception; and the various non-canonical legends about the feats and fates of the early apostles.[2]

In the past fifty years, two important ancient libraries have been un-earthed and their contents have been added to the list of apocryphal writings. The "Dead Sea Scrolls" is the term used for Jewish documents found in the Judean Desert; the "Nag Hammadi library" refers to a trove of over forty documents found near Luxor in Egypt that preserve noncanonical Christian writings. These noncanonical gospels, acts of the apostles, apocalypses, and tracts from ancient Jewish and Christian sects, testify to the rich diversity of legends and doctrines among early Jews and Christians. Many of these texts are crucial to our investigation of Satan.

Regardless of these disputed books, all versions of the Christian Bible—Protestant, Catholic, and Orthodox—preserve the Jewish scriptures (*TaNaK*) in their entirety. However, there is one more important difference between the Christian Old Testament and *Tanakh*. The early Christians began with the contents of the Hebrew Bible and then added their own sacred documents. In the course of producing Episode 2 (the New Testament, the Christian sequel to the Episode 1, a.k.a., the Jewish Bible), the Christian version of *Tanakh* underwent some sequence editing.

The sequence of the *Torah* is the same in both Jewish and Christian Bibles: Genesis, Exodus, Leviticus, Numbers, and Deuteronomy. The contents of the second and third sections of the Jewish Bible, the *Nevi'im* and *Ketuvim*, the Prophets and Writings, are also preserved in the Christian Bible, but their order has been rearranged. The most important changes relate to the Prophets.

The second section of the Jewish Bible, *Nevi'im*, the Prophets, contains two different sets of materials, traditionally known as the Former Prophets and the Latter Prophets. The Former Prophets, so-called because they tell stories about an earlier era, include Joshua, Judges, Samuel (divided into two parts, 1 Samuel and 2 Samuel in modern Bibles), and Kings (now 1 Kings and 2 Kings). The Latter Prophets consist of the Major Prophets—Isaiah, Jeremiah, and Ezekiel—and the Minor Prophets, also called the Book of the Twelve, denoting twelve shorter books, from Hosea to Malachi.

It is within the Prophets section that Jewish and Christian Bibles, identical in content, offer different sequences. From the Jewish perspective, both sections of the *Nevi'im*, the Former Prophets in Joshua-Kings and the Latter Prophets in Isaiah-Malachi, are equally "prophetic"; that is, they offer a religious interpretation of history. But the types of writing are very different. The Former Prophets tell a continuous story from the emergence of the Israelites in Canaan (around 1200 B.C.E.) to the exile of many Jews from Judah to Babylon (around 580 B.C.E.). The priestly historians who authored this chronicle couch their prophetic spin—their homilies, prayers, and moralisms—through historical narratives that illustrate both the benefits of faithfulness to *Torah* and the dire consequences of unfaithfulness.

The Latter Prophets mainly consist of the collected speeches and writings of the Hebrew prophets, important religious leaders from the eighth to fourth centuries B.C.E. The varying textures of these two sections of the Prophets section, the storytelling in Joshua-Kings and the speechifying in Isaiah-Malachi, is impossible to miss and may explain why in Christian Bibles these two subsections of the Jewish Prophets have drifted apart. In the Christian Old Testament, the Former Prophets immediately follow the Genesis-Deuteronomy sequence, just as in the Jewish Bible, allowing for Moses to hand the baton of leadership to Joshua and for the book of Deuteronomy to lead directly into the book of Joshua, uniting the *Torah* and *Nevi'im*.

But in Christian Bibles, the Latter Prophets have moved to the end of the Old Testament. We do not know if this alteration in the order of biblical books is a Christian innovation or not. Nevertheless, whether the early church adopted a variant Jewish sequence or created its own, it found the placement of the Latter Prophets at the end of the Old Testament to be a congenial arrangement. It understood the Gospels, the first section of the New Testament, to represent the fulfillment of the hopes of the Hebrew prophets.

The order of the books of the *Ketuvim*, the Writings, also differs in Jewish and Christian Bibles. The order of books in Jewish Bibles roughly reflects the chronological order in which the various scrolls emerged and were accepted as sacred: the Law by 500 B.C.E., the Prophets by roughly around 300 B.C.E., and the Writings by 100 B.C.E. The order of books in the Christian Old Testament, by contrast, is according to literary genre. Books among the Writings that have a historical texture (Ruth, 1 and 2 Chronicles, Ezra, Nehemiah, Esther) have been inserted among the Former Prophets, which have the same kind of chronological narrative.[3]

The other most significant difference between the Jewish Writings and the corresponding section of the Christian Old Testament has to do with the book of Daniel. In Jewish tradition, Daniel, with its daytime tales about Diaspora heroism (Daniel in the lion's den; the three Hebrew youths in the fiery furnace) and nighttime visions about cosmic battles that overturn empires and reward the righteous, is one of the Writings. This is because it was written relatively late in the centuries before the common era, long after the contents of the Law and Prophets were in circulation. But in Christian Bibles, Daniel is in the prophetic section, between Ezekiel and Hosea. This placement mirrors the Christian elevation of the book of Daniel from among the miscellany of the Writings to the status of a major prophetic work, on the order of the books of Isaiah and Jeremiah. And for Christians, the fevered end-of-time scenarios of Daniel, combats among God, the angels, and hybrid chaos monsters, are fulfilled and their ongoing adventures narrated in the New Testament book of Revelation.

The shifting of the order of books in the Jewish Bible to their location in the Christian Bible changes the entire trajectory of the plot. This is best illustrated by the respective ways that the Jewish *Tanakh* and the Christian Old Testament end. The concluding verses of each book offer a distinctly partisan exit. The final verse of the Jewish Bible is a call for Jewish exiles in Babylon to return home to Jerusalem.

> Thus says King Cyrus of Persia: The LORD, the God of heaven, has given me all the kingdoms of the earth, and he has charged me to build him a house at Jerusalem, which is in Judah. Whoever is among you of all his people, may the LORD his God be with him! Let him go up. (2 Chr 36:23)

This call for a pilgrimage to Jerusalem, for a "going up" (an *aliyah*), resonates in Judaism to this day, for instance, when families at their Passover Seder vow "Next year in Jerusalem," or when someone expresses their commitment to Jewish faith and identity by immigrating (the ultimate *aliyah*) to the state of Israel.[4]

In contrast, the final verses of Malachi in the Christian Old Testament highlight the return of Elijah, the coming Day of the Lord, and a subsequent revitalization of community life: "[The LORD] will turn the hearts of the parents to their children and the hearts of the children to their parents" (Mal 4:6). This exit from what for the Christians is the Old Testament leads smoothly into the second section of the Christian canon, the New Testament, which begins with Matthew's Gospel. Christian readers move from Elijah to John the Baptist, from Yhwh to Jesus, and from the promised restoration of postexilic Jewish life to the realization of that promise in the coming of the Christ. (See Table 1.1.)

The New Testament

The New Testament is a collection of four independent accounts of Jesus' life (the Gospels), a chronicle of the Christian heroes of the first post-Easter generation (the Acts of the Apostles), twenty-one epistles (letters attributed to Paul, Peter, John, and others), and an apocalypse (the book of Revelation). Just as was true with the Hebrew Bible, the authorship of these texts is a debated issue. Christian tradition has assigned an author to each book, in every case one of Jesus' original disciples or a renowned figure in early Christianity. Scholars who are guided more by historical methodology than traditional dogmas look at these traditions with skepticism and assume a far more complicated evolution of these texts.[5] (See Table 1.2.)

The Letters of the Apostle Paul

Among the earliest Christian documents are letters written by Paul, the Jewish missionary to the Gentiles who is responsible for the spread of Christianity beyond the shores of Palestine. Although thirteen letters are ascribed to him, it is likely that only seven are from his hand: Romans, 1 Corinthians, 2 Corinthians, Galatians, Philippians, 1 Thessalonians, and Philemon. Because the other six letters differ in style and reflect the concerns of a later

Table 1.1 Order of the Hebrew Bible Canon (with Abbreviations)

Hebrew Bible	Protestant Bible	Catholic Bible
Genesis (Gen)	Genesis (Gen)	Genesis (Gen)
Exodus (Ex)	Exodus (Ex)	Exodus (Ex)
Leviticus (Lev)	Leviticus (Lev)	Leviticus (Lev)
Numbers (Num)	Numbers (Num)	Numbers (Num)
Deuteronomy (Dt)	Deuteronomy (Dt)	Deuteronomy (Dt)
Joshua (Josh)	Joshua (Josh)	Joshua (Josh)
Judges (Judg)	Judges (Judg)	Judges (Judg)
1–2 Samuel (1–2 Sam)	1–2 Samuel (1–2 Sam)	Ruth (Ruth)
1–2 Kings (1–2 Kgs)	1–2 Kings (1–2 Kgs)	1–2 Samuel (1–2 Sam)
Isaiah (Isa)	1–2 Chronicles (1–2 Chr)	1–2 Kings (1–2 Kgs)
Jeremiah (Jer)	Ezra (Ezra)	1–2 Chronicles (1–2 Chr)
Ezekiel (Ezek)	Nehemiah (Neh)	Tobit (Tobit)
Hosea (Hos)	Esther (Esth)	Judith (Jud)
Amos (Amos)	Job (Job)	Esther (Esth)
Micah (Mic)	Psalms (Ps)	1–2 Maccabees (1–2 Macc)
Joel (Joel)	Proverbs (Prov)	Job (Job)
Obadiah (Obad)	Ecclesiastes (Eccl)	Psalms (Ps)
Jonah (Jonah)	Song of Solomon (Song)	Proverbs (Prov)
Nahum (Nah)	Isaiah (Isa)	Ecclesiastes (Eccl)
Habakkuk (Hab)	Jeremiah (Jer)	Song of Solomon (Song)
Zephaniah (Zeph)	Lamentations (Lam)	Isaiah (Isa)
Haggai (Hag)	Ezekiel (Ezek)	Jeremiah (Jer)
Zechariah (Zech)	Daniel (Dan)	Lamentations (Lam)
Malachi (Mal)	Hosea (Hos)	Baruch (Bar)
Psalms (Ps)	Joel (Joel)	Ezekiel (Ezek)
Job (Job)	Amos (Amos)	Daniel (Dan)
Proverbs (Prov)	Obadiah (Obad)	Hosea (Hos)
Ruth (Ruth)	Jonah (Jonah)	Joel (Joel)
Song of Solomon (Song)	Micah (Mic)	Amos (Amos)
Ecclesiastes (Eccl)	Nahum (Nah)	Obadiah (Obad)
Esther (Esth)	Habakkuk (Hab)	Jonah (Jonah)
Daniel (Dan)	Zephaniah (Zeph)	Micah (Mic)
Ezra-Nehemiah (Ez-Neh)	Haggai (Hag)	Nahum (Nah)
1–2 Chronicles (1–2 Chr)	Zechariah (Zech)	Habakkuk (Hab)
	Malachi (Mal)	Zephaniah (Zeph)
		Haggai (Hag)
		Zechariah (Zech)
		Malachi (Mal)

Table 1.2 The New Testament (with Abbreviations)

The Gospels	*Other "Pauline" Letters*
Matthew (Mt)	2 Thessalonians (2 Thess)
Mark (Mk)	Colossians (Col)
Luke (Lk)	1–2 Timothy (1–2 Tim)
John (Jn)	Titus
	Ephesians (Eph)

Acts of the Apostles (Acts)

Authentic Pauline Epistles	*Other Apostolic Letters*
	Hebrews (Heb)
Romans (Rms)	James (James)
1–2 Corinthians (1–2 Cor)	1 Peter (1 Pet)
Galatians (Gal)	2 Peter (2 Pet)
Philippians (Phil)	1, 2, 3, John (1,2,3 Jn)
1 Thessalonians (1Thess)	Jude (Jude)
Philemon (Philem)	
	Revelation (Rev)

time in Christian history, it is likely that these were written in Paul's name by his followers sometime after his death.[6] The earliest of the seven authentic Pauline epistles is 1 Thessalonians, written in 50 C.E., which makes it the oldest complete Christian document, older even than the Gospels. Whatever accounts of Jesus' sayings and activities in circulation around 50 C.E. were either oral or in fragmentary documents that did not survive.

By all accounts, Paul seems to have been a tireless missionary, committed to spreading the good news about Jesus. A former persecutor of early Christians, Paul was transformed by a visionary encounter with the risen Jesus (Gal 1:11–17; Acts 9:1–9; 22:3–11; 26:12–19; see also 1 Cor 15:8). Paul's letters are designed to address specific problems and issues within the early Christian communities he founded, mostly in Asia Minor. He seems to have encountered some staunch opposition, both from the remaining Jerusalem apostles (particularly Peter) and from outside factions who disagreed with some of his teachings.

The Gospels

The Gospels (from a Greek word meaning "good news") tell the story of Jesus of Nazareth through the eyes of the four authors (or Evangelists): Matthew, Mark, Luke, and John. Written between 70 and 95 C.E., the Gospels take the form of biographical descriptions of Jesus' life; they cannot, however, be compared to modern biographies.[7] The Gospels can best be described as theological biographies that tell the story of Jesus from a faith perspective. For example, other than the brief stories of Jesus' birth in Matthew and Luke—and one short scene of Jesus as an older child, being left behind during a family pilgrimage—there are no stories of Jesus' childhood or his life before we meet him in the Gospels as an adult. Today modern readers often wonder: Where was he all those years? What did he look like? Was he married? The Gospels are silent on such details because these questions are unimportant in the story the Evangelists wanted to tell. Incidentally, stories about Jesus' early life and family did become the subject of non-canonical, apocryphal gospels written within a century of the official Gospels. The "official stories" about Jesus did not satisfy the curiosity of the early Christians, so unofficial versions were produced to fill the narrative gaps.

The first three canonical Gospels, Matthew, Mark, and Luke, contain similar stories that generally follow the same order. Because the three are so similar, they are often called the Synoptic Gospels (synoptic is from a Greek word meaning "like-view" or "to see together"). The three Synoptic Gospels not only provide a similar chronology of events in Jesus' life, but also share many of the same themes or concerns, including the emphasis on Jesus as teacher, worker of miracles, and exorcist. In the Synoptics, Jesus proclaims the Kingdom of God is at hand, and he reaches out to the poor and disenfranchised.

The fourth Gospel, the Gospel of John, however, is quite different, both in the way in which Jesus is presented and in its theology. The Gospel of John is more verbose, more patently symbolic, and more philosophic than the Synoptics, which have a relatively straightforward narrative style. For instance, compare the opening sequences of Mark with that of John.

The beginning of the good news of Jesus Christ, the Son of God. (Mk 1:1)

And then a mere two verses later, we are in the middle of the story: "John the baptizer appeared in the wilderness . . ." (Mk 1:4).

The Gospel of John, in contrast, opens in majestic style, with abstract theological terms and philosophic turns of phrase.

> In the beginning was the Word, and the Word was with God, and the Word was God. He was in the beginning with God. All things came into being through him, and without him not one thing came into being. What has come into being in him was life, and the life was the light of all people. The light shines in the darkness, and the darkness did not overcome it. (John 1:1–5)

John the Baptist also appears a few verses later, just as he did in Mark's account, but in the Gospel of John, this prophetic figure is described in symbolic terms and with highly nuanced expressions.

> There was a man sent from God, whose name was John. He came as a witness to the light, so that all might believe through him. He himself was not the light, but he came to testify to the light. The true light, which enlightens everyone, was coming into the world. (John 1:6–9)

Still, regarding the major aspects of Jesus' life, all four Gospels agree: Jesus was detained by the Roman authorities, condemned, crucified, buried, and rose from the dead.

Acts of the Apostles

Acts of the Apostles, the book that follows the Gospel of John in the canon, is the second of two volumes written by the author of the Gospel of Luke. Acts chronicles, in ideal fashion, the adventures of the early Christian community following the resurrection of Jesus. Acts begins in Jerusalem and ends in Rome with Paul carrying the "good news" to the heart of the Roman Empire. The spread of Christianity, the work of the Holy Spirit, the relationship between Judaism and Christianity, and the nonviolent nature of the Christian movement are among Acts' central themes. Most scholars agree that Acts was written sometime between 80 and 85 C.E.

The Book of Revelation

The Bible's final book, Revelation, was written by a man named John (not the author of the Fourth Gospel), a Christian exiled to the island of Patmos (Rev 1:1, 4, 9; 22:8). Revelation is an example of apocalyptic literature—a style of writing popular during this period—that employs highly symbolic language to describe the "end time." The title "Revelation" is the Latin translation of the original Greek title of the book, "the Apocalypse."

Revelation, the last book admitted into the Christian canon, describes a series of strange, symbolic visions and cosmic battles between the forces of Good (led by Christ) and Evil (led by Satan). Although this book is often misunderstood and misapplied by those who fail to recognize the symbolism inherent in the text, it is an important book in any serious study of Satan. Indeed, it is in Revelation where we find the fullest (and most terrifying) biblical portrait of Satan.

The End Result

The Bible began as the collection of sacred scrolls written and edited over the course of a thousand years by the Jewish people, stored in temples, and handled by scribes. In its maturity, the family feud among first- and second-century C.E. Jews and the breakaway sect of Christians led to the emergence of two rival Bibles. We cannot confidently state when it was that the Jesus sect crossed the boundary from being one more fractious camp within early Judaism to that of major world religion.[8] But surely the production of the New Testament (which existed in some form by around 200 C.E.) was a decisive break. (By the way, in the same general time period, the Jewish community was producing its own sequel to the *Tanakh*, the rabbinic writings we know best as the Mishnah and the Talmud.)

The New Testament was modeled after the Jewish Bible. The four Gospels of the New Testament, like the five books of the *Torah*, mixed stories and sayings to tell the basic story of the faith. The Acts of the Apostles and the Epistles of Paul had the same function in the Christian Bible that, respectively, the Former and Latter Prophets did in the Jewish Bible: chronological narratives about the fortunes of the community (Acts is analogous to Joshua-Kings) followed by the collected writings of leaders (the Pauline letters are analogous to the oracles of the Latter Prophets). The Christian sequel included the book of Revelation, a set of densely coded visions and end-of-time scenarios, that built off the fevered Diaspora visions of the Hebrew (and Aramaic) book of Daniel in the *Tanakh*. Only the poetic books of the Jewish Bible—Psalms, Proverbs, Ecclesiastes, Song of Songs, and Job—did not inspire Christian revisions. The poetry, prayers, hymns, adages, and yearning expressions of these books among the Jewish writings, the *Ketuvim*, had universal and timeless qualities that made them accessible to Christians as well as Jews.

The Debates about the Bible

The Bible belongs neither to pious guardians of theological orthodoxy nor to skeptical, historically minded scholars. The Bible belongs to the world and is wide-open for interpretation. For many, the Bible is the oracle through which the God of Jewish and Christian faiths speaks to them. Whether the question is profound and universal in scope ("Is capital punishment just?") or highly personal and provisional ("Should I quit my present job to embark on a sojourn of itinerant preaching and healing?"), many people either systematically thumb through their Bibles or dramatically open them at random to find answers to life's perplexities.

There are vast libraries of commentary, both Jewish and Christian, reflecting every conceivable point of view, to guide readers who prefer swimming close to the shores of their given tradition, sect, or denomination. At the same time, the Bible can be read in intensely private ways. Synods may forge ethical programs for their communities on the basis of reasoned debates about biblical texts that lead to consensus about the divine will. Serial killers may adopt the persona of an avenging angel—the Bible includes plenty—to normalize their delusions. It is customary for professors of biblical studies to disparage idiosyncratic schools of interpretation—imagining accounts of angels as extraterrestrial visitations, splicing the headlines from today's newspapers between the lines of the visions of Daniel and Revelation in order to produce scenarios about the end of time—but that has little effect on the ongoing, ever-growing phenomenon of Bible interpretation, with its dizzying diversity of styles and ideologies.

This book treats the Bible like any other piece of literature. That is, we read it with measures of sympathy and suspicion, with curiosity about its authors and their times, and with full appreciation for its profundities and full attention to its primitive features. We indicated our religious affiliations—Roman Catholic and Protestant—in the preface, although neither of us pretends to be definitively or officially Catholic or Protestant. We are writing for a mixed multitude of Christians and Jews, whether back-slidden or at the forefront of the saints when they go marching in. We are also addressing persons of other or no religious affiliation who are simply curious about Satan. We will certainly disappoint those readers for whom the Bible is beyond analysis, a divine document to be trusted and obeyed but never subjected to interpretation. We hope that, in the end, we also disappoint readers who want to see the Bible exposed as antiquated and primitive, a cultural superego from which modern persons need liberation.

We seek to understand the communications of these ancient Jewish and Christian communities whose struggles were both so different from and so similar to our own. In order to understand what they wrote, we will pay close attention to the meaning of their words, the structures of their speech, and the circumstances of their lives. Beyond these philological and historical facets, great ambiguities remain. What is unambiguous, however, is the fact that Satan's birth took place within the pages of Bible.

What's in a Name?

As we move forward in our search for Satan, it seems prudent at this juncture to mention that throughout history, the figure known as Satan has been known by many other names. (Those that appear in the Bible, the Apocrypha, and early Jewish and Christian literature are discussed in later chapters.) For example, in the New Testament, the Devil goes by these names: Satan, Devil, Beelzebub, the Evil One, the Prince of this world, Belial, Abaddon, and Apollyon.[9] Most readers will be familiar with Prince of Darkness, Lucifer, and Mephistopheles. But how many of the medieval popular names, collected by scholar Jeffrey Burton Russell, are familiar?[10]

Old Horny, Old Hairy, Back Bogey, Lusty Dick, Dickon, Dickens, Gentleman Jack, the Good Fellow, Old Nick, and Old Scratch

Viewers of medieval dramas would have seen a legion of diabolical characters on stages, with a dazzling array of names:

Dark Lord, Sathanas, Mammon, Belphegor, Asmodeus, Behemoth, Berith, Astaroth, Inferus, Baal, Ammon, Moloch, Tenebrifer (shadowbearer), Cocornifer (hornbearer), Schonspigel (pretty mirror), Ragamuffin, Ribald, Cacodemon, Crooked Nose, Snakey

and dozens more.[11]

The term "devil" is from the Greek, *diabolos,* a translation of the Hebrew word *śaṭan,* itself the source of the term "Satan." The Greek word *diabolos* and the Hebrew word *śaṭan* mean the same thing. They refer to a character in opposition, an adversary, enemy, or slanderer. Russell offers a convincing explanation for how the Devil has come by so many names, noting a basic axiom of diabology ("the study of the devil"), namely that one era's deities become the next era's demons.

Historically, when a culture replaces one set of gods with another, it tends to relegate the losing set to the status of evil spirits. The Christians made demons out of the Olympian deities of Greece and Rome, just as the Olympian religion had earlier transformed the earthbound Titans into evil spirits.[12]

This principle is at work in the classic satanic tale, *Paradise Lost,* in which the names of the members of Lucifer's underworld cabinet are drawn from the roster of ancient Israel's neighboring religions: Moloch, Chemos, Baalim, Ashtaroth, Asorteth, Astarte, Thammuz, Dagon, Rimmon, Osiris, Isis, [H]orus, Belial, and others (*Paradise Lost* 1: 390–505). In Christian polemics through the ages, Satan has been rechristened in this manner countless times, assuming the name of whatever rival deity happened to appear on the horizon. Armed now with at least a basic understanding of the Bible and a host of names to invoke and chant as needed, let us move forward to investigate Satan's humble beginnings.

chapter 2

unsystematic theology

The Nature of God in the Hebrew Bible

There's too much tendency to attribute to God the evils that man does of his own free will.

—*Agatha Christie*

Judaism and Christianity are polished gems of thought that have been crafted by rabbis and philosophers, clerics and theologians for centuries. But for all the devout industry of these divines and the alpine pile of tractates and treatises produced as guides to the perplexed, a single disquieting truth endures: The God of the Bible is a moving target and remains impossible to pin down.[1]

Although the pious, quite rightly, rationalize the elusive nature of the biblical God as more evidence of God's grandeur, there is something more. The God of the Hebrew Bible, Yhwh by name, confounds and surprises, and repels and attracts.

The Divine Name

The Hebrew Bible uses many different words to refer to God. The two most common names have been translated into English as "God" and "the LORD." "God" is our translation of the Hebrew word *elohim*. This word *elohim* presents two ambiguities. First, the form is grammatically plural; that is to say, the *-im* ending on nouns in Hebrew is analogous to a final *-s* on a noun in English. The word for "God" in biblical Hebrew, thus, could mean "gods." The other ambiguity about the form *elohim* is this: Since biblical Hebrew did not have capital letters, biblical interpreters must decide on a case-by-case basis whether to translate *elohim* as "god" or "God." The single Hebrew word *elohim* could mean "god," "gods," "God," or "Gods."

The opening words of the Ten Commandments illustrate many of these ambiguities.

In the King James Version, Ex 20:1–3 reads,

> And God spake all these words, saying,
> I am the LORD thy God, which have brought thee out of the land of Egypt,
> out of the house of bondage,
> Thou shalt have no other gods before me.

Now let us render the same passage without translating the three examples of *elohim*.

> And *elohim* spake all these words, saying,
> I am the LORD thy *elohim*, which have brought thee out of the land of
>   Egypt,
> out of the house of bondage,
> Thou shalt have no other *elohim* before me.

In these verses, the single word *elohim* is used as a name for God ("and God/*elohim* spake"), as a title or epithet ("thy God/*elohim*"), and as a plural form referring to gods other than the biblical deity ("other gods/*elohim*"). We did not have to venture very far in our discussion—we are merely talking about the deity's name—to encounter the complexity of the biblical portrait of God.

The other most common name for God in the Hebrew Bible is the Tetragrammaton, a Greek term that means "the Four Letters." Those four letters in Hebrew are, successively, *y, h, w,* and *h.* The Hebrew word *yhwh* is translated in English Bibles as "the LORD," and the latter word is often doubly marked as special in printed Bibles by rendering it in all capitals and by adjusting its font so that the final three consonants are smaller than the initial one.

The reason for these stylistic flourishes is that, early in the course of the development of Judaism, it became taboo to pronounce the divine name out of respect for its gravity (although scholars have reconstructed its likely pronunciation as "yahweh"). The common practice among Jews was to substitute a different word altogether, such as the phrase "my Lord," Hebrew *adonai,* for *yhwh* when voicing it. In manuscripts of the Hebrew Bible, the spelling of this divine name is a hybrid form. Its consonants are *y-h-w-h* (from an original *yahweh*), but its vowels are those from a different word, *adonay,* as a way of reminding biblical readers that they are supposed to say "Adonai," "my Lord," instead of "Yahweh."

The word "Jehovah," a common name in medieval usage for the Old Testament deity, is actually an erroneous translation of the Hebrew spelling of the Tetragrammaton, made by European Christians who did not understand this coded way of spelling. The form "Jehovah" represents a straightforward vocalization of the consonants from *yahweh, y* (in German *j*), *h, w* (or *v*), and *h,* and of the vowels from "adonay," *a* (or *e*), *o,* and *a.* But there was never a deity named Jehovah in antiquity. There was a deity shrouded in mystery named Yhwh whose form was unimaged (Ex 20:4) and whose name was unpronounced.

In summary: The two most common names for God in the Hebrew Bible are *elohim* and *yhwh.* Elohim can mean either "God" or "gods," depending on context. Yhwh means one thing and one thing only; it is the special name of the deity who made a covenant with the people Israel. This word Yhwh was considered too sacred to pronounce so, instead, the word "Adonai," "my Lord," was used. In English editions of the Bible, the form *yhwh* is translated as "the LORD."

We discuss the meaning of the name Yhwh later. For now it is sufficient to note that nothing, not even the names by which we refer to and address this deity, is simple. The God of the Hebrew Bible is complicated, inscrutable, and mercurial. And this truth was just as apparent to the ancients as it is to us. Furthermore, this truth may be an important factor in the birth of Satan. Recall, for example, that it is Yhwh, the frenetic artist, who creates all forms of life in the first two chapters of Genesis, only to then destroy his flawed masterpiece in a catastrophic flood. It is Yhwh, in the Exodus tale, who inflicts unimaginable horror on the Egyptians in the form of deadly plagues, but then parts the sea so the Israelites (his undisputed favored ones, at least in this story) can cross dry shod to escape Pharaoh's army. And let us not forget that it is Yhwh who dictates the ruinous destruction of Jerusalem and the exaggerated punishment of the Exile—but then, in an about face (the Divine snit apparently over), offers the hope of restoration to the demoralized exiles as they prepare to return to the Promised Land.

But as we move ahead, let us remember that we are in the realm of religious language here. Before we get swept up in the transcripts of conflicting testimony about Yhwh and Old Scratch that have been entered into the proceedings of the biblical courtroom, we must keep our bearings. It is a matter of religious faith whether there is a God, and whether that God is known as Yhwh, and whether the scriptures of Jews and Christians are accurate reflections of ultimate reality. This book will proceed to tell our version of the biblical story and will not pause to take reality checks after each account of a biblical marvel or massacre. Guided by their religious sympathies or skepticism, readers will have to decide for themselves how much, if any, of the Bible they can accept. Warning: Common side effects of biblical study include visual flashes, deep remorse, and (unless reading Song of Solomon) decreased libido. The authors accept no responsibility for what readers do with our products after they take them home.

Two Problems with Biblical Monotheism

The hallmark of Jewish and Christian faith (and Islamic, too) is that there is one God, although Christians have a funny way of explaining this and the slightest slip in dogmatic exposition can make it sound as if there are three. In many ways, the birth of Satan is tied, directly or indirectly, to the triumph of this idea in biblical religion. We refer to the "triumph" of monotheism because there was competition involved; Yhwh was not always alone in the hearts and minds of the people.

Even casual observers of religion can easily understand that the Bible is capable of diverse interpretations and has been the arena of pitched denominational rivalries. All the various human communities that swear by the Bible and, at the same time, virulently and (sometimes) violently disagree with each other illustrate this. Proponents of a certain religious practice or ethical imperative offer their proof-text from scripture while their opponents offer another. For example, Baptists and Methodists may respectively accuse each other of misunderstanding the biblical truth about the method of baptism (immersion versus sprinkling) but the more important problem is that the Bible itself, like the Gershwin brothers' happiest unhappy couple, says *po-tate-oh* on one page and *po-taht-oh* on the next.

The testimony about monotheism is among the most conflicted in the Hebrew Bible.[2] On one hand, biblical religion is characterized by its proclamation that there is one God. On the other hand, there are numerous references in the Bible to gods other than the One. The Hebrew religious geniuses whom we know as the prophets, from the ninth to the sixth centuries B.C.E., sharpened and honed an idea attributed first to Moses: "Hear, O Israel, the LORD, your God, is one" (Dt 6:4).[3] This is the first line of the *Shema*, the prayer as central to the practice of Judaism as the "Our Father," the Lord's Prayer, is to Christianity. According to prophet Amos, a hard case who spoke in the eighth century B.C.E.:

Does disaster befall a city,
unless the LORD has done it? (Amos 3:6)

Municipal disasters came in many sizes: disease, drought, shakedowns from superpowers seeking tribute. The latter is probably what Amos had in mind. The roar of the Assyrian army, on the prowl through the Fertile Crescent from the Tigris to the Mediterranean under lion-festooned standards, caught Amos's attention. The prophet heard something no one else did. While his peers imagined that the Assyrian advance was fueled by territorial avarice, Amos claimed that God (Yhwh), not the Assyrian deity, Assur, was behind the imminent oppression of Israel.[4] The Assyrian army was merely God's tool, whether a hoe to prune, a club to punish, or a poker to stoke an annealing fire in Israel. This austere theology, the prophetic faith nurtured in the highlands of Israel, was its own kind of high-and-lonesome. Yhwh alone was the source of all blessings and curses, rewards and punishments.

A prophet during the Babylonian exile, two centuries later, also claimed that all events, whether beneficial or detrimental, were under Yhwh's control.

> I am the LORD, and there is no other.
> I form light and create darkness,
> I make weal and create woe;
> I the LORD do all these things. (Isa 45:6–7)

Mainstream Jewish and Christian theology are both heirs to the prophetic insight that the universe is ultimately a unified field, but these kinds of clear statements about who is in charge and where the buck stops are not universal in the Bible. The most damaging categories of evidence to the Hebrew Bible's own case for monotheism are twofold. First, the Bible contains a multitude of references to deities other than Yhwh. These are the rival gods and goddesses (such as Baal, Astarte, and Molech, whose names will become epithets for Satan in *Paradise Lost*) of neighboring peoples whose attractiveness to Israel elicits the passion of its jealous God:

> The Israelites again did what was evil in the sight of the Lord, worshipping the Baals and the Astartes, the gods of Aram, the gods of Sidon, the gods of Moab, the gods of the Ammonites, the gods of the Philistines. Thus they abandoned the LORD and did not worship him. (Judg 10:6)

> . . . because of all the evil of the people of Israel and the people of Judah that they did to provoke me to anger. . . . They set up their abominations in the house that bears my name, and defiled it. They built the high places of Baal in the valley of the son of Hinnom, to offer up their sons and daughters to Molech.[5] (Jer 32:32–35)

> You shall tear down their altars, break their pillars, and cut down their sacred poles for you shall worship no other god, because the LORD, whose name is Jealous, is a jealous God. (Ex 34.13–14)

In addition, there are references and allusions in the Bible to divine or semidivine beings among Yhwh's entourage. As biblical scholar Jack Miles writes,

God has "a divine social life" in the Bible.[6] We return to these problems—in shorthand, the gods and the angels—later in this chapter, for both of these classes of beings, the deities of Israel's neighbors and the semi-divine angels, will figure in the development of satanic lore. In fact, the names of Yhwh's competitors will become alternative names for the Devil after the biblical period. As for the angels, they will be divided into classes, good and evil, celestial and infernal, serving as messengers, lackeys, and agents for their respective kingdoms. But we are getting ahead of ourselves and must first review what the Bible has to say about the nature of the divine personality.[7]

The Divine Personality in a Nutshell

Moses gets so many of the great lines in the Hebrew Bible. There is the *Shema,* as mentioned earlier:

Hear, O Israel, the LORD your God is one. And you shall love the LORD your God with all your heart, and with all your soul, and with all your might. (Dt 6:4–5)

There is also the revelation of the divine name in Ex 3:13–15. In that story, Moses was reluctant to leave goat herding in the wilderness in order to return to Egypt and demand that Pharaoh release the Hebrews from slavery. Furthermore, Moses was not even sure that the Hebrews themselves would fall in line behind him, so he asked God,

If I come to the Israelites and say to them, "The God of your ancestors has sent me to you, and they ask me, 'What is his name?' what shall I say to them?" God said to Moses, "I AM WHO I AM."

"I-am-who-I-am." The Hebrew words might also mean "I-will-be-who-I-will-be" or, best (we think), "I-cause-to-be-what-I-cause-to-be."[8] This phrase, "I-cause-to-be-what-I-cause-to-be" (in other words, "I-make-everything-happen," as clear a statement of monotheism as you will find), gets formulated as a single word in Hebrew, God's first name, God's special name: Yhwh.

Yhwh is a third-person form in grammar, and means literally "He is" (or "He Causes/Creates") despite the fact that it is more customary to refer to this God as the great and august "I am." As previously mentioned, wherever you encounter the form "the LORD" in this book or in an edition of the Bible, it is translating the Hebrew word Yhwh, a term that became taboo to pronounce.

Another greatest hit of Moses is the text in Ex 34:6–7, where God reveals the essence of the divine personality. In the story that precedes it, Moses has gained a special intimacy with God. In the course of his forty-day sojourn on Mount Sinai, dictating all 613 commandments of the written Law (and only the rabbis of old know how much additional off-the-record deep background, i.e., the Oral Law), Moses and the LORD have become downright friendly.[9] Moses makes a playful request of God: "Can I see your glory?" The glory of God is the aura, the garment of light that was thought to surround the deity.

God agrees but takes precautions. The divine glory is like the most intense sunlight, indispensable to life yet toxic if viewed directly. So God hides Moses in a cave ("the cleft of a rock") and announces that he will pass by. The text itself does not describe what Moses saw, except to say that Moses saw only "the backside of God." Then, shortly afterward, in Exodus 34, the LORD flashes Moses again "and proclaim[s],"

> The LORD, the LORD,
> a God merciful and gracious,
> slow to anger,
> and abounding in steadfast love and faithfulness,
> keeping steadfast love for the thousandth generation,
> forgiving iniquity and transgression and sin, . . .

For a moment, it is as if Moses were back in Eden where before time God went for afternoon strolls through Paradise (Gen 3:8). In this passage that begins with Moses seeing "the flanks" of Yhwh (Ex 33:23) and ends with Moses hearing Yhwh proclaim (or sing) the divine name in poetic diction (Ex 34:6–7), Moses gets as close to the deity as any mortal does in the Hebrew Bible.

So far, so good, but there is another stanza to the poem.

... forgiving iniquity and transgression and sin, ...
yet by no means clearing the guilty,
but visiting the iniquity of the parents upon their children
and the children's children,
to the third and the fourth generation.

Exodus 34:6–7—and variants of it occur throughout the Hebrew Bible—is the Bible's basic declaration of what Yhwh is like.[10] The divine personality is overwhelmingly gracious and life-giving, reliable and generous *as well as* not to be trifled with; never, ever letting the guilty make a clean getaway. This, if anything, is the systematic theology of the Hebrew Bible: God as both friend and avenger. In our legal terms, God as judge, jury, prosecutor, and defense counsel. We might imagine these as separate functions, but for God's chosen people the shoulder that bears us when we pull up lame is connected to the long arm of the law that apprehends us when we run from the scene of our crimes.

This formula does not state that the admixture of adjectives is balanced. There is no Yin and Yang here, no fifty-fifty split of attractive and repellent features. To the contrary, Yhwh, the creator of the universe and the source of all the blessings of life, is overwhelmingly gracious and merciful, extending steadfast love to the *thousandth* generation. But, at the same time, those who pursue courses of actions contrary to the divine will and later translated into legal codes through the Mosaic *Torah* or "teaching," are clearly courting disaster. The consequences of their follies threaten not only them but also their descendants, to the *third and fourth* generations. Already you can feel the tension in such a view of God.

The Divine Godfather

The most prevalent image of God in the Hebrew Bible, for better or for worse, is God as patriarch. It is a grave mistake to imagine this great patriarch as the kind of father we may know best. God was a certain kind of father, the kind of father figure known to the ancient cultures around the eastern Mediterranean, as the biblical scholar David Schloen has pointed out.[11] God was conceived as the Great Father, the patriarch above all patriarchs. Bounteous, good-natured, forgiving, wise, strong, but also fiercely—even savagely—protective of his clan. Furthermore, this godfather was inordinately concerned that he be shown the proper *respect* and was ready to teach the disrespectful a lesson should his will be opposed.

The Bible contains many images of and metaphors for God; the kind of Mediterranean-style godfather is merely one metaphor, although it is among the most common. There are even places in the Bible, especially in the poems of Isaiah, where God is compared to a mother.[12] Personally, we believe that God has maternal and paternal aspects, as well as facets that cannot be contained with any kind of familial image. But much of the imagery about God in the Hebrew Bible begins from the idea of God as the ultimate father figure.

Although this image of God as patriarch does not directly affect our understanding of the birth of Satan, it does help us to understand many aspects of the portrait of God in the Hebrew Bible, especially those aspects modern readers might find off-putting: the deity who leads his clans into battle; the deity whose anger is aroused by careless rites and betrayals, by a lack of respect.[13]

With this review of two crucial ideas for understanding the portrayal of God in the Hebrew Bible, we can now return to the main focus of this chapter: how strong tensions in the idea of monotheism served as labor pains for the delivery of Satan.

Are the Other Gods Real?

The first bit of conflicting testimony regarding monotheism that the Bible offers is the shadowy presence of rival deities.[14] The *Shema*, the grand statement of monotheism, can be found near the beginning of the scroll of Deuteronomy (Dt 6:4). Near the end of the same scroll is a poem attributed to Moses that seems to suggest that, while the LORD may be One, the LORD is not the only one.

> When the Most High apportioned the nations,
>   when he divided humankind,
>   he fixed the boundaries of the peoples

according to the number of the gods;
the LORD's own portion was his people,
Jacob his allotted share. (Dt 32:8–9)

This text can be translated and interpreted in ways that are congenial to monotheism, and it is poetry, after all, so we must allow it some rhetorical flexibility.[15] Still, it suggests that Yhwh is the God of Jacob (an alternative name for Israel in the Bible), but that other peoples have their own gods.

We cannot read the minds of the ancient Israelites; we can only read the literary legacy they left to us in the Bible. When the First Commandment, in Ex 20:3, says, "You shall have no other gods before me," we cannot penetrate behind that word, "gods." Did the early Israelites understand these gods to be unreal and without substance? Or did they understand them to be cosmic figures of some import but who were out-of-bounds for them?

We read in the book of Judges, for instance, that the Israelites had "abandoned the LORD, the God of their ancestors, who had brought them out of the land of Egypt" and "followed other gods, from among the gods of the peoples who were all around them" (Judg 2:11–12). The simplest reading of texts such as these (and there are many more) is that perhaps some Israelites held that while Yhwh was the God of Israel, Yhwh was not the *only* god. There may well be other deities for other peoples, but Yhwh is the sole God who deserves Israel's awe and singular devotion.

Should we call such belief polytheism, a slippery word that denotes belief in many deities? But even polytheists often reserve special devotion for the power that functions as their personal god, their contact deity in the divine government. Perhaps a more useful term to describe the religious culture in these texts is henotheism, the worship of a single god without denying the existence of other gods.

The prophetic movement in Israel sharpened this understanding, so eventually monotheism triumphed over henotheism, at least in the writings of the leading Hebrew religious thinkers. The ninth-century B.C.E. prophet Elijah took on the prophets of Baal in a kind of priestly Olympics on Mount Carmel, bested them in prophetic feats, and then ridiculed their supposed deity:

"[Maybe Baal] has *wandered away* [taken a bush stop!] or he is on a journey, or perhaps he is asleep and must be awakened" (1 Kgs 18:27).

The eighth-century B.C.E. prophet Amos indirectly countered the idea that all peoples had their own national deity. It was Yhwh—not Dagon, not Baal Hadad—who presided over not merely the exodus of the Israelites but also the respective exoduses of the Philistines and Arameans, and gave them the lands in which they now reside:

> Are you not like the Ethiopians to me,
> O people of Israel? Says the LORD.
> Did I not bring Israel up from the land of Egypt,
> and the Philistines from Caphtor and the Arameans from Kir? (Amos 9:7).

But it was the anonymous sixth-century B.C.E. prophet whose poems were appended to the scroll of Isaiah (whom some call Second Isaiah or Isaiah of Babylon) who stated matters most clearly. This Israelite prophet, who lived among the temples and pantheons of Babylon, addresses the gods in one speech:

> You, indeed, are nothing
> and your work is nothing at all;
> whoever chooses you is an abomination. (Isa 41:24)

and elsewhere sweeps all other deities from their pedestals with this declaration.

> For I [Yhwh] am God, and there is no other;
> I am God, and there is no one like me. (Isa 46:9)

We do not know whether the form of henotheism practiced in ancient Israel involved grudging respect for other gods or agnosticism about them. We only know this: The end result was a faith that involved complete devotion to Yhwh.

This triumph of monotheism over a form of henotheism did not take place overnight, however, but appears to have been a slow evolution over centuries, and cannot be dated confidently before the period of the Babylonian Exile in the mid-sixth century B.C.E.

This makes sense because it was during the Exile that the displaced Jewish community discovered that its faith was as alive and vital in a foreign land as it had been in Jerusalem. Furthermore, the life the people planted in alien soil and the blessings they received there convinced them that Yhwh was more than the patriarch of a clan at home in Judah and Ephraim (another name for the northern kingdom usually called Israel) but was the God of what for them was an ever-expanding world. The daily interactions of Jewish priests and prophets with Babylon's rich tapestry of cult and monumental religious art forced them to sharpen their critique of the gods and broaden their view of the scope of Yhwh's governance.

What does this triumph of monotheism have to do with the birth of Satan? We can only say one thing for certain: It is in biblical writings that emerge after the Exile—after this triumph, in the books of Zechariah, Job, and 1 Chronicles—that Satan makes his most vivid appearances in the Hebrew Bible. Satan does appear in one pre-exilic book, in Numbers, chapter 22, and we discuss all these texts in subsequent chapters. The Satan (in Hebrew, *hassatan,* "the Adversary") who appears in these postexilic books is hardly the arch-opponent of God that we encounter in the New Testament, but is a figure who will develop into the cosmic Adversary. Thus, Satan begins to appear with more frequency in the Bible *after* the triumph of monotheism.

To point toward one more conclusion, although it may be premature, the consolidation of all divine powers into Yhwh may have had an unexpected side effect. That is, before the adoption of monotheism, the misfortunes suffered in life were often blamed on other gods or evil forces. In a monotheistic system, however, Yhwh alone is responsible. Because Yhwh embodies both good and evil, it seems likely that many people find it difficult to embrace a deity that intentionally inflicts suffering.[16] This brings us to the age-old question of theodicy, and it also demands that we explore people's existential frustration as a contributing factor in the birth of Satan. Put simply, unable to reconcile faith in a God who is both benevolent and, at the same time, is the playwright of the entire human drama, whether tragic or comic, the ancient mind sought an alternative explanation for evil in the world: Evil does not come from God at all, but from a malignant being who acts in opposition to the goodness of God. This proved to an attractive idea to many.

The poetry in the book of Job hints at the existential frustrations inherent in a monotheistic faith. Job, the Hebrew Everyman, finds himself in the

Catch–22 position of asking God to rescue him from the very source of his oppression—God.[17] Clearly, the fullness of Yhwh—all in all, defender, avenger, source of darkness and light—presented believers with an existential frustration. And although the birth of Satan, like the triumph of monotheism itself, would take centuries, some Jews and many more Christians would come to resolve this tension by ascribing their rescues to God and their oppressions to Satan.

The Heavenly Throng

Jack Miles's statement bears repeating: In the Bible, God has a divine social life.[18] The Bible itself does not explicitly catalog the ranks of divine or semidivine beings, but it alludes to them throughout. Here we review some of these biblical allusions to angels, demons, sprites, divine courtiers, and the chaos monsters that serve as cosmic border guards.[19]

There is another category we must consider as well: the rich vocabulary of circumlocution the biblical writers developed. At times, these phrases—for instance "the Angel of the LORD," when a visit from the LORD was reported, or "the hand of the LORD," when a cosmic caning was administered—may simply represent poetic license, a colorful, varied repertoire of epithets used in storytelling. But such statements can also serve as distancing devices: "It was not *God* who punished me; it was *the hand* of God."

We are moving now from the sidelines in our search for Satan and wading into the fray. Our first important and some might say, startling discovery is that we do not have to look very far. Satan, it would appear, is right under our noses. For it is among these beings and these personifications of often unpleasant divine aspects that we discover Satan's traits, Satan's DNA, if you will.

Angels

We know from reading the texts of ancient Egypt, Babylon, Sumer, Assyria, Phoenicia, Syria, and Anatolia, to name only the cultures that abutted ancient Israel, that most peoples of the Near East and eastern Mediterranean imagined a divine government of senior administrators, rival deities vying for influence, and their junior functionaries, who served as bodyguards, messengers, gofers, lackeys, and hitmen. The Bible, however, gives us no such Olympian soap opera or three-dimensional board game in which the moves on one level of the board, the heavenly, determine the results on the two below, the earth and the underworld.

Still, a variant of this picture seems to be in the back of the minds of the biblical authors, if not the front. The Bible refers to a divine council, which meets in a heavenly throne room.[20] So the idea of a heavenly throng begins right in the first chapter of Genesis: "Let *us* make humankind in *our* image" (emphasis added) and it continues through the scenarios of prophets who support their truth-claims by saying that they had eavesdropped on the very deliberations of this body.[21] This heavenly courtroom is the place from which cosmic messengers—in Hebrew, *mal'akim;* in Greek, *aggelos,* "angels"—are dispatched on errands. Some of these messengers, these angels, reveal messages to barren couples (Judges 13) or prophets (2 Kgs 1:3; Zechariah 4–5), deliver food to folks stranded in deserts (1 Kgs 19:4–9), or publish good tidings, that help is on the way, that God is not angry anymore, that happy days are here again.

Those are the kind of tasks that have angels energetically volunteering "Here am I, Lord; send me."[22] The Bible also mentions "evil messengers," not in the sense that they are evil—they are simply following orders—but in the sense that they have unpleasant tasks.[23] These messengers conduct reconnaissance of cities whose noisome evil has disturbed the peace, the *shalom* (Gen 18:1–19:24). They trail behind when God marches out to war, dealing out "plague and pestilence" even after the battle is over (Lev 26:25, Dt 32:23–24, Hab 3:5). These messengers whisper bad advice into the ears of false prophets and vain kings, just to mess with them (1 Kgs 22:19–23; 2 Kgs 19:7). In a vision of Ezekiel, these messengers mark idolaters in Jerusalem for execution (Ezek 9:1–11).

The Bible sometimes refers to the ranks of this heavenly host as *benay elohim,* "sons of God," that is, "[minor] divine beings" (Gen 6:2, 4; Job 1:6, 2:1, 38:7; Ps 25:1; 82:6, 89:7). Most are anonymous. A few, such as Michael (Dan 10:13, 21; 12:1) and Gabriel (Dan 8:16, 9:21), are named. Most of these heavenly lackeys and gofers do whatever tasks they are assigned. A few, such as the Cherubim, who guard cosmic boundaries such as the gates of Paradise (Gen 3:24; Ezek 28:14) and the Inner Sanctum of Solomon's Temple in Jerusalem (1 Kgs 6:23), and "Goodness" and "Mercy," who providentially guard the steps of those who walk the path of righteousness (Ps 23:6), develop specialties. There are two heavenly beings, however, with very specialized portfolios who deserve particular attention: *Mashit*, the Destroyer, and *hassatan*, the Adversary.

The Destroyer

Mashit is a menacing agent unleashed by God to kill large numbers of people, usually by inflicting a plague. In this context, the Destroyer distinctly appears in three passages: Ex 12:23, 2 Sam 24:16, and 1 Chr 21:15, each of which is discussed briefly below. They point to a macabre shadow-side of God, to the type of primeval maliciousness that inundated Noah's world and toppled Babel's ziggurat.

The first biblical reference to "the Destroyer" appears in Ex 12:23. Here the LORD sends ten plagues upon Egypt in order to pressure Pharaoh to release the enslaved Hebrew people. The final plague, the death of all Egyptian firstborns, makes the hail of frogs and swarms of locusts look like child's play. Cecil B. DeMille's film *The Ten Commandments* vividly portrays the Destroyer moving through the neighborhoods of Egypt, striking houses that do not bear a mark of lamb's blood on their doors and "passing over" (hence the term "Passover") the houses of the Hebrews who had marked their doors in this ritual way. What the film does not make clear is that the Destroyer does not act alone. Indeed, the Bible tells us that the Destroyer has a handler:

> For the LORD will pass through and strike down the Egyptians; when he sees the blood on the lintel and on the two doorposts, the LORD will pass over that door and will not allow the [D]estroyer (*Mashit*) to enter your houses and strike you down. (Ex 12:23)

Yhwh and his Terminator-like accomplice complete their mission. Perhaps the most frightening aspect of this is that it is *Yhwh* who controls this cosmic devourer. There is a similar scene in the book of Ezekiel, where one heavenly messenger inscribes an "*X*" on the foreheads of the righteous (Ezek 9:4).[24] Only those with such a mark are spared execution—"destruction" according to Ezek 9:6, the verb that corresponds to the noun "Destroyer"—at the hand of avenging angels (Ezek 9:1–11). The term "Destroyer" is not used in Ezekiel but the cognate verb is. And the modus operandi is the same as in the Passover account in Exodus. Neither the Destroyer in Exodus nor "the Seven" in Ezekiel get paid to make decisions, accept plea bargains, or trifle with details.[25] These agents of divine punishment are mute, unfeeling, and murderous. They can be trained, just barely, to recognize the most basic binary symbols—marked, unmarked—but once they are released from their cages or unleashed from their restraints, they dumbly, numbly fulfill their contract.[26]

The Destroyer also appears in 2 Sam 24:16 and 1 Chron 21:15: Yhwh, who commissions all disasters (and our idiom for hurricanes and floods as "acts of God" reflects this) and authors all woes, is reported to have sent plagues in both of these biblical reports about the same incident. The plague was punishment for a sin committed by David, namely ordering a population census.

> So the LORD sent a pestilence on Israel from that morning until the appointed time; and seventy thousand of the people died, from Dan to Beersheba. (2 Sam 24:15)

We will debate neither the historicity nor the ethics of this account. The priests and prophets who justified the ways of God to Israel were perennially suspicious of royal trespasses into their sphere. Behind the royal census were governmental designs for taxation and conscription. The religious leaders in ancient Israel championed contrasting practices, the tithe under priestly control and the muster of troops behind prophetically inspired judges. We also must always remember the deep logic of monotheism: If God was the author of weal and woe, then God was ultimately responsible for pestilence. That leads to the next link in the chain of casuistry: Why did God send the disaster? It was the job of religious leaders to divine the order in this chaos. In this case, one specialist probably came up with the diagnosis that carried the day: The germ of this communicable disease resulted from David's attempt to take a census.

To continue with the story in 2 Samuel 24, the agent or harbinger of the catastrophe is described through several terms: as "pestilence" (or "Pestilence"), as "the angel" (*mal'ak*), as "the angel who was bringing destruction" (*ham-mal'ak hammashit*), and as the "smiting angel." It takes only a small amount of linguistic flexibility to allow that "the destroying angel" of 2 Samuel 24 is referring to the same figure known in Exodus 12 as "the Destroyer."

The text of 1 Chronicles narrates the same story as that of 2 Samuel 24: A Davidic census leads Yhwh to send Pestilence/an angel/the destroying angel against Israel. In 2 Chr 21:16, however, we are treated to a few more details. For example, the physical appearance of this angel is described, as gigantic and brandishing a sword:

> David looked up and saw the angel of the LORD standing between earth and heaven, and in his hand a drawn sword stretched out over Jerusalem. (1 Chr 21:16)

For now it is enough to emphasize what these stories have in common: the description of the Destroyer or the Destroying Angel whose specialty is indiscriminate slaughter, under divine control. But there is an additional astounding difference between the two accounts of David's misguided census. The text of 1 Chronicles 21, for the most part faithful to the earlier version of the story in 2 Samuel 24, includes a change whose theological implications dwarf even the gigantic Angel of Death. For while the story in 2 Samuel 24 begins

> And the anger of the LORD was kindled against Israel, and he [i.e., the LORD] incited David . . . [to] count the people (2 Sam 24:1)

the parallel account in 1 Chronicles 21, written several centuries later, begins

> Satan stood up against Israel and incited David to count the people. (1 Chr 21:1)

This change sends a small shiver down our spines: Here he is, directly in our sights, Satan, *hassatan,* the Adversary, being given responsibility for an action that the Bible had previously attributed to the LORD.

Personifications, Epithets, and Euphemisms

For the most part, the biblical portraits of angelic characters remain shadowy and insubstantial, as if they were impossible to dispense with altogether but undeserving of focused attention. The primary focus of the Hebrew Bible is on the supreme God. Yet God too remains clothed in mystery. One way the Bible expresses a kind of deferential reticence about using the name "God" or "the LORD" is to change, within a single account, the terms used for the heavenly ambassador. For instance, in Gen 32:22–32, the famous account of Jacob's encounter with an opponent at the river Jabbok, the otherworldly figure is described in successive lines first as a man and then as God. And throughout the Hebrew Bible, we have accounts that in one line refer to the angel of the LORD and in the next—talking about the precisely same subject—as the LORD God himself.[27]

According to author Rivkah Schärf Klüger, the phrase *mal'ak Yhwh,* "the angel of the LORD," was a figurative expression, a way to express "the side of Yahweh turned toward man . . . but only one side, one aspect of his being."[28] That the Bible is characteristically vague in its descriptions of these figures is perplexing. It is often not clear whether the cosmic agent is an independent being, an aspect of Yhwh, or something in between.

Whereas other ancient Near Eastern religions describe divine functionaries in unambiguous terms, the biblical writers, more often than not, present an ambiguous portrait of them. These minor cosmic beings were so embedded in popular lore that they could not be excised from the accounts penned by biblical writers. At the same time, however, they were unworthy of detailed treatments and of expanded narratives. We should note that outside the official canon, in the extrabiblical Jewish literature we discuss in chapter 5, certain Jewish groups were very interested in the angels, in their origins, names, and functions. It may have been that discourse about angels was eschewed only in the official religion, reflected in the writings of biblical prophets and scribes.

Another category of indirect speech about God is the rich repertoire of epithets used in the Hebrew Bible to indirectly refer to the deity, such as the Name (*Shem*), the Glory (*Kabod*), and, in postbiblical Jewish literature, the Presence (*Shekinah*).[29] These are divine traits that become terms of veneration in their own right, and can be addressed or spoken about as if they were entities. Other similar traits—or "hypostases"—are almost reminiscent of what we would today call the dissociative states of a sociopath: "the Wrath [of the LORD]" (Dt 29:20; Jer 4:4, 21:12; Ezek 5:13, 7:19), "the Arm" (Ex 15:16; Dt 4:34; Isa 30:30, 51:9), "the Hand" (Dt 2:15, Judg 2:15), and "the Sword" (ouch!) (Isa 34:5–6; Jer 12:12, 47:6).

As we will see, over time descriptions of these unattractive aspects began to move farther and farther from the core of the divine personality. In Ex 34:6–7, Yhwh saves and judges, extends mercy and exacts punishment. In the prophetic figures of speech just mentioned, it is Yhwh's "hand" or "arm," an element on the periphery of the divine form that performs the punishing functions. Ultimately, this impulse eventually leads to Yhwh's disassociation from many of the unpleasant but necessary tasks of world management and the assignation of these functions instead to a separate being, Satan.

Repellent Aspects of Yhwh

The subject of this book leads us, again and again, to examine the most peculiar and distasteful aspects of the Bible and its God. Many readers over the centuries (and certainly most in our own) are appalled by the holy wars under divine directive in the books of Joshua and Judges. Our generation would not to be first to ask if everyone of Noah's generation deserved to die in the Flood (Gen 6:5–13). Or could not God find ten righteous folks in Sodom and Gomorrah, the kind who would take in strangers and give an honest measure in the bazaar (Gen 18:22–32). We could go on and on about the barbarities and subethical goings-on commissioned by God in the pages of Holy Writ: laws that condone slavery and subjugate women; religious attitudes that suggest that foreigners are subhuman and their cultural practices polluted.[30]

Interpretive strategies developed by ethically sensitive Jews and Christians allow believers to separate the wheat from the chaff in their faiths and build humanitarian programs out of ethically ambiguous materials. Modern folks who require a pure religion, uncontaminated by gross misunderstandings and shameful eras, will have to build one from scratch. The sad truth is that any religion with deep roots in human history has a checkered past.

Ancient readers had their own complaints with the God of the Bible, although those complaints may have been different from ours. For example, it is doubtful that many Judahites were troubled by the accounts of holy wars in Joshua. Their Patriarch could become quite riled up if his people's welfare were at stake. The LORD is a *gibbor*, a hero, a warrior, according to Ex 15:3. But was the Exile fair, as Second Isaiah hints and the book of Job indirectly asks?[31] Did God booby-trap the law, as Ezekiel suggested, making it impossible to follow and so easy to misunderstand, just to expose the people's ineptitude?

> Moreover I gave them statutes that were not good and ordinances by which they could not live. I defiled them through their very gifts, in their offering up all their firstborn, in order that I might horrify them, so that they might know that I am the LORD. (Ezek 20:25–26)

Did God use people, as Jeremiah claimed he had been, to accomplish tasks with no concern for their personal welfare?

> O LORD, you have enticed me,
> and I was enticed;
> you have overpowered me,
> and you have prevailed.
> I have become a laughing-stock all day long;
> everyone mocks me.
> For whenever I speak, I must cry out,
> I must shout, 'Violence and destruction!'
> For the word of the LORD has become for me
> a reproach and derision all day long. (Jer 20:7–8)

And how many laments and psalms echo some variant on "Why?" "How long?" and "Where are you?"

So it is a matter of perspective: What is it about Yhwh that is inscrutable and capricious, or cruel and vain? Is it his tendency to play favorites (as with Jacob, Joseph, and David) or his sudden impulse to extend compassion to foreigners who never earned his love in the first place (this is Jonah's complaint)? It does seem safe, however, to say this: Even if the nature of the complaint differs, according to time and place, every generation that has, like Jacob, wrestled with the LORD (Gen 32:22–32) has experienced some form of dislocation.

It might be helpful to stand back and look at biblical religion from the detached perspective of the history of religions. If we look at biblical faith alongside its contemporary religions of the ancient world, we cannot help but observe that Yhwh came up the hard way.[32] The biblical God first emerged in written records in the late Bronze Age and "his" best-known portraits, in the Five Books of Moses, were sketched during the Iron Age. It has taken centuries of attention from, first, priestly and prophetic stylists and, later, rabbinic and scholastic salonists to make this deity presentable in polite company.

Yhwh began among the ranks of the warrior deities of the eastern Mediterranean and Near East, a rival of gods like Zeus, Baal, Hadad, and Marduk. Yhwh in those days appeared with all the subtlety of a violent thunderstorm.

> The God of glory thunders, . . .
> The voice of the LORD is powerful . . .
> The voice of the LORD flashes forth flames of fire.
> The voice of the LORD shakes the wilderness,
> The voice of the LORD causes the oaks to whirl,
> and strips the forest bare. (Ps 29:3–9)

It took prophets such as Elijah to soften this image into "a still, small voice," as in the account of his experience on Mount Horeb:

> And, behold, the LORD passed by, and a great and strong wind rent the mountains, and brake in pieces the rocks before the LORD, but the LORD was not in the wind: and after the wind an earthquake; but the LORD was not in the earthquake: and after the earthquake a fire; but the LORD was not in the fire: and after the fire a still small voice. (1 Kgs 19:11–12, KJV)

It took generations of priests and prophets to translate the "voice of God"—in Hebrew, *qol elohim,* their idiom for thunder—into sentences of ethical imperatives and paragraphs of fluid case laws.

From this perspective, it is remarkable that Yhwh ever made it from the ranks of Semitic warrior deities to become, in Judaism, *Melech HaOlam,*

"King of the Universe," and, in Christianity, *Pater Noster,* "Our Father." As it turns out, there was more to Yhwh than the ancients knew. Yhwh was more than another thunder-clapping, zephyr-snorting storm god and more than a territorial clan godfather zealously protective of his people and honor. Still, these early features in the portrait of the biblical God were not deleted but remained and remain active in the tradition. The biblical writers, for whatever reasons, did not attempt to candy-coat or suppress God's unsavory side. The God in the still, small voice remained free to return in a whirlwind in the book of Job. The divine superhero warrior God remained free to retake the field, bearing the epithet "Lamb," to combat the Red Dragon in the book of Revelation. This is the unsystematic but potent nature of the God we discover in the Bible.

Moving Forward

As we move to examine in some detail the biblical passages that directly refer to Satan, we carry from this chapter the conditioning factors that led to his birth and growth. Prophetic monotheism, always more honored in theory than in practice, was a profound idea, a cosmic unified field theory. But it is unclear how long this insight, championed by the Hebrew prophets from at least the ninth century B.C.E. and classically isolated by Second Isaiah in the laboratory of sixth century Exile, remained stable once it was exposed to real-life conditions. As if the One were not enough, a number of mediator figures began to emerge in postexilic biblical writings, including Wisdom, the archangels Michael and Gabriel, and the Adversary, *hassatan.*

Another seed from which the idea of Satan took root was the tangled and prolific jungle of cosmic lackeys, murderous spirits, and shadowy personifications that populate the margins of the Bible. These bits and pieces of myth and folklore that never amounted to much on their own were capable of being combined, over time, into single terrifying incarnations of malevolence, their ranks organized into demonic legions. Eventually, the jumbled lore about these characters was capable of being sorted into stories about primeval cosmic rebellions, fallen angels, and spheres of influence.

The triumph of monotheism and the complicated plentitude of Yhwh, author of weal and woe, sketches the profile of a deity one might think was hard to get close to, although millions have. For some of the people all of the time, and for all of the people some of the time, the immeasurable breadth of this span of divine aspect would prove to be a stretch. The fall-back position, known in psychology as projection, was to deny repellent aspects of the divine personality and ascribe them to another being, or to remove unpleasant but necessary functions from the divine portfolio—say the intrusive moral audits of human virtue and the sending of plagues—and assign them to a cosmic being other than God. Indeed, a single figure will be assigned both roles: that of cosmic attorney general, assayer of moral mettle, "Devil's advocate" in building the case-against when it is time to see what the superficially righteous are made of, and that of death-dealer (as in 1 Chr 21:1). The name of this figure is Satan.

chapter 3

the devil is
in the details

Satan in the Hebrew Bible

We may not pay Satan reverence, for that would be indiscreet, but we can at least respect his talents.

—*Mark Twain*

As we have already pointed out, the triumph of prophetic monotheism was a slow and evolutionary process and not without its share of problems. It is clear that the shift from many gods to a singular Lord of the Universe gives rise to an existential frustration among God's chosen people as they grapple with the reality of a God who creates both weal and woe. It would appear that, over time, an exorcism of sorts takes place; the negative aspects of Yhwh are cast out and assigned to alternative beings, such as the Destroyer (*Mashit*), the "smiting angel" (*hammal'ak hammashit*), and, of course, *hassatan*. Eventually it is *hassatan*, "the Adversary," who will become the embodiment of evil, but this, too, is a slow, evolutionary process, with many more twists and turns to explore.

We have seen that in the Hebrew Bible, the Adversary is still a mere youth, a heavenly "minor," one of the benign sons of God, his career just beginning. Indeed, the elusive Satan is not yet fully formed; we catch only brief glimpses and cannot yet bring him into focus. Even his traditional accoutrements—horns, tail, red color, pitchfork, and hellish abode (an amalgamation of appurtenances borrowed from a legion of adversaries from many cultures) would not materialize for centuries. It is almost as if Satan lurks outside the house, rattling the windowpanes and peering inside, but never actually crosses the threshold. Who would have guessed: Innocuous little Satan, who begins as one of the gaggle of Yhwh's adoring footmen, someday becomes the concierge of a fiery postmortem torture chamber.

Although the Satan of later imagination is generally absent in the Hebrew Bible, there are tantalizing clues that hint at his future metamorphosis. These clues act as signposts on a circuitous path that leads us away from Satan's role as divine lackey to that of a malevolent, independent being with his own agenda.

In this chapter, we investigate the specific references to the term "Satan" in the Hebrew Bible. Generally speaking, "Satan" appears there both as a terrestrial adversary and as a celestial one. We begin with the former. Here at the end of the chapter, we move to a different but related subject. There are two other motifs in the Hebrew Bible that play a role in the development of Satan, although they lack a specific reference to the name "satan" or "*hassatan*" themselves. Those two motifs are "the serpent," first introduced in Genesis 3 and later associated with the Devil, and the child-devouring deity Molech, a Phoenician/Canaanite deity mentioned in the Bible who also came to be associated with the Devil in some traditions.

Satan as a Terrestrial Adversary

Four out of the five appearances of the term "satan" in reference to an earthly adversary occur in biblical passages associated with King David or his son, Solomon. David, the quintessential Renaissance man—the sensitive musician warrior king—is a towering biblical figure, who, despite his many flaws (in particular, his predilection for other men's wives) is nonetheless favored by the LORD. In fact, David is favored to such a degree that he and his kingship become the proverbial yardstick by which all future kings are to be measured. Unfortunately, few are able to measure up, not even his own son and successor, King Solomon, the visionary architect of the first-ever temple to Yhwh (who sadly shares his father's weakness for "forbidden women"—although in Solomon's case, this means, foreign women).

Satan's first appearance is in 1 Samuel 29 in one of the so-called Davidic outlaw tales. These tales—an Iron Age anticipation of the Wiley Coyote and Road Runner cartoons—feature a paranoid King Saul (Israel's first king) pursuing an upstart David in a vain attempt to eliminate the competition, which is what paranoid kings did in those days. The ever-resourceful David, however, always manages to stay one step ahead of his pursuer. And, although he could have killed Saul on more than one occasion (David once happened upon Saul in the very vulnerable position of relieving himself in a cave—the king was, at it were, on his proverbial throne), for a variety of reasons, David chooses to remain on the run.

In any case, because of Saul's vendetta, David decides to hide himself among Israel's most hated enemy, the Philistines (the enemy of my enemy is my friend). David pretends to be a turncoat, and even fights alongside the Philistines in several battles. When it is clear that a battle is brewing between the Philistines and Israelites and, however, the Philistine commanders become concerned about David's loyalty. It is all well and good to have David fight with them against mutual enemies, but would he bear arms against his own people? This is a legitimate concern, given the fact that David was once considered one of Israel's most courageous and cunning soldiers. And so, fearful that the mercenary David will turn against them when confronted with warfare against his kinsmen, the Philistines demand that David be sent away, lest "he become an adversary [*satan*] to us in the battle" (1 Sam 29:4).

Used in this way, the word "satan" is simply a noun meaning "adversary" within a military context.[1] It is a way of suggesting that David's presence among the Philistines might be a stumbling block (another definition of "satan") to victory in the battle against Israel.

In 2 Sam 19:17–24, the term "satan" is also used to indicate a human adversary. David, now king of Israel, returns to Jerusalem after defeating his own son, the rebellious Absalom, in battle. As David approaches the city, he is greeted by Shimei, an old man who seeks absolution from David for doing the unthinkable: cursing the king. Sometime earlier, during the conflict between David and Absalom, David was forced to flee the city. At that time, Shimei, clearly aligned with Absalom, hurled stones at David and cursed him (2 Sam 16:1–14). With the defeat of Absalom and the restoration of David's kingship, however, Shimei regrets his actions and prudently begs for forgiveness.

Although David may be inclined simply to "forgive and forget," his nephew (and bodyguard), Abishai, has other ideas. Abishai, himself a member of the royal court, does not easily forget Shimei's disrespectful behavior. In fact, Abishai suggests to David that Shimei be put to death for cursing the king. David, for whom *Realpolitik* always takes precedence over honor feuds, responds: "What have I to do with you . . . that you should today become an adversary [*satan*] to me?" (2 Sam 19:22). Some scholars assert that David's use of the word "satan" should be understood in the context of a *legal accuser* because Abishai is actually a member of the royal court and therefore assumes the functional role of accuser (or prosecutor). Furthermore, Abishai's accusation is justified: Shimei *did* curse the king.[2]

This position is compelling in this particular context, but it seems more likely that David's response indicates that *Abishai*—not Shimei—has become an adversary [*satan*] to David for suggesting the execution of an old man (who is clearly not a threat to David or his kingship) in the first place. David has more important things to worry about right now, and Abishai's suggestion is a distraction. Used in this way, the term "satan" is little more than an epithet; that is, David is essentially telling his nephew, "You are a troublemaker" (another meaning of the word "satan").

A similar use of the word "satan" appears in the books of Kings, where the term is used as a way to refer to one's enemies but also as a means to designate adversaries sent by God to harass King Solomon. King Solomon, who ascends the throne following David's death, is perhaps best known for building the First Temple. In 1 Kgs 5:4, Solomon requests that King Hiram of Tyre (in southern Lebanon) send workers to help Israel build the Temple. Solomon notes that the Temple could not be built during his father's reign because David was too preoccupied with the defense of his nascent nation. Solomon, however, is not plagued with such issues and reports, "the LORD my God has given me rest on every side; there is neither adversary [*satan*] nor misfortune" (1 Kgs 5:4). In essence, there are no vexing adversaries [*satans*] to threaten Solomon's building campaign, so now seems to be the ideal time for constructing a temple to the LORD. Put simply, the mention of "satan" is this passage is generic and refers to any potential enemy of Israel.

Although the "satan" in 1 Kgs 5:4 is nonspecific, the term "satan" in 1 Kgs 11:14 is used to refer to specific individuals sent by Yhwh to cause trouble for King Solomon: "Then the LORD raised up an adversary [*satan*] against Solomon, Hadad the Edomite; he was of the royal house in Edom."[3] Here Hadad of Edom is "a satan" to Solomon. We really do not know very much about Hadad of Edom, other than the fact that he fled to Egypt after he was defeated in a battle with David. Hadad returns to Edom during Solomon's reign (1 Kgs 11:14–22, 25b), probably still in pain from wounds inflicted by David—which, of course, would give him good reason to despise Solomon, David's son. Apparently, the feeling was mutual.

The second adversary mentioned is Rezon:

> God raised up another adversary [*satan*] against Solomon, Rezon son of Eliada. He was an adversary [*satan*] of Israel all the days of Solomon, making trouble as Hadad did; he despised Israel and reigned over Aram. (1 Kgs 11:23; 25)

Not much is known about Rezon either, except that he seems to be the leader of a band of outlaws and is an even bigger troublemaker than Hadad. Interestingly, during the period between the final writings of the Hebrew Bible and the initial writings of the New Testament, Satan is also described as the leader of a legion of outlaws who wreak havoc and cause trouble for individuals and groups of people.

What is most compelling about 1 Kings 11, however, is not the historical background of Hadad or Rezon but the fact that it is *God* who stirs up these adversaries [*satans*] against Solomon. Modern (and we assume, ancient) readers might logically wonder why God would do such a thing. Even a casual reading of Kings, however, reveals that God indeed has probable cause.

Apparently, Solomon instigates the divine harassment through his own unrestrained sexual proclivities. Yet Solomon is not punished simply because he is a ladies' man. (As we mentioned, so was David.) Indeed, the Bible is not so prudish as to deny the kings of Judah their harems. The problem is Solomon's *foreign* wives:

> King Solomon loved many foreign women, along with the daughter of Pharaoh: Moabite, Ammonite, Edomite, Sidonian, and Hittite women; from the nations of which the LORD had said to the Israelites, "You shall not enter into marriage with them, neither shall they with you; for surely they will incline your heart to follow their gods." (1 Kgs 11:1–2)

Their foreignness is not the issue (after all, David's own grandmother Ruth was a Moabite); the problem with mixed marriages during this time is that wives often bring their religious background with them. A foreign wife, such as the Moabite Ruth, who converted ("your God will be my God," Ruth 1:16), poses no problem. But the Bible tells us that Solomon's wives lead the king's heart astray and that he even worships—right alongside his foreign wives—strange (and forbidden) gods and goddesses (1 Kgs 11:1–8). It is not surprising then, that jealous Yhwh flexes his muscle and sends a few troublemakers (*satans*) to stir things up a little for Solomon. Granted, it is not exactly a horse's head in the bed, but the sending of adversaries is designed as a warning: shape up, or else.

The final "earthly" appearance of Satan in the Hebrew Bible occurs in Psalm 109[4]:

> Do not be silent, O God of my praise.
> For wicked and deceitful mouths are opened against me,
> speaking against me with lying tongues.
> They beset me with words of hate,
> and attack me without cause.
> In return for my love they *accuse* [emphasis, added] me,
> even while I make prayer for them.
> So they reward me evil for good,
> and hatred for my love.
> They say, "Appoint a wicked man against him;
> let an accuser [*satan*] stand on his right." (Ps 109:1–6)

In Psalm 109, the writer (or psalmist) seeks deliverance from slanderous enemies who falsely accuse him (Ps 109:4) and thus incur his extended curse (Ps 109:6–19). The role of *satan* in Psalm 109 seems to be in the context of a legal proceeding in which the psalmist envisions his enemies facing charges of slander.[5] In this way, the *satan* in Psalm 109 is similar in context to the *satan* of the other four passages.

Although all the references to the term "satan" reviewed thus far (1 Sam 29:4; 2 Sam 19:17–24; 1 Kings 5:4; 11:14, 23, 25; Ps 109:1–6) vary in context and meaning—from a purely legal or military figure, to a violator of the divine will—all of these passages refer to beings in the terrestrial realm. These earthly satans hardly resemble our modern understanding of Satan. But, there is another *satan* who appears in the heavenly realm, and it is to this celestial *satan* that we now turn.

Satan as an Angelic Adversary

Balaam's Smart Ass

The story of Balaam and the ass (Num 22:22–35) marks the first appearance of a nonhuman *satan* in the Hebrew Bible. In later stories, Satan is the grand chameleon and assumes many forms. In this account from the book of Numbers, however, we should still understand the term "satan" in the lower case. In other words, *satan* in the Balaam story does not refer to the Devil, who in pre-exilic biblical narratives does not yet exist.

Balaam, a legendary Jordanian prophet known from extrabiblical sources, incurs God's wrath because he undertakes a journey that is in opposition to the divine will (Num 22:22).[6] In anger, God sends a sword-brandishing messenger (*mal'ak Yhwh*, or "Angel of the LORD," whom we first met in chapter 2) to block Balaam's path. Even though Balaam was a renowned seer in ancient Syrian legends, he gets portrayed as a blind buffoon in the Hebrew scriptures, whose writers, by and large, regard foreign visionaries as quacks (Num 22:23). Balaam is unable to see the angel blocking his path. Fortunately, his astute donkey spies the angel and maneuvers Balaam out of the way and into a nearby field—a saving action that is rewarded by a whipping from her ungrateful, unknowing, unseeing master (Num 22:23), who is angry because their journey has been sidetracked. Balaam cannot see the angel and therefore thinks the donkey is merely being "mulish."

Not easily deterred, the angel blocks the narrow pathway into which Balaam has guided the donkey in an effort to resume his journey, and once more, the ass makes a defensive move to spare her master from the angelic impediment (Num 22:24–25). Unfortunately, the donkey's maneuver results in a minor injury to Balaam's foot, for which the donkey is again beaten (Num 22:25). Ever persistent, the angel reappears, this time successfully blocking the donkey's travel through a narrow passage (Num 22: 26). The donkey, admitting defeat, simply lays down, thus incurring yet another beating from her master (Num 22:27).[7]

It is at this point that the LORD opens the donkey's mouth so that she can finally address her abusive master: "What have I done to you that you have struck me these three times?" (Num 22:28). Not seeming to find a talking donkey at all unusual (which rather calls into question his sobriety), Balaam instead launches into a defense of his brutality, indicating that, had he had a sword in hand, the poor beast would have been slaughtered (Num 22:29). Whereupon the donkey reminds Balaam of her faithful service to him: "Am I not your donkey, which you have ridden all your life to this day? Have I been in the habit of treating you this way?" (Num 22:30). Balaam concedes that the donkey has been a good animal, and then the LORD opens his eyes so that he, too, is able to view the sword-wielding messenger (Num 22:31). At this, Balaam falls to the ground, even as the angel takes him to task for his brutish behavior toward the donkey and proceeds to reveal that he (the angel, or *mal'ak*), has "come forth as *a satan* [emphasis added] because Balaam's journey was undertaken hastily" (Num 22:32–33). Balaam admits his guilt, pleads ignorance, and is allowed to continue on his journey under the condition that he speak only when he is told to do so (Num 22:34–35).

What is most striking about the *satan* in this particular narrative is the way in which he functions as a literal obstacle or stumbling block, as the term implies. So, in a very real sense, the story of Balaam's ass supports the notion that Satan is always a character of opposition; indeed, this is his primary role in the Bible and beyond.

Hassatan in the Book of Job

The book of Job is perhaps the Bible's most bizarre masterpiece. Readers both ancient and modern cannot help being moved to ask the eternal question, "Is God fair?" a question that brings us right back to the question of theodicy.[8] Job, a faithful and pious man, is tested beyond human endurance. Despite his faithfulness to the LORD, Job suffers unimaginable losses. First, Job is divested of his wealth and livelihood; next, his ten children all die in a freak storm; and finally, he suffers serious health problems that render him incapacitated. Job, a man who is described as "blameless and upright, one who feared the LORD and turned away from evil" (Job 1:1), is a good, just man and certainly does not deserve such suffering. Perhaps that is why centuries of devout Christians and Jews have turned to Job in times of personal crisis. Not so much for answers (for the reasons for Job's suffering—or, indeed, suffering in general—is never fully explained in the story) but for comfort. Job's undeserved pain speaks to the heart of all those who have loved and lost—to the countless souls who have cast questioning eyes to the heavens for answers as to why the just must suffer—and to those who want to hold onto their faith when reason tells them it is all a sham.

Assuming that the book of Job was written after the Exile, somewhere between 530 and 400 B.C.E., it represented a way for a Hebrew dissident to wrestle with the question of whether God had treated Israel justly.[9] Such a question could not be addressed directly—or if someone did, that story did not get by the scribal sentries guarding the contents of the canon. Instead, the author of Job gave us a hypothetical, a fairy-tale-like story about a legendary character who suffered unjustly. But although the Job of the story was from the land of Uz, and its main character was a kind of Jordanian Abraham, we cannot help but think of him as the Hebrew Everyman, grappling with the question of God's fairness.[10]

Why are we so preoccupied with the book of Job in a book about Satan? Because the most developed and sustained appearance of the cosmic troublemaker, *hassatan* (Satan's direct biblical ancestor) is found in the book of Job.[11] And here, *hassatan*'s role is to test the integrity of a righteous man, to find out what this model of patriarchal piety is really made of.

The action in the story shifts between the earthly realm and God's heavenly abode; causing misery and creating mayhem, *hassatan* moves with ease between both spheres. We first meet *hassatan* at a gathering of the heavenly council: "One day the heavenly beings came to present themselves before the LORD and Satan [*hassatan*] also came among them" (Job 1:6). At first glance, *hassatan* appears to be simply one more member of the heavenly court, one of "the sons of God," the divine courtiers assembled in the throne room of the cosmic monarch.[12]

"Where have you come from?" (Job 1:7), God asks *hassatan*. *Hassatan* replies: "From going to and fro on the earth, and from walking up and down on it" (Job 1:7). *Hassatan*, it appears, has a special function in the divine government: to audit human virtue. *Hassatan* does not seem to be stirring up trouble on earth—at least not yet—but merely reporting in to his supervisor.[13]

God's next question, however, changes the dynamic and launches the subsequent tragedy.

> "Have you considered my servant, Job? There is no one like him on earth, a
> blameless and upright man who fears God and turns away from evil." (Job 1:8)

Remember: This is God talking. God invites the Adversary, the cosmic attorney general, to open a file on Job. And God cannot resist bragging about his favored one, his apparent "pet."[14]

As in many scripts, the villain's lines are the most memorable: "Does Job fear God for nothing?" *hassatan* asks God (Job 1:9). The "fear of God" in the Hebrew sense does not mean that Job is afraid of God; rather, it denotes awe, loyalty, and respect for God. *Hassatan* assumes Job's piety is less than heroic. After all, it is easy to love and worship God if one has a charmed life, one abundantly blessed by good fortune.[15] *Hassatan*'s subsequent rhetorical question goes straight to the heart of the matter: "Does Job fear God for naught," for nothing, for free? As far as *hassatan* is concerned, the answer is obviously no. Job fears God because virtue and piety have proved profitable for him. Job's lavish abundance has not escaped the Troublemaker's notice, and so *hassatan* addresses the LORD:

> "Have you not put a fence around him and his house and all that he has on
> every side? You have blessed the work of his hands, and his possessions have
> increased in the land." [16] (Job 1:10)

The term "fence" in the above mentioned text reminds us that Job is the recipient of God's special protection.[17] Metaphorical "fences" include Job's family, estate, and social standing, all of which have made him impregnable, protecting his serene patriarchal life from chaos. His life of humane generosity means that he has plenty of capital in the social "favor bank" on which to draw should the need arise. As for Job's credit with God, consider what Job 1:5 suggests:

> [H]e would rise early in the morning and offer burnt offerings according to the number of . . . all [his children]; for Job said, "It may be that my children have sinned and cursed God in their hearts." This is what Job always did.

Every morning Job rises before dawn and performs ritual on behalf of his children. With cultic mortar and pestle, Job mixes good medicine for his children each morning to inoculate them against divine punishment. Job's credit with the Almighty is so good that his children could draw on it.

Job's world is safe and protected, his "fences" secure—that is, until the Troublemaker, *hassatan,* offers a challenge to God to remove those fences, to see what Job is made of behind all that insulation. "But stretch out your hand now and touch all that he has, and he will curse you to your face" (Job 1:11), *hassatan* volleys back to God.[18] And so the great game begins. God allows *hassatan* to remove Job's fences. But *hassatan* is prohibited, in the first round at least, from one move: *Hassatan* is not permitted to harm Job himself (Job 1:12).

One by one the fences fall: Job's livestock are stolen by raiders, his herds and field hands are incinerated in a brushfire, his camels and stablehands are lost to a marauding band; finally, unspeakably, Job's ten children, assembled for a family occasion, die in a tornado (Job 1:13–19).

Job's reaction to the complete ruination of his life reflects the grief customs of his day: He tears his garment, shaves his head, falls to the ground, and affirms God's sovereignty (Job 1:20–21)[19]:

> "Naked I came from my mother's womb, and naked shall I return there; the LORD gave, and the LORD has taken away; blessed be the name of the LORD." (Job 1:22)

Job, it seems, had been preparing for this crisis every day of his life. He was truly righteous, he was like a tree planted by the waters and he would not be moved (cf. Ps 1:1–3), not by any loss, no matter how tragic. Job could put it all in perspective, somehow, and stay on the path of righteousness. Hence, Job passed the first test and God won round one of the contest.

There is an interesting connection between Job's first test and the 2005 film, *Constantine*. The film, based on the comic book, *Hellblazer*, features the adventures of a supernatural detective, John Constantine, played by the actor Keanu Reeves. John Constantine acts as a sort of superhero exorcist, ridding the world of nefarious demons who possess unsuspecting humans and threaten world security. Although there are other connections between Satan's story and *Constantine* (we explore these in later chapters) one particular connection deserves brief mention. In the film, God and Satan make a wager for the souls of humans and each agree that these souls may be won through influence, rather than through physical contact.

Such a wager is reminiscent of the first agreement between God and *hassatan* in first round of Job's testing: "The Lord said to *hassatan*, 'Very well, all that he [Job] has is in your power; only do not stretch out your hand against him!'"(Job 1:12). In Job's case, the initial agreement proves to be temporary.

Round two follows the same pattern, but this time *hassatan* will not be content to leave Job with any fences. God once again boasts, "Have you considered my servant Job? There is no one like him on earth, a blameless and upright man who fears God and turns ways from evil" (Job 2:3; 1:8). The repetition serves to heighten the tension between God and the Adversary, and the reader cannot help but wince at the fact that God's victory is at Job's expense.

God apparently blames *hassatan* for Job's reversal of fortune: "He [Job] still persists in his integrity, although you [*hassatan*] incited me against him, to destroy him for no reason" (Job 2:3c), but careful readers should not buy these goods. It was *God* who provoked *hassatan* to consider Job in the first place, and it was *God* who granted *hassatan* permission to dismantle the structures of this righteous man's life.

Unhappy with the loss of the first round, *hassatan* seeks to score with a knockout in round two[20]:

Then Satan answered the LORD,
"Skin for skin! All that people have they will give to save their lives.
But stretch out your hand now and touch his bone and his flesh, and he will
curse you to your face."[21] (Job 2:4–5)

This is the final fence around Job's soul: his physical flesh, his bones, his skin.[22] And God agrees to these terms, with one important proviso: *Hassatan* may not take Job's life (Job 2:6).[23] Reminiscent of the first challenge, the Troublemaker once again departs the heavenly realm and returns to Job's earthly home (cf. Job 1:12 and 2:2).

Hassatan wastes no time in adding to Job's misery, inflicting "loathsome sores on Job from the sole of his foot to the crown of his head" (Job 2:7). There is little Job can do to ease his suffering. He sits in an ash pit, scraping his boils with a potsherd (Job 2:8).[24] Job, his skin peeling, flayed by *hassatan*, heroically passes this second test too. The text of Job 2:10 offers the official report: "In all this Job did not sin with his lips," although the wording of the final phrase ("with his lips") leaves this doorway into the remainder of the book of Job ajar. The rest of the book includes over thirty chapters of anguished conversation in which Job's three "friends," Eliphaz, Bildad, and Zophar, assert that, despite Job's protests of innocence, his suffering must be the result of sin. The normally patient and pious Job soon rages against the prevailing wisdom that we somehow get what we deserve, and he challenges God to offer an explanation. In response to Job's challenge, God makes a dramatic appearance in the whirlwind. God spends three chapters (Job 38–40) reminding Job of the wonders and mysteries of creation, effectively giving a nonanswer to the question Why? on the lips of countless suffering Jobs from the beginning of time.

Most germane for our purposes, however, is that the catalyst for all the early action, *hassatan*, the prosecutor who went off the deep end and enjoyed his job too much, disappears entirely after the initial scenes. The Adversary does not even return for a curtain call in the final chapter, Job 42, where a new crop of Job's children, last seen in Job 1 buried under a collapsed house, appear so that easily beguiled readers can go home with a smile.

Although Job 1:1–2:10 reveals the most complete portrait of Satan in the Hebrew Bible, it is clear that this figure is far from the demonic tempter who would later appear in the desert to test the spiritual mettle of Jesus in the Gospels. *Hassatan*'s function in the Prologue of Job seems merely to administer the tests, to aid the LORD by finding out if mortal virtue is more than skin deep. *Hassatan* does not act without the LORD's permission, and must play by the Almighty's rules. Maybe, *maybe* there is something more in the perverse energy and brilliance of *hassatan*'s machinations. This ancestor of Lucifer, the Adversary of Job 1–2, may have only limited powers, may have only a little light, but he is going to let it shine, shine, shine on the innermost depths of a good man. Who could stand up to such scrutiny? Job cannot. *Hassatan* may disappear from Job early on, but the image of the gleeful zeal with which he has prosecuted will live on in the imaginations of readers, like the grin of the Cheshire Cat.

Of course, the notion of being "tested" or "punished" by God is not an alien concept in the Bible.[25] But what is wholly different in this story of testing and misfortune is that God employs a lieutenant to carry it out. This marks a significant turning point in our exploration of Satan. We now have evidence of the satan figure acting on behalf of the deity, but just one step away from acting alone. For although *hassatan* in Job is still featured as a member of the heavenly court, he also appears to be a somewhat independent figure, roving the earth, wreaking havoc and disrupting the life of a good and pious man, and daring to make wagers with the Almighty himself. There is even a certain arrogance and audacity associated with this character—and if God is testing Job, one could just as easily argue that *hassatan* is testing God.

The Accuser Accused

The book of Zechariah is generally dated to around 520 B.C.E., making it roughly contemporaneous with the book of Job. The bulk of the book of Zechariah consists of eight nocturnal visions, the fourth of which includes the appearance of a figure called "the Satan" (Zech 3:1–7). Zechariah's prophecies are densely coded apocalyptic commentaries on the restoration program under way in Jerusalem following the Exile. These visions represent idealized pictures of a political reality: a future of shared political-priestly leadership. Israel would be ruled by both a king—from the line of David—and a priest in the LORD's service.[26] This unlikely alliance, however, would never come to fruition.

The setting in Zechariah 3, like much of the Prologue of Job, is in the heavenly realm at a gathering of the divine council: "Then he showed me the high priest Joshua standing before the angel of the Lord, and Satan standing at his right to accuse him" (Zech 3:1). We can see that this group, the heavenly council, includes the now-familiar "sons of God," the LORD, and *hassatan*, "the Accuser" or "the Adversary." In this depiction of the divine council's proceedings, the scene also includes a human being named Joshua, the very priest whom Zechariah hoped would serve as coregent in the new, postexilic regime.

It is clear that a cosmic court proceeding is under way, and the context suggests that we have joined the scene near its end. Zechariah's candidate has been the subject of an ancient version of a congressional hearing for presidential appointees. *Hassatan*'s role, we must assume, has been to act as "Devil's advocate," to probe and test and accuse and dig up whatever dirt he could on this candidate for high priest. The minutes of the proceeding have not been revealed in scripture. We enter the hall just in time to hear the LORD say, in effect, "Enough is enough."

> The LORD rebuke you, O Satan [i.e., *hassatan* the Adversary]!
> The LORD who has chosen Jerusalem rebuke you! (Zech 3:2)

The LORD continues his rebuke by adding: "Is not this man a brand plucked from the fire?" (Zech 3:2), which is God's way of pointing out that Joshua, who has already endured the suffering of the Exile, has been spared by God's favor.[27] According to Zech 3:3, Joshua "was dressed with filthy clothes." Since soiled clothing is probably a metaphor for individual or communal sin, we can assume that *hassatan* had at least scored a few points before God calls an end to the proceedings.

Another angel in the scene commands some other heavenly lackeys to remove Joshua's filthy clothes and then says to the future high priest, "See, I have taken your guilt away" (Zech 3:4). The Judge has spoken; Joshua's sins have been forgiven; he has been found sufficiently righteous to merit the position of high priest. That rebuke is all we hear about *hassatan* in the vision.

Taken together with the description of *hassatan* in the book of Job, the portrait in Zechariah 3 confirms the image we had there: *Hassatan* is a member of the divine government with the thankless but essential job of examining the moral integrity of superficially pious mortals. What we cannot confirm, however, is the tone of the divine voice here. Is this divine rebuke of *hassatan* like the vocal hostilities of rival backbenchers who scream at each other in chambers only to sip sherry together in hotel suites later on? Or is this more than intramural sparring, more than the inevitable but provisional residue of an adversarial hearing? Indeed, the genesis of a cosmic separation of powers?

If the latter is the case, then we have—for the first time in the Hebrew Bible—*hassatan* acting as God's opponent in a forensic setting.[28] And although Satan is not yet a fully developed, independent being here in Zechariah 3, we can see the beginnings of what would later become the perennial confrontation between Satan and God.

How David Came to His Census

The story of David's census, mentioned briefly in chapter 2, is worth revisiting and discussing in more detail. The Bible contains two versions of the story. The tale was first told in 2 Samuel 24 and was retold in 1 Chronicles 21. Both stories detail a census taken by David, a practice forbidden in the *Torah* (Ex 30:11–16).[29] Judging by the response, it would appear that God is deadly serious about the prohibition against numbering the people. In fact, David's census so angers the LORD that the deity unleashes a plague that kills 70,000 innocent people. A repentant David then builds an altar to the LORD. We might be tempted to cite this tale as yet another example of God's punishing wrath, but the story contains much more.

Although the stories in 2 Samuel 24 and 1 Chronicles 21 are very similar, there is one glaring difference—a difference that is crucial in our investigation of the birth of Satan. In the version presented in 2 Samuel 24, it is *God* who moves David to number the people:

> Again the anger of the LORD was kindled against Israel, and he incited David against them, saying, "Go and count the people of Israel and Judah" (2 Sam 24:1).

In the later version of the same story, however, it is not God who incites David to number the people, but Satan:

> Satan stood up against Israel, and incited David to count the people of Israel. (1 Chron 21:1)

Why does the author (or authors) of Chronicles change the instigator of the census from God to Satan? The Chronicler is retelling Israel's history—including a rehash of the story in 2 Samuel 24—through the lens of his own theology and at a later date.[30] The Chronicler rewrites the events and "updates" them. For example, we know that the Chronicler is concerned with the rehabilitation of David, whom he presents not as the politically brilliant but flawed king of Samuel and Kings, but as a sort of priestly leader who establishes Jerusalem as the center of worship.[31] But if the Chronicler is wont to omit some of David's more unsavory transgressions—for example, he makes no mention of David's exploitation of Bathsheba (2 Samuel 11)—he is unable to gloss over David's census taking. So how could he present this story in a more positive light?

First, it is important to note one of the more striking aspects of the Chronicler's version of events, specifically, the terrifying wrath of Yhwh. When the author of Chronicles came to the census episode in his sourcebook, 2 Samuel, he was confronted with an account of the deity at his most murderous, in the mode of his bipolarity farthest from "merciful and gracious, slow to anger, and abounding in steadfast love" (Ex 34:6). This, of course, poses a problem for the Chronicler as he pens his account of the events because "the Chronicler could not accept a Yhwh who inflicts both sin and punishment."[32]

The Chronicler, then, reflects the growing existential frustration of a monotheistic people who find it difficult to accept a God who is the author of both good and evil. Hence, in the Chronicler's tale, *it is not Yhwh but Satan* who orders the census, and when Joab, David's right-hand man, fails to complete the census (1 Chr 21:6), Yhwh's subsequent wrath seems justified (1 Chr 21:7ff).[33] (By the way, there is nothing new about Joab taking a fall for David. That was his primary role in 2 Samuel and 1 Kings, too.) Moreover, by assigning blame to Satan, the Chronicler, in a stroke of sheer genius, is able both to preserve David's integrity and to keep Yhwh's reputation unblemished.

Finally, we observe the Chronicler's use of the designation "Satan," minus the definite article (this is not *hassatan,* but *Satan*).[34] For the first time in the canonical Hebrew Bible, "Satan" appears as a proper noun.[35] It is as if Satan is stepping from the shadowy ranks of the heavenly host at the back of the stage, chanting their "Holy, Holy, Holies," to emerge front and center as a character in his own right. Satan—no longer God's lackey as in the book of Job—stands alone in Chronicles, acting apart from the divine council.[36] According to Rivkah Schärf Klüger, this separation is expressed linguistically through the use of Satan as a proper noun.[37] Perhaps even more important is that this satanic verse of 1 Chron 21:1 represents "the detachment and becoming visible of the dark side of God."[38] In other words, the cosmic personality split seems well under way.

Two Other Diabolical Motifs:
The Serpent and Molech

Even casual readers of the Bible have heard about the story of the Garden of Eden (Genesis 2–3). The first man and woman, Adam and Eve, lived in a primeval paradise with the animals, without clothes, without work, and without conflict. That changed when Eve first, then Adam violated the divine prohibition against eating fruit from one of the trees in the garden, the Tree of the Knowledge of Good and Evil:

> And the LORD God commanded the man, "You may freely eat of every tree of the garden; but of the tree of the knowledge of good and evil you shall not eat, for in the day that you eat of it you shall die." (Gen 2:16–17)

As a result of this primeval trespass, Adam and Eve were expelled from childlike Eden into History, where snakes do not talk but they bite, humans are self-consciously aware of their nakedness and vulnerabilities, and the agonies of childbirth and the burdens of food production put a damper on the tropical holiday mentality.

Many casual readers of the Bible assume two things about this story: that the fruit that Eve took a bite from was an apple and that the serpent who enticed Eve to disobey the divine commandment was the Devil. Neither assumption has any basis in the Hebrew Bible. Both represent later—centuries later—interpretations. Regarding Eve's apple, the Bible itself solely uses the generic term "fruit":

> The woman said to the serpent, "We may eat of the fruit of the trees in the garden; but God said, 'You shall not eat of the fruit of the tree that is in the middle of the garden, nor shall you touch it, or you shall die.'" (Gen 3:2)

> So when the woman saw that the tree was good for food, and that it was
> a delight to the eyes, and that the tree was to be desired to make one wise,
> she took of its fruit and ate; and she also gave some to her husband, who was
> with her, and he ate. (Gen 3:6)

The identification of the fruit as an apple emerges in the early centuries of
the common era, as the Bible began to be interpreted in and translated into
Latin. In Latin, the word for "bad" is *malus* and the word for "apple" is
malum. The identification of this fruit, which led to the entrance of all that
was bad into the world, with the apple, of *malus* with *malum*, proved irre-
sistible to ancient punsters.

The identification of the serpent in Genesis 3 with the Devil, although
without any foundation in the original story, emerged in the final centuries
before the common era. We discuss this era, which we refer to as the Intertestamental Period, in chapter 5. Let us simply mention here that it was
during the Intertestamental Period, between 200 B.C.E. and 200 C. E.,
that the Devil in all his macabre glory appears in Jewish and Christian literature. The account in Genesis 3 about the serpent in Eden, written in the
Iron Age (anywhere from 300 to 700 years before the Intertestamental Period) assumes that the serpent was one of the wild animals and that the serpent was ultimately subservient to the LORD God, since God made it:

> Now the serpent was more crafty than any other wild animal that the LORD
> God had made. (Gen 3:1)

The LORD God determined its manner of life:

> The LORD God said to the serpent, " . . . upon your belly you shall go, and
> dust you shall eat all the days of your life." (Gen 3:14)

Nowhere in the Hebrew Bible is there any identification made between
the serpent and the Devil/Satan; furthermore, the Hebrew Bible does not in-
vest snakes, as a species, with any special qualities of evil. The appearance of
the serpent, as opposed to some other animal, in the role of tempter in the
Garden of Eden story is probably influenced by creation stories from other
cultures. For instance, in the Gilgamesh epic, a Babylonian narrative poem
(which we discuss in chapter 4), a serpent appears in a scene that also includes

a plant of life (which compares with the Tree of Life in the biblical story) and an explanation for why snakes shed their skins (which compares with the explanation for why snakes crawl on their bellies in our story). The writer of Genesis has completely rearranged these motifs of a plant of rejuvenation, a snake, and the etiology of serpentine behavior. Nevertheless, the fact that all three motifs were stock elements of ancient Near Eastern stories about the olden days is the most likely explanation for the role of the serpent in the story of Genesis 3. But in Jewish and Christian literature of the Intertestamental Period, the serpent did come to be identified with Satan. For instance, in the Life of Adam and Eve, a rewritten account of the Adam and Eve story from the first century C.E., Eve declares, "The devil answered me through the mouth of the serpent" (Life of Adam and Eve 17:4).[39]

In another work from the same general period, the Wisdom of Solomon, a scroll that is among the contents of the Apocrypha, the serpent is indirectly connected to the Devil: "Through the devil's envy death entered the world" (Wisdom 2:24).

The most explicit statement of this identification of the serpent with Satan, an interpretation that has endured to this day, appears in the New Testament book of Revelation. As if to remove any doubts, the text of Rev 12:9 reads: "that ancient serpent, who is called the Devil and Satan," and the text of Rev 20:2, "the dragon, that ancient serpent, who is called the Devil and Satan."

But this common interpretation of the Garden of Eden story, which associates the crafty serpent with the cunning Devil, is merely that, an *interpretation*. In this study, we are moving through the Bible one text at a time, one era at a time, historically charting the development of the character Satan. According to that approach, we cannot say that Satan appears in Eden, any more than we can say that Eve offered Adam a bite from an apple. Both of these ideas appeared many centuries later, long after the scroll of Genesis was first committed to parchment.

The second diabolical motif found in the Hebrew Bible is that of "Molech." Molech was the name of a Canaanite deity to whom child sacrifices were made.[40] These rituals were forbidden in biblical law:

> "You shall not give any of your offspring to sacrifice them to Molech, and so profane the name of your God: I am the LORD." (Lev 18:21)

Any of the people of Israel, or of the aliens who reside in Israel, who give any of their offspring to Molech shall be put to death; the people of the land shall stone them to death. I myself will set my face against them, and will cut them off from the people, because they have given of their offspring to Molech, defiling my sanctuary and profaning my holy name. And if the people of the land should ever close their eyes to them, when they give of their offspring to Molech, and do not put them to death, I myself will set my face against them and against their family, and will cut them off from among their people, them and all who follow them in prostituting themselves to Molech. (Lev 20:2–5).

Later the biblical prophets would issue their own stern warning against such practices:

And they go on building the high place of Topheth, which is in the valley of the son of Hinnom, to burn their sons and their daughters in the fire—which I did not command, nor did it come into my mind. Therefore, the days are surely coming, says the LORD, when it will no more be called Topheth, or the valley of the son of Hinnom, but the valley of Slaughter: for they will bury in Topheth until there is no more room. (Jer 7:31–32)

You took your sons and your daughters, whom you had borne to me, and these you sacrificed to them to be devoured. As if your whorings were not enough! You slaughtered my children and delivered them up as an offering to them. (Ezek 16:20–21).

Despite the legal prohibitions and prophetic condemnation of child sacrifice, the practice continued in the very environs of the holy city of Jerusalem in a valley just outside the city, the Valley of Hinnom. The Aramaic form of "Valley of Hinnom" is *Ge Henna,* which evolves into the word *Gehenna,* a synonym in New Testament times for hell. And, perhaps even more appalling, some of Judah's kings (the Bible specifically mentions Kings Ahaz and Manasseh, but there were probably others) offered their own children as burnt offerings:

In the seventeenth year of Pekah son of Remaliah, King Ahaz son of Jotham of Judah began to reign. Ahaz was twenty years old when he began to reign; he reigned for sixteen years in Jerusalem. He did not do what was right in the sight of the LORD his God, as his ancestor David had done, but he walked in the way of the kings of Israel. He even made his son pass through fire, according to the abominable practices of the nations whom the LORD drove out before the people of Israel. (2 Kgs 16:1–3)

Manasseh was twelve years old when he began to reign; he reigned fifty-five years in Jerusalem. . . . He did what was evil in the sight of the LORD, following the abominable practices of the nations that the LORD drove out before the people of Israel. He made his son pass through fire; he practiced soothsaying and augury, and dealt with mediums and with wizards. He did much evil in the sight of the LORD, provoking him to anger. (2 Kgs 21:1–2;6)

In the Bible, Molech is nowhere associated with Satan. Still, the grim specter of this "horrid king, besmeared with blood of human sacrifice, and parents' tears" (John Milton, *Paradise Lost* 1:392–93) will shadow Satan as he develops into a rapacious underworld tyrant. In the Middle Ages, "Molech" or "Moloch" is another name for Satan.[41] In Milton's *Paradise Lost* (1:392–405), "Moloch" is the name of one of Lucifer's chief officers.

The term "satan" appears in the Hebrew Bible in several contexts, but there is no hint in any of them of the Titan of Evil who will emerge after the writing of the Hebrew Bible, in the subsequent Intertestamental Period. In First Temple biblical literature—those scrolls written before the exile to Babylon and the destruction of Solomon's Temple (i.e., before 586 B.C.E.)—the term "satan" can refer to an agent of obstruction or of punishment, either divine or human, sent by God. In these texts, such as in the story about Balaam in Numbers and in the many stories about the early kings of Judah and Israel in the books of Samuel and Kings, there are many different "satans." The term is still in the lowercase, as it were, in spelling; "satan" refers to a category, those angels and persons sent by God on missions of opposition.

In biblical texts from the Second Temple period, from after the Exile (from 530 to 200 B.C.E.), such as Job and Zechariah, "satan" has evolved into "*hassatan*," "the Adversary," "the Opponent." *Hassatan* is clearly one of the divine beings, and not human. This figure remains part of the heavenly entourage and has the job of testing humans and reporting back to God about their righteousness.

Even later in the Second Temple period, such as in the texts from Chronicles (composed after the Exile) that overwrite earlier texts from 1–2 Samuel about David's reign, Satan emerges in yet another form, that of the instigator of David's ill-conceived census. This Satan, glimpsed briefly in 1 Chr 21:1, is the transitional figure who authors a disaster and lures an honest man, King David, to embark on a tragic course that will eventually lead to the deaths of thousands (1 Chr 21:14). The satan figure in 1 Chronicles is the avatar of later characterizations of Satan. The more mature, developed Satan—the familiar Devil and tempter in the New Testament and beyond—will not emerge in any recognizable form for many more years. And, as we shall see, Satan's final portrait is sketched by many artists, each of whom adds definition to the final product.

chapter 4

the influence of israel's neighbors on the development of satan

Men create gods in their own image.

—*Xenophanes*

Satan's climb to biblical eminence did not take place in a vacuum and certain external factors undoubtedly helped it along. Divisions within postexilic Judaism, the foreign domination of Palestine, and the popularity of apocalyptic literature all dovetail at just the right moment; change is afoot in Israel, as previously held truths and ideas are challenged. But in addition to these internal factors, Satan's birth is assisted by a host of foreign midwives. The religions of Mesopotamia, Canaan, Egypt, Persia, and Greece—Israel's closest neighbors—influenced the development of the idea of Satan in Jewish religion and added elements to his character. These nations had their own explanations for evil and their own malevolent deities.

Our central interest in the religious stories of Israel's neighbors has to do with the role of supernatural evil beings and cosmic adversaries, for these will also be Satan's roles. Because of its antiquity and the fact that this story was apparently known in ancient Israel, the best starting point for this inquiry is the ancient Mesopotamian tale the Epic of Gilgamesh.

Mesopotamian Influences on Satan

Dating to the turn of the second millennium or earlier, the Epic of Gilgamesh was written in the Babylonian language, Akkadian, on twelve clay tablets.[1] There were multiple occasions, over the course of a millennium, when the Hebrew people might have been exposed to this Mesopotamian classic. A fragment of Gilgamesh (dated to 1550–1150 B.C.E.) has been found during excavations at Megiddo (located in northern Israel).[2] Jewish exiles would have almost certainly have come into contact with it during their sixth-century B.C.E. sojourn in Babylon. The names of the hero of the epic and of its main monster, Gilgamesh and Humbaba, respectively, are mentioned in Aramaic fragments among the Dead Sea Scrolls.

The epic describes the adventures of a hero, Gilgamesh, legendary king of the city-state Uruk, and his hirsute sidekick Enkidu. On one level, the Gilgamesh epic is an amazing adventure story. Gilgamesh and Enkidu raid, love, drink, and brawl their way across a fantastic landscape that includes alpine forests guarded by monstrous sentries, the Cave of the Sun, an enchanted island, and the arid steppes of ancient Iraq. Gilgamesh and Enkidu encounter goddesses, scorpion-men, worldly wise saloon girls, prostitutes with hearts of gold, and several species of monsters. Motifs first seen in the Gilgamesh epic later appear in the Bible, Homer, the Arabian Nights, and, in fact, virtually every larger-than-life adventure tale ever told, written, or filmed.

The Epic of Gilgamesh makes four important contributions to the development of the idea of Satan. The first is the motif of a supernatural opponent of the hero. This appears in the account of Gilgamesh and Enkidu's raid on the Cedar Forest, the paradisiacal retreat of the great god Enlil. Gilgamesh and Enkidu are met there by a monstrous sentry named Humbaba:

> Humbaba—his roaring is the storm flood,
> His mouth is fire, his breath is death![3]

One of the oldest examples of a supernatural adversary in literature, Humbaba is an appropriate starting point in any examination of the influence of Israel's neighbors on the emergence of Satan. Like Satan, Humbaba is the guardian of a dark and foreboding place that induces fear in humans. Both Satan and Humbaba are described as physically terrifying and have associations with fire and death. Because we possess only a portion of ancient Near Eastern literature—surely much more was written than has been uncovered by archaeologists—it would be unwise to assume that the Babylonian Humbaba was a direct ancestor of the Hebrew Satan. Our contention is that Humbaba is *representative* of the kind of supernatural adversary that existed in ancient narratives and that this type of monster contributed to the development of the idea of Satan in Jewish belief.

There are also biblical echoes of Humbaba, the Mesopotamian monster who guards the entrance to a divine forest of the high god, in the image of the terrifying cherubim in Gen 3:23–24 assigned by Yhwh to guard the gates of Eden (or, more specifically, to keep the banished Adam and Eve from trying to return to Paradise): "the LORD God sent him [Adam] forth from the Garden of Eden . . . and . . . placed the cherubim, and a sword flaming and turning to guard the way to the tree of life."

The second contribution of the Gilgamesh epic to our study is its description of the permeability of the border that separates our terrestrial landscape from a terrifying and fantastic netherworld. Besides traveling into the Cedar Forest and encountering Humbaba, Gilgamesh must also make his way past the scorpion-men (other monstrous cosmic border guards), to traverse a fiery cavelike tunnel. Still later, Gilgamesh takes a ferry from Land's End across a sea that devours every oar that breaks its surface, to arrive on an island whose inhabitants, the Noah-like character Utnapishtim and his wife, never die. These specific locations do not directly reappear in satanic lore, but this view of landscape does. In the human imagination, Satan enters our world and we fall into his through such mythological manholes in our symbolic-geographic landscapes.

A third contribution from the epic is its portrayal of the trickster god Enki (also known as Ea). Enki appears in many Mesopotamian myths, always as a member of the divine court mischievously ready to break ranks with his peers. In the Gilgamesh narrative, Enki is mentioned by Utnapishtim, the Noah-like survivor of the primeval flood. The Mesopotamian pantheon forbade its heavenly council members to warn humans about the approaching flood. But Enki broke ranks with his peers and cunningly whispered warnings of the deluge through Utnapishtim's bedroom wall. Although Enki could not talk to humans about the secret directives of the divine government, the *wall* could talk, and talk it did, instructing Utnapishtim to build a boat and take his family on it, along with "the beasts of the field, [and] the creatures of the wild."[4] Although this Mesopotamian divine character Enki/Ea is usually not mentioned as an ancestor of the Judeo-Christian Satan, the motif of a member of the divine entourage with a mind of his own, artfully adept at circumventing the divine will, is reminiscent of *hassatan*'s role in the divine court of Yhwh.

A fourth contribution of the Gilgamesh epic to our study is the underlying similarity between it and Jewish and Christian apocalyptic writings. The biblical books of Daniel (from the Hebrew Bible) and Revelation (from the New Testament), as well as several non-canonical Jewish apocalyptic texts (such as 1 Enoch and Jubilees from the intertestamental period), refer to a cosmic battle between good and evil. Such battles are often described in highly symbolic language, including the use of beasts, monsters, and evil beings. In particular, as Neil Forsyth notes in his book, *The Old Enemy*, Gilgamesh's struggle is profoundly related to the Christian narrative: "It is true that Gilgamesh is a god-man who tries to overcome death, that he tries to do so by liberating his people from a monstrous tyrant, that he collects companions to help him, and that after death, Gilgamesh lives on as a figure of worship."[5]

In essence, these apocalyptic stories in Jewish and Christian tradition adopt the template of ancient epic adventures such as Gilgamesh, borrowing plot lines while shifting the stage from earth to heaven (reminiscent of the Prologue of Job). The epic human adventure becomes the ultimate cosmic adventure as a divine hero, the Son of Man in Daniel, the Lamb in Revelation, does battle with the final enemy.

On a deeper level, beyond the excitement of its storytelling, the Gilgamesh epic also manages to address virtually every great theme of human existence. The contrast between the two main characters, the valiant, almost-godly hero Gilgamesh and his animalistic soul mate Enkidu, captures the contradictions of human nature. The interactions between these men prone to violent sprees and the women in the epic who attempt to civilize, domesticate, and humanize them create an arena for a primeval battle of the sexes. In Gilgamesh's final adventure, his lonely heroic search for immortality and his ultimate resignation to the sorrows and joys of mortal life, the epic reaches a rare place in heroic literature: the intersection of soaring adventure and the deepest explication of the human condition. If Gilgamesh typifies the literary model of a courageous hero, his actions seem to speak to something deeper within the human heart. Perhaps we are able to see our own struggles embodied in Gilgamesh's wrestling with the beast: our own fear of death, our own quest for truth, and our own fervent desire to believe that, ultimately, good triumphs over evil.

Canaanite Influences on Satan

Moving from the Mesopotamian highlands to ancient Syria and Lebanon, the cultures of which we refer to here as Canaanite, even more astonishing connections to Satan emerge. The discoveries at Ras Shamra (the site of the ancient city of Ugarit), located along the northern coast of modern-day Syria, have provided a great deal of information about Canaanite religion.[6] Although members of the Canaanite pantheon such as Baal and Asherah are mentioned in very unfavorable terms in the Bible, we must be cautious in accepting the biblical condemnation of Canaanite religions as ritually and ethically debased. From an anthropological view, Canaanite and Israelite cultures were remarkably similar. In fact, it was probably this similarity, this kinship that led biblical writers to seek to exaggerate the differences between their societies, because it is common for the most intense rivalries to appear among cultures that are most similar.

The poetic myths found at the site of the ancient Syrian city of Ugarit give us an inside view of Canaanite religion, free from the polemics of the biblical authors. The Canaanite pantheon was a fractious family led by the great father, El, a name that the Bible itself uses for its God and that is linguistically related to Enlil of Mesopotamian religion, Elohim of Israelite religion, and Allah of Arabic religion. Traces of "El" can also be found in the names of several popular biblical figures, including Ishma*el*, Isra*el*, and Ezeki*el*, and the term "El" itself was considered appropriate for God in Hebrew usage. Among El's sons are Baal, the god of fertility, and Mot, the god of the underworld. The Canaanite pantheon also included three major goddesses: Asherah and

Ashtarte were goddesses of love and war, and Anat was a "tomboy" goddess, an adolescent maiden, with a taste for warfare that rivals that of the Hindu goddess Kali.[7]

Although Baal functions in the Bible as the LORD's chief rival for Israel's affections, it is El's other son, Mot, who plays a greater role in the development of Satan. Mot is a dark and loathsome god; as god of the underworld, he also represents sterility and death.[8] He carries "a scepter of sterility," as he sits on his throne named "Low," in his town, "the Pit," and his land, "Filth."[9]

The part of the Ugaritic mythic cycle most relevant to this investigation includes a battle between Baal and Mot. Apparently, Mot has been terrorizing the earth, so Baal descends to the underworld in order to subdue him. A battle ensues, and Baal is killed during the fight. Baal's sister, Anat, goes in search of his body, finds it, buries it, and then exacts revenge. In a murderous rage, Anat goes down to the underworld and kills Mot, grinding his body like grain and scattering his remains in a field:

> She seizes the Godly Mot—
> With sword she doth cleave him,
> With fan she doth winnow him—
> With fire she doth burn him.
> With hand-mill she grinds him—
> In the field she doth sow him.[10]

This action brings about a resurrection of Baal and returns fertility to the soil (which had been barren since his death).[11] Mot, too, is ultimately resurrected, and the two gods continue their feud, remaining locked in a life-and-death battle for all eternity.

The Anat-Baal texts are important in our exploration of Satan for several reasons. First, the themes of good triumphing over evil, and life over death, that resonate throughout the poem are themes consistently associated with tales about Satan. Second, the shadowy, terrifying underworld inhabited by the evil character Mot is highly suggestive of Satan's own terrifying abode. Third, Mot is a son of the high god, El. This reminds us of Satan's beginnings, in the form of *hassatan*, as one of the "sons of God" (Job 1:6). Fourth, and perhaps most important, Mot is the adversary who must be conquered by the "good god," Baal. This conflict, of course, anticipates Jesus' battle against Satan in the New Testament. It also echoes the struggle between Humbaba and Gilgamesh, as well as that between Set and Horus in the Egyptian Osiris myth to be discussed.

The Ugaritic texts yield another figure, Habayu, who may also have contributed to the development of the biblical Satan. Habayu is a terrible netherworld demon who sports horns (often a symbol of power in the ancient world) and a tail, physical characteristics that will later be associated with the Christian Satan. Habayu appears in a story that features El in an advanced state of inebriation during a celebratory feast connected with the cult of the dead.[12] In his drunkenness, El sees Habayu in an "infernal vision" in which Habayu apparently douses El in urine and excrement.[13] Although the figure of Habayu is not as developed as Mot, the possible influence of Habayu on the development of Satan cannot be ignored. In fact, some scholars suspect that the origins of the traditional depiction of Satan with horns and a tail ultimately can be traced back to the physiognomy of Habayu.

Egyptian Influences on Satan

Like Canaan, Egypt was an immediate neighbor of ancient Israel, and there were economic, military, and political dealings among these cultures. In addition, both in the earliest period of Israelite history, as suggested by the narratives in Exodus, and in the postexilic period, Hebrew/Jewish communities lived in Egypt. Moreover, there were numerous opportunities for ideas to move back and forth across the permeable Afro-Asiatic border that separated Egypt and Israel.

In Egyptian mythology, all gods and goddesses are considered manifestations of the one true god. All things—including good and evil—emanate from the same divine source, and evil is as much a part of the universe as good. Even so, evil actions disrupted the natural order of the cosmos, or *ma'at*, and were to be avoided.[14] Egyptians believed that each individual was responsible for his or her own actions and would be held accountable for these actions in the afterlife.

In the Egyptian underworld, into which all mortals descended after death to be judged, the deceased's soul was weighed on a scale by Anpu (or

Anubis), the jackal-headed god often featured in Egyptian funerary art. Because pharaohs were considered deities, they alone were exempt from judgment. If a person were judged to be good, he or she would continue to exist in this shadowy necropolis; but if the person were judged to be evil, then he or she would be subjected to torture before being consumed by fire or by hungry demons.[15]

The story of Isis and Osiris is one of the more popular tales in Egyptian mythology and is critical to our investigation of Satan. The Isis and Osiris myth contains a variety of powerful themes, including sibling rivalry, death and resurrection, love, revenge, and the struggle between good and evil. The central focus of the story concerns the murder of the great Egyptian god Osiris by his brother Set (or Seth); the search by Isis to recover the body of her brother/husband; and the subsequent revenge that Horus, their son, takes against Set.[16]

Isis, often depicted wearing horns, can assume many forms and is considered to be both an enchantress and a protector of the dead. Osiris, the symbol of resurrection, eternal life, fertility, and prosperity, develops an enviable following among humans. This apparently causes his evil brother, Set, to plot against him. Set throws a party and, during the festivities, produces a beautiful sarcophagus. He offers to give the sarcophagus to the person who best fits into it (having secretly designed the coffin as a perfect fit for Osiris). The guests take turns, trying on the sarcophagus for size. When Osiris takes his turn and steps into the coffin, Set and his seventy-two co-conspirators slam the lid, nail the coffin shut, and toss it into the Nile.

The coffin floats down the Nile (and apparently into the Mediterranean Sea) before coming ashore in the town of Byblos (in Lebanon), where it miraculously grows into a fragrant tree. The tree is cut down by the king of Byblos and used as a pillar in his home. Isis, the wife of Osiris, who has been mourning the loss of her husband, searches for his body. She learns that her husband is entombed in the pillar. She rescues his body, puts it aboard a barge, and brings it home. On the way home, she lies on top of the body and conceives a son, Horus.

Despite the fact that Set succeeds in killing Osiris, the deceased deity is still able to produce life. This powerful resurrection myth then segues into a story about Set's implacable spite and Isis' undying love, both directed toward Osiris. Isis hides and guards the body of her beloved, but Set finds it and tears it into fourteen pieces, scattering Osiris's body parts throughout Egypt. Isis searches for Osiris's lost limbs; each time she finds a piece of Osiris, she buries it and builds a shrine over it.[17]

Osiris is considered a god of the dead, a ruler and judge of the underworld. And although his story offers the promise of life after death, there is a demonic or ghoulish association with Osiris, perhaps because of his connection to the physical process of death and decay.[18] In Egyptian art he is usually featured with green skin.[19]

In resonance with Egyptian beliefs, early Israelite religion held that good and evil emanated from a single divine source. In addition, the Egyptian notion of personal responsibility for sin and subsequent judgment is also a persistent biblical theme. The final place of this judgment is a shadowy underworld known in Egyptian mythology as Tuat; in the Hebrew Bible, as Sheol, the dark subterranean place of the dead.

Later, in Second Temple religion, this Shadelands acquires a moral dimension. Sheol morphs into "Gehenna." Gehenna (the Aramaic name for the Valley of Hinnom outside of Jerusalem) was known both as a refuse heap, ever aglow with burning piles, and as a place where the illicit religious practice of child sacrifice had been practiced in the Iron Age (ca. 1000–500 B.C.E.).[20] This wholly real, geographic place became symbolically associated with the place where the unrighteous would be judged in the afterlife. By the time of the New Testament, the term "Gehenna" was sometimes used as another name for "hell" (Mt 10:28; 23:33), Satan's abode.

Thus, in the atlas of the underworld, Egyptian Tuat and Hebrew Sheol refer to the same land of the dead. But in Egyptian religion, only the righteous, those whose hearts balanced against "the feather of truth" on the scales of justice, the scales of *ma'at*, entered this benign netherworld. In ancient Israelite religion, both the righteous and unrighteous entered Sheol. The fate of the wicked in Egyptian eschatology included annihilation by Amamet, a monster with the forelegs of a crocodile, the body of a lion, and the hindquarters of a hippo. If a soul was deemed evil or burdened by guilt, it was devoured by Amamet. This idea may have influenced the Second Temple Jewish idea of Gehenna, and of the Christian hell, where the wicked were often tortured by flames or demons.[21]

But beyond even these connections are the intriguing similarities between the wicked god, Set, and the biblical notion of Satan (there is no etymological connection, although the names are similar in English transcription). Set, like Satan, is not a mortal. And although Set is never viewed with quite the contempt and fear eventually associated with Satan, he does represent the closest thing to an evil being in Egyptian mythology. Set's artistic representations, like those of Satan, are frightening. The god of the desert—of scorching heat—he is usually painted red, a color Egyptians associated with evil. Red, of course, would also become the favored color for Satan. Set, like Satan, is engaged in a battle of good and evil, first with his brother, Osiris, and then with his nephew, Horus.

Some artistic depictions of Set and Horus show their heads resting upon a single body, while other depictions show two separate gods. In earlier dynasties, it appears that the two were worshipped together, representing two halves of the divine personality.[22] This dual aspect may parallel a similar tension within early Hebrew religion, which understood God as author of both good and evil, and the later adoption of monotheism that would assign evil to a wholly separate source, Satan.

Horus and Set both have roles in the ever-mutating story of Satan. An artistic motif associated with Horus, "the all-seeing-eye," or "the eye of Horus," from the Egyptian Book of the Dead was adopted by various European secret societies beginning in the eighteenth century, such as the Illuminati and the Freemasons (both groups are discussed in great detail in Dan Brown's blockbuster, *The Da Vinci Code*).[23] The "Temple of Set" became the name of a religious group that spun off from Anton LaVey's Church of Satan in 1975.[24] In the 2004 film *National Treasure*, the Eye of Horus is the subject of great interest, especially in its most vivid contemporary expression, on the Great Seal of the United States. Throughout the last two centuries, many conspiracy theorists have read great significance into the use of this arcane ancient symbol on American currency. Their scenario is that elite members of a secret society—whether Jews, Communists, atheists, New Deal Socialists, Roman Catholics, Freemasons, or transgovernmental cabals and commissions—have inserted their codes into the mainframes of contemporary society as part of their mission to dominate the world. As we have mentioned before, and detail in the next chapter, such conspiracy theories represent secularized versions of the ancient lore surrounding Satan in that both types of story purport to reveal an evil universal conspiracy. The modern versions merely substitute elite human cabals for the ancient demons.

Persian Influences on Satan

Nowhere was the designation of a separate principle of evil clearer than in the dualistic religious system of ancient Persia. A radical new understanding concerning the origin of good and evil, Persian dualism emerged around 600 B.C.E. with the teachings of Zarathustra (or Zoroaster).[25] In what is modern-day Iran, the teacher and prophet Zarathustra claimed that there was only one true God, a creator God named Ahura Mazda ("Wise Lord"). This strict monotheism was a fairly radical concept in the ancient Near East; even Israel's exclusive worship of Yhwh did not preclude the possibility that there were other gods worshipped by other peoples. Aside from this early form of monotheism, Zoroastrianism has other elements in common with Israelite religion. Ahura Madza, like Yhwh, was envisioned as the leader of a divine council, surrounded by a heavenly throng of angelic creatures, reminiscent of Yhwh's own divine court.[26]

But, for our purposes, the most important contribution to our investigation of Satan's evolution comes from one of the most profound teachings of Zarathustra: the revelation that evil does not emanate from God (Ahura Mazda) at all, but rather comes from a separate, malignant being, called Ahriman, "fiendish spirit" (or, sometimes, Angra Mainya, "the evil spirit"). Information about these teachings come to us from the Gathas (or hymns), the sacred scriptures of Zoroastrianism, believed to have come from Zarathustra himself.[27] Zoroastrian teachings are highly ethical in nature and center on the concept that human beings are involved in a constant struggle between good (light) and evil (darkness). These two opposing forces are embodied in two beings: a good god, Ahura Mazda, and an evil being, Ahriman who is the destructive personification (and creator) of evil, the harbinger of death, disease, and lies.[28] Even more exciting is the possible influence of Zoroastrianism in books such as Job, Zechariah, and Chronicles, all of which feature a satan figure and all of which can be dated to the Persian period.[29]

Ahriman is described as an evil spirit, and not a creation of Ahura Mazda, but wholly separate from him.[30] Both Ahura Mazda and Ahriman are "original in being themselves uncreated representative of contradictory principles."[31] Further, the Gathas make it clear that humans are to choose one of two paths: the path of goodness and light, as manifest in Ahura Mazda, or the path of darkness and evil, following the ways of Ahriman:

> Well known are the two primeval spirits correlated but independent; one is the better and the other is the worse as to thought, as to word, as to deed, and between these two let the wise choose aright. [32]

And Ahriman is not alone in malicious activities, but is assisted by a host of other demonic figures who help him to lure humans astray.[33] Ahriman's second in command, Aheshma (the demon of wrath), is said to move about the earth, "polluting it and spreading disease and death."[34] Ahriman remains locked in constant battle against those who are lined up on the side of goodness, but in the end, good will triumph over evil.

There are some interesting parallels between the plot lines of Zoroastrian and Christian narrative. In Zoroastrianism, those who choose the path of righteousness will reap rewards, while those who follow Ahriman will be subjected to suffering. Each of these paths also included a postmortem judgment that would determine one's eternal fate. Those whose lives were devoted to good deeds would enter a paradise, similar to the Christian concept of heaven, while those who engaged in disreputable behaviors would be banished to the torments of hell. The Zoroastrian hell is a particularly horrifying place, and many scholars feel it may have contributed to Christian understanding of hell as a posthumous place of unremitting pain and suffering.[35] A vivid description of the Persian hell is found in the Vision of Arda Viraf written sometime between 226 and 641 C.E.[36] In this tale, the hero of the story, the pious Arda Viraf (sometimes the name is rendered "Arda Wiraz"), is given a tour of sorts, of heaven, hell and of an in-between place similar to the Christian concept of limbo called *Hammistagan* ("place of the Motionless Ones").[37] His description of hell is one of the more chilling accounts in literature:

> I saw the greedy jaws of hell: the most frightful pit, descending, in a very narrow, fearsome crevice and in darkness so murky that I was forced to feel my way, amid such stench that all who inhaled the air, struggled, staggered, and

fell, and in such confinement that existence seemed impossible. Each one thought: "I am alone."

I saw also, the soul of a man, the skin of whose head was being flayed . . . who in the world had slain a pious man. I saw the soul of a man into whose mouth they poured continually the menstrual discharge of a woman while he cooked and ate his own child. . . . "While in the world," I was told, "that wicked man had intercourse with a menstruating woman."[38]

According to Zoroastrianism, the present age is a time of great crisis, but "Saviors will come from the seed of Zoroaster, and in the end, the great Savior" shall restore all goodness.[39] One such savior, according to Zoroastrian teaching, will be born of a virgin, bring about the resurrection of the dead, and make humankind immortal.[40] It is not difficult to see connections between the anticipated Zoroastrian savior and the Christian savior, Jesus.

According to Lewis M. Hopfe and Mark R. Woodward, authors of *Religions of the World,* the teachings of Zoroastrianism surely influenced the development of Satan. Most notably, it is only after the Exile that we find mention of a satan-figure in the Hebrew Bible (with the possible exception of *hassatan* in Numbers 22).[41] Moreover, according to Hopfe and Woodward:

> In the intertestamental literature, Satan and his demons are mentioned frequently; in the New Testament literature, they are accepted as a regular part of life. Jesus is confronted by Satan as he begins his public ministry, and a large part of that ministry is devoted to exorcising demons. Pre-exilic biblical books have no mention of a resurrection of the body, little concern for life after death in either heaven or hell, no reference to God's plan for bringing the earth to an end, only an occasional mention of angels, and no word about a day of judgment. Each of these themes, which were part of the teachings of Zoroastrianism, developed in Judaism after the exile, and each had become a vital part of the religion of by the time of Jesus.[42]

Although it is clear that Zoroastrian religious beliefs—especially regarding the evil demon Ahriman—had much to do with Satan's evolution, it is the Greek god of the underworld, Hades, and his terrifying dwelling that perhaps is most familiar to modern readers. Let us now turn to the Greek religion in search of clues to Satan's startling metamorphosis.

Greek Influences on Satan

Greek myths, too, contain a sort of dualism similar to the teachings of Zarathustra, but with some distinct differences. For example, under the influence of Pythagoras, a dualistic understanding developed called *Orphism*, which held that the soul was immortal but is confined to a body that is mortal. In Persian dualism, the conflict is between good and evil forces or spirits; Orphism, on the other hand, taught that the conflict is to be found within ourselves—between the soul, considered to be divine and immortal, and the body, which must be evil. According to Jeffrey Burton Russell, "In Orphism the dualism of matter and spirit, body and soul, is first clearly enunciated: its influence upon Christian, Gnostic, and medieval thought was enormous, and it is one of the most important elements in the history of the Devil."[43]

Followers of Orphism, like followers of many of the Eastern religions, believed in the transmigration of souls, or reincarnation. A karmic principle seems to be operative in Orphism in that the actions in this life affect future lives.[44] It seems likely that the influence of Orphic dualism contributed to the Greek understanding of good and evil, an understanding clearly embodied in their deities.

The gods of the Greeks are ambivalent, possessing qualities of both good and evil, emanating as manifestations of the one God.[45] Thus, the complexity of the Greek deities may be due to a sort of hodgepodge synthesis of elements found in surrounding cults, including the Near East.[46] But if all Greek gods and goddesses seem to possess a dichotomistic nature, particular Greek deities such as Hermes, Pan, and Hades may have influenced the development of Satan more than others.

The god Hermes, known as the winged messenger of the heavenly court, is called Hermes Psychopompos (*psyche*, meaning "shade," and *pompos*, meaning "guide") in some myths, and is known as the god who escorts dead souls to the underworld.[47] Hermes' son, in some accounts, is Pan, a hairy, goatlike creature with hooves and horns, who, like his father, is a god of sexual desire. Both father and son may well have helped to shape the evolving notion of how Satan ought to appear, with the winged god Hermes influencing the medieval tradition of a winged Satan (as in John Milton's *Paradise Lost*) in much the same way that his son, Pan, contributed to

Satan's depictions in art and literature as a monstrous, hairy being with horns and hooves.[48] But it is the Greek god Hades, the god of the underworld, who contributed most to the popular depiction of Satan and to the symbolic chthonic landscape that would be assigned to him.

One of the best-known myths in all of Greek mythology, Homer's Hymn to Demeter, tells the story of the abduction of Persephone, a goddess of fertility, by Hades and the negotiated deal, brokered by Zeus, that resolved the crisis. Persephone would spend part of the year, the winter, in the underworld with her husband, Hades, and part of the year, the growing seasons, in the upper world. We see here a plot line similar to the myth of Baal's capture by Mot in Canaanite religion.

Hades, the Greek equivalent to Mot, causes sterility, and only the most energetic intercessions of the heavenly gods, whether Zeus and Hermes in Greek myth or Anat in Canaanite myth, limit death's reign to an annual season. The underworld gods of the eastern Mediterranean were perennially eager to bring more of the cosmos under their sterile domain. But what of Persephone's husband, Hades? What are the possible connections between Hades and Satan? Hades is perhaps the most underdeveloped god in the Greek pantheon, but here is what we do know about him. He is a cold-hearted god who has the ability, with the aid of a special helmet, to render himself invisible. Hades is a solitary, enigmatic deity, famed only for his kidnapping of Persephone, and wholly dreaded by the Greeks. Satan, like Hades, gained the reputation of lurking about unseen. And, as Satan will, Hades lives in a place of fear and torment where the souls of the deceased journey after death. Concerning himself neither with earth nor heaven, Hades remains fixed in his subterranean abode, symbolizing the permanence of death. There, of course, his path diverges from that of the biblical Satan, who is preoccupied with the goings-on of earth, always interested in disrupting human activity and causing misery in any way he can.

The Greeks had a vision of the underworld that bears striking similarities to both the Jewish Sheol and the Christian hell. Hades is not alone in his underworld kingdom; in addition to the souls of the deceased, three terrifying goddesses, called *Erinyes* (sometimes referred to as the Furies or the daughters of Hades in Greek poetry), and the goddess Hecate (usually associated with ghosts and black magic), round out his underworld entourage. The Erinyes are particularly fearsome, depicted as being clad in "black cloaks soaked in blood, wielding whips of scorpions, and with snakes instead of hair."[49] As terrifying as these underworld figures may be, however, it is perhaps the physical structure of the Greek underworld that is most frightening.

The underworld has a tripartite structure wherein the deceased may spend eternity. The highest level, known as the Elysian Fields, is usually reserved for those who accomplished great things in life, such as war heroes, who will enjoy a peaceful repose, similar to the Christian notion of heaven. The second level is called the Asphodel Fields, a sort of purgatory for those who were neither great nor evil. But the lowest level of the underworld, Tartarus, is a place of pure darkness, located in the deepest recesses of the earth. This particular level is the dwelling place for criminals and other evildoers who are condemned to suffer eternal torture and punishment for their disreputable lives on earth.

Hesiod wrote that an anvil would take nine days and nights to fall from heaven to earth, and nine days and nights to fall from earth to Tartarus. Were we to add fire to Tartarus, it would closely resemble the Christian concept of hell. In fact, Tartarus is said to have been the very inspiration behind Dante's *Inferno* and the prototype for the Christian hell (see chapter 7).

The Significance of Foreign Influences on the Birth of Satan

These discussions of Mesopotamian, Canaanite, Egyptian, Persian, and Greek conceptions of underworld gods, divine tricksters, cosmic combats, and realms of the dead provides us with a bird's-eye view of the world that surrounded biblical Israel. We cannot draw straight lines between these foreign gods and ideas and Jewish and Christian ideas about Satan, Sheol, Gehenna, and hell. However, we can infer that these foreign ideas were in the air that biblical writers and Jewish and Christian apocalypticists breathed. By circuitous paths, through direct or indirect means, over long periods of contact, these (and other) foreign ideas contributed to the development of the Jewish Satan (see Table 4.1).

For example, Humbaba, Mot, Habayu, Set, Ahriman, and Hades, like Satan, are supernatural beings feared by humans. All of these figures have an initial connection (mostly familial) with a high god, and most are engaged in a battle with an opposing good god. Humbaba is appointed to guard the secret forest by the high god Enlil; Mot is a son of the high god El; Set is the brother (or in some versions of the myth, son) of the god Osiris; Ahriman, in some versions, emanates from a creator god along with Ahura Mazda; Hades is a brother of Zeus. In addition, Humbaba, Mot, Habayu, Ahriman, Hades, and Satan all dwell in a forbidding place; and Mot, Habayu, Ahriman, Hades, and Satan, in particular, make their home in a subterranean abode where souls are judged.

Finally, many of the characters in these myths have likely contributed to Satan's physical appearance: the fire breath of Humbaba; the horns and tail of Habayu; the red color of Set; and the sheer ugliness of Hades. Perhaps the Greeks contributed most to Satan's appearance: the horns and hairiness of Pan; the wings of Hermes; and even the trident (which would become Satan's pitchfork) carried by the Greek god Poseidon. (See Table 4.1.)

The key principle in the incorporation of "pagan" elements into the Judeo-Christian Satan, as we have mentioned, is that all deities from all foreign systems are fair game and can be incorporated freely into portraits of the Devil. The orthodox may demonize the old gods and the foreign gods using satanic epithets, while at the same time, incorporating the symbols of these gods into their own diabology. By a similar method, those who wish to express contrary religious values—or simply to register their opposition to mainstream culture—borrow names, rites, and symbols from ancient religions and hammer them into whatever shapes they please. Whether they are nineteenth-century Romantic poets and Gothic novelists, early twentieth-century British occultists, post–World War II American biker gangs, or rock and roll bands (like "Black Sabbath,") we have witnessed a recycling of pagan elements throughout history.

Since the dawn of recorded history, people have sought answers to the big questions in life: Why are we here? Who created the world? Why must we die? Why is suffering so much a part of life? Religious stories attempt to answer these questions. And the evil beings at play in these stories not only create a critical level of suspense that helps to make the narrative more memorable, but they also help us to grapple with the reality of sin and suffering.

Table 4.1 Supernatural Beings and Satan: Shared Aspects

Supernatural Being	Source	Relation to Deity	Frightening Appearance	Subterranean or Dark Abode	Associated with Death	Feared by Humans	Battle or Trickery Involved
Humbaba	Mesopotamia	Appointed by Enlil to Guard Cedar Forest	Giant monster	Dark Cedar Forest	Breathes fire and death	Feared by all	Battle with Gilgamesh
Mot	Canaan	Son of El	Demon	Underworld god	God of death and sterility	Feared by all	Baal must subdue him
Habayu	Canaan	El sees Habayu in a drunken vision	Horns and tail	Underworld	Connected with cult of the dead	Fear-inducing	Defiles El with excrement and urine
Set	Egypt	Son of goddess Nut and god Re	Head of black jackal-like animal; forked tongue; tail	Storm god; dwells in scorching desert	Associated with desert heat and death	Feared by all	Murders Osiris through trickery
Ahriman	Persia	Uncreated	Fearsome demon	Underworld god	Causes death and destruction	Feared by all	Perpetual battle with Ahura Mazda

(continues)

Table 4.1 Supernatural Beings and Satan: Shared Aspects

Supernatural Being	Source	Relation to Deity	Frightening Appearance	Subterranean or Dark Abode	Associated with Death	Feared by Humans	Battle or Trickery Involved
Hades	Greece	Son of Zeus	Odious and ugly; fearsome	Underworld god	Brings death to the land; lives in land of the dead	Feared by all	Kidnaps Persephone and takes her to underworld
Satan	Israel	Originally one of the *benay elohim*	Later Christian representations show horns, tail, red, hairiness	Commander of hell	Causes death and destruction	Feared by all	Battles Jesus for the Kingdom

The themes concerning the triumph of good over evil and life over death, recurrent in all of these religious stories and perhaps most clearly conveyed in Persian dualism, point to a type of Judeo-Christian "modified dualism" that allows Satan to flourish in the first place. There is no denying the fact that looking at the world through a dualistic lens provides a set of answers to our most troubling existential questions. And so perhaps God's chosen people, in their quest for truth, came to reject a God who sent misery and joy in equal measure. One can almost hear the cry of their epiphany: *Surely God would not allow this to happen to us! Our misery must be the result of a malevolent force opposed to the goodness of God.*

chapter 5

satan between
the testaments

Evil draws men together.
—Aristotle

the slow evolution of the Devil—from low-level cosmic lackey, to the repository of God's negative aspects, to beneficiary of the inevitable religious syncretism of the ancient Near East—suddenly shifts into overdrive as we step into a chaotic arena of political unrest, religious factionalism, and apocalyptic writings. The impetus behind this shift can be found in the Jewish intertestamental literature, written during the roughly three- to four-hundred-year gap between the Hebrew Bible and the New Testament. The era between the composition of the final writings of the Hebrew Bible (the book of Daniel in the early second-century B.C.E.) and the composition of the final writings that made up the New Testament (the book of Revelation, around 100 C.E.) was a period of amazing religious fecundity in western Asia and the eastern Mediterranean. Donald Harman Akenson has described Palestine in this period as a virtual petri dish hosting every form of religious vitality.[1] Rabbinic Judaism and Christianity would evolve and grow to maturity from this matrix. Until the twentieth century, the shadows cast by these massive bodies of religious thought eclipsed the scores of other religious sects and movements—Jewish and Christian—that had emerged. But now, thanks to the hard work of countless archeologists who have unearthed great caches of ancient libraries and the painstaking research of contemporary philologists, we have a more complete picture of the fractious, unruly, and creative period that produced Judaism and Christianity.

This turbulent period also marks the adolescence of Satan. In previous chapters we glimpsed only snapshots of the Devil's infancy, usually only in the background of group photos from the Hebrew Bible where the central focus was on another subject altogether. In the Intertestamental Period, however, Satan acquires articulation and definition; the Devil comes of age and begins to act independently, apart from the divine court. Satan now has his own agenda and his own band of cosmic lackeys.

What factors led to all this religious ferment? We must first recall the radical social changes experienced by the Jewish people during this period, their dispersion throughout the ancient world, and the frustrations of centuries of demeaning colonial life. In the Diaspora (the scattering of Jews beyond their homeland of Israel), the Jewish people, on one hand, were forced to sharpen their identity as a way to differentiate themselves from others. In order to sing the Lord's song in foreign lands, the Jewish people became even more expert and inventive in the expression of their tradition. On the other hand, the contact with other cultures had a profound effect on God's chosen ones. Themes and strains from other religious tunes were in the air, and many of these found their way into Jewish thought.

The dizzying dance of differentiation and assimilation produced an array of options for sectarian religious expression. Furthermore, based on the vast accumulation of religious writings—and this body of literature will undoubtedly continue to grow as more ancient documents are discovered and deciphered—the Intertestamental Period was rich in the very act of writing. If we ignore for the moment the contents of what is called the pseudepigraphical literature, (those ancient writings that are not part of the Bible or Apocrypha), the contents of the Dead Sea Scrolls from the Jordan Valley, the Nag Hammadi library from the Nile Valley, as well as the myriad documents preserved in translated form in Ethiopic, Old Church Slavonic, Greek, Coptic, Aramaic, and Latin, we must marvel at the sheer *quantity* of religious literature produced between 200 B.C.E. and 200 C.E.[2] Each polemic and apocalyptic scenario, each putative patriarchal vision and renegade gospel, each community constitution and liturgical vision sparked another. Nothing was settled in this literature, everything was up for grabs, and virtually every idea, symbol, and ritual of the later faiths can be traced back to this period.

Something dramatic took place between the "First" Testament accounts in Job and Zechariah—which feature a heavenly prosecutor known variously as *hassatan,* the Adversary—and the "Second" Testament accounts about the cosmic opponent of God named Satan (the Hebrew name) or the Devil, *diabolos* (the Greek name). The outlines of that drama can be sketched by sampling the outpouring of Jewish literature from the final two centuries before the common era and the first two centuries of the common era. It was during this period that Satan moved from the shadowy ranks of the cosmic courtiers to centerstage as their fallen prince.

Above, we used the word, "apocalyptic" and before proceeding we must pause to understand the term in more depth, because the character "Satan" and the literary genre "apocalyptic" are as intertwined as cowboys in Westerns and unlikely lovers in romantic comedies. The word "apocalyptic" is Greek in origin and means "revelatory." Apocalyptic thinking and writing, then, unveils or reveals something hidden from view. Many types of thinking and writing conceivably could be defined as "apocalyptic" or "revelatory," but since the latter word is more common in English, we reserve the former, more unusual term for special cases, when cosmic or supernatural forces are credited or blamed for causing the phenomenon.

For instance, if a tabloid announced that the child born to a Hollywood starlet had been sired by a handsome president, that would certainly constitute a revelation. But we would reserve the term apocalyptic for the tabloid story that announced that the child born to a Hollywood starlet had been sired by a demon from hell or an alien from outer space.

Jewish apocalyptic thought emerged between the Testaments, between 200 B.C.E. and 100 C.E. This type of storytelling sought to reveal the reason for the frustrated hopes of a people who could not reconcile their misfortunes with their theology. If the descendants of Abraham and Sarah were partners to a covenant with the Architect of the Universe, then why had their cultural and political properties been condemned by a parade of

Near Eastern tyrants? The response of the Jewish apocalypticists was to construct a new theory that explained this conundrum. They built the theory from pieces of Jewish folklore, puzzling biblical passages, and the myths of surrounding cultures. The theory revealed a cosmic conspiracy at work, led by a supernatural criminal mastermind (Satan) who controlled a vast, nefarious network of demonic forces dedicated to frustrating the divine purpose at every turn.

The apocalyptic repertoire also included stories that inspired hope and offered discouraged people the imaginative leverage to cope with degrading social conditions. Jewish apocalyptic also revealed that God has his own secret service of angels, led by Gabriel, Michael, Raphael, and others. The good angels protected the righteous in the short term, and in the long term, they engaged in a spy-versus-spy combat with the fallen angels. At some imminent date, always communicated in code ("the end of days," "a time, two times, and half a time," "seventy weeks," "the thousand three hundred thirty-five days," all from the biblical book of Daniel), the Grand Army of the Jordan would triumph over the Demonic Confederacy, and the righteous would receive their reward. This story and a thousand fantastic variations of it have thrived ever since. Since its emergence in Second Temple Jewish culture, the apocalyptic story has become one of the central narratives of Western culture, and this ancient style of thought was perfected by early Christians who embraced it long after its decline in Rabbinic Judaism. Satan is a product of this style of narrative and so we must begin this account of the formative stage of Satan's development by looking at the apocalyptic book, Daniel, probably the final book of the Hebrew Bible to be composed.

Satan in Daniel

The book of Daniel was written in the second century B.C.E. to encourage Jews living in the Diaspora to maintain their faith in the face of foreign domination. The stories in Daniel chapters 1 to 6 sketch the daytime world of Diaspora Judaism with edifying tales about how a Hebrew youth named Daniel and his friends kept their faith (and kept kosher) during the Babylonian Exile. The second section of the book of Daniel, chapters 7 to 12, sketches the nighttime world of Diaspora Judaism, where years of deferred dreams and frustration over the triumphs of tyrants led to fevered visions of cosmic reversals and battles in which "a Son of Man" (Dan 7:13), or the angelic princes Gabriel (Dan 8:16) and Michael (Dan 10:21; 12:1), would defeat the tyrants of the world personified as chaos monsters.

Although Daniel lacks direct references to supernatural evil beings (i.e., Satan), there are "adversaries" in Daniel. These enemies are the foreign rulers occupying Israel, whom Daniel describes (in highly apocalyptic language) as monstrous beasts. Daniel makes it clear, however, that those who endure in faith will survive the difficulties of the present age (Dan 12:1–3).[3]

In Daniel 4 there are three allusions to a class of cosmic beings called "the watchers" (the plural form is in Dan 4:17; the singular form "watcher" is in Dan 4:13, 23). The word "watchers" (sometimes called the "watcher angels") seems to be synonymous with the term "angels" for Daniel, and no special attention is given to these figures who, like other low-level cosmic beings, act as heralds of divine decrees and agents on divine missions. Still, the mention of the Watchers in the book of Daniel is significant because, as we shall see, these beings will occupy a central role in Satan's continuing drama in other Jewish texts from the same period.

Enoch and the Watchers

The apocalyptic book of Enoch (also known as 1 Enoch or Ethiopic Enoch) contains a variety of material dating from between 200 and 60 B.C.E.[4] Particularly relevant in the development of Satan is a collection of visionary tales included in the Enoch material known as the "book of the Watchers."[5] One such tale narrates how the *benay elohim*, or "the sons of God" (called "the Watchers" in Enoch) fell from their divine posts within the heavenly court. Before we explore the Enoch tale, it seems prudent to mention a strange passage in Genesis in which the *benay elohim* come to earth in order to mate with human women:

> When people began to multiply on the face of the ground, and daughters were born to them, the sons of God saw that they were fair; and they took wives for themselves of all that they chose. Then the LORD said, "My spirit shall not abide in mortals forever, for they are flesh; their days shall be one

hundred twenty years." The Nephilim were on the earth in those days—and
also afterward—when the sons of God went in to the daughters of humans,
who bore children to them. These were the heroes that were of old, warriors
of renown. (Gen 6:1–4)

In Genesis, the children born from this odd coupling are heroes and legendary warriors. This fragment from Genesis, one of the most bizarre and
inscrutable passages in the Hebrew Bible, serves as the launching pad for
the apocalyptic fantasy of 1 Enoch with its astral characters and scenarios.
According to Enoch, in the beginning, God appointed certain angels to
watch over the universe (the Watchers).[6] One of the watchers, Semyaz,
mustered a group of two hundred "lust-filled" angels who descended to
earth in order to mate with human women (cf. Gen 6:1–4).[7] Among Semyaz's lieutenants is an angel named Azazel who dominates the subsequent
narrative. This angelic trespass of a cosmic border results in a race of giants
(the *nephilim,* or "fallen ones") who, in turn, bring forth demonic spirits.
These terrifying demons are voracious monsters, devouring everything in
sight, including people.[8] The whole terrible scenario unleashes such violence and corruption in the world that God is forced to send good angels
down to put a stop to things. Under the leadership of these good angels
(and under the direction of God), a cosmic combat ensues, and God deliv-
ers a prediction for the future: After seventy generations, the demonic in-
surgents will be defeated and condemned to eternal torment, and the earth
will enter into a period of rest and peace.[9]

The story of the Watchers is the stuff of apocalyptic literature. The use
of symbolic language, cosmic battles, end-time predictions, the combat between good evil, and the emphasis on evil's hold over the present age are all
hallmarks of this literary genre.[10] Moreover, the Enoch material serves to
explain the cause of evil in the world: Evil is the result of an evil being. It
is not difficult to see connections between the Watchers and the combat
myths of Mesopotamia, Egypt, Canaan, Persia, and Greece (see chapter 4),
all of which describe, in one way or another, the battle between good and
evil. But what are the connections to Satan?

As we discussed in chapter 3, Satan in both Job and Zechariah is one of
"the sons of God," that is, one of the heavenly beings. As God's emissary,
Satan is involved in roving the earth and observing activities in the terres-

trial sphere. What is different about the *benay elohim* (or Watchers) in Enoch, however, is that a leader emerges among the disgraced angels, variously called Azazel, Semihazah (sometimes, Semyaza or Semjaza), and later, Satan.[11] This leader commands a gang of unsavory comrades who do very little "watching" but instead cause quite a bit of trouble. In fact, the leader makes a pact with the Watchers to stick together as they embark on their evil mission to earth. During this mission, not only do they have sexual intercourse with human women, but they proceed to teach their human wives the forbidden art of magic. We can also hear echoes of the cranky views of the sectarians who invented these stories: Among the forbidden arts that the Watchers teach humans is cosmetology. "The beautifying of the eyelids" (1 En 8:1) receives special censure. And, as already mentioned, their offspring, the *nephilim*, turn on humankind and wreak destruction and death. Azazel is specifically credited with teaching men how to make weapons, tempting them to violence, vanity, and injustice.[12]

In the Watchers myth it is important to note that the battle between Azazel and the archangels sent to subdue him reflects the social, political, and religious struggles occurring in late Second Temple Judaism.[13] Even more significant is the fact that Enoch credits the existence of sin not to God or humans, but to Azazel: "The whole earth has been corrupted though the works that were taught by Azazel: to him ascribe all sin" (1 En 9:6; 10:8).[14] Azazel is more than simply a cosmic troublemaker. In fact, he seems more like the Satan we know today: the author of sin, the corrupter of humanity, and the antithesis of God.

Interestingly, while the name "Azazel" is used throughout the text in Enoch, the name "Satan" appears only in the final chapters (1 Enoch 37–71). This is a significant detail. By the time the final chapters were written (in the first century B.C.E.), apparently the name "Satan," rather than "Azazel," had become the popular designation for the Evil One.[15] Demonstrating a fine-tuning of the Devil's character, Satan is now a fearsome demon and the embodiment of evil. Moreover, in the actions of the Watchers, we can observe that these evil agents are now several steps removed from God, acting on their own (instead of following divine orders like the *benay elohim* in Zechariah and Job) and thus clearly oriented toward evil.[16] According to Jeffrey Burton Russell, "Enoch has safely removed them beyond the limits of the Divine nature itself, and this in turn allows him and his fellow apocalyptic writers a free hand in bringing out their evil nature."[17]

The myth of the Watchers would become foundational in the history of diabology. One of the central motifs in the Watchers myth is the element of taboo sexuality; that the Watchers were born from illicit sexual intercourse between mortals and angels. Strange sexual encounters are part of nearly every subsequent satanic narrative. Legends about evil spirits, male *incubi* and female *succubae,* who have intercourse with humans in their sleep, are common themes in diabology. During European and North American witchcraft hysterias, this motif mutated into accounts of Black Sabbaths, Witches' Sabbaths, and the like, in which female participants had intercourse with demons or even with the Horny One himself. This motif persists in twentieth and twenty-first-century stories about women giving birth to demonic children (the subject of several successful feature films during the 1960s and 1970s, including *Rosemary's Baby* and *The Omen*), in fantastic tales about humans coupling with aliens, and in folkloristic accounts about "breeders," women abducted by satanic cults for the purposes of breeding newborns that are then (with a touch of the Moloch legend mixed in to gruesome measure) ritually sacrificed.[18]

In bringing out the evil nature of the Watchers, the apocalyptic writers of Enoch contribute to the growing chasm between God and some of his "sons," the *benay elohim*. This separation is critical in understanding the emergence of Satan, for not only does the separation preserve God's goodness, but it also clears the way for a single being to become the antithesis of God. Eventually, this being, Satan, will become Jesus' opponent. But for now, the saga of the Watchers continues in another important text.

The Book of Jubilees

Written between 160 and 140 B.C.E., the book of Jubilees is a significant source in our investigation.[19] Its author was troubled by the internal conflicts brewing among various Jewish groups concerning Jewish assimilation into Gentile culture.[20] These conflicts, according to Jubilees, are the result of an evil being the author calls, variously, *Mastema* ("hatred"), *Beliar* ("without light"), and, toward the end of the text, *Satan*.[21]

Written in the apocalyptic style of 1 Enoch, the book of Jubilees claims that the Watchers descended to earth not because they were attracted by the sight of human women (as in 1 Enoch), but for a noble cause: to teach humans justice and righteousness. Unfortunately, they soon abandon their didactic mission for an erotic one. Like the Watchers in Enoch, the angels in Jubilees have intercourse with human women, and thus disaster is unleashed. Once again a race of giants results from these ill-fated unions, and these giants beget murderous offspring.

In a very real sense, Jubilees is to Genesis-Exodus what Chronicles is to Samuel-Kings.[22] As already noted, Chronicles revisits the events of Samuel-Kings, and the author (or authors) rewrites much of Israel's history from his own theological perspective. Hence, the Chronicler's version of events differs somewhat from the events presented in Samuel-Kings. Recall that in 1 Chronicles 21, it is *Satan*, not *God*, as in 2 Samuel 24, who incites David's census. In much the same way, when the author of Jubilees rewrites his version of the events in Genesis and Exodus, he credits the more unsavory deeds of God to a malicious, evil being. For example, when the author of Jubilees relates the terrifying events of Genesis 22 (the demand from God that Abraham sacrifice his only son Isaac, and offer him as a sacrifice to the LORD), it is *Mastema*, not God, in the Jubilees version (Jub 17:15–18) who issues the appalling decree. And in the bizarre story found in Ex 4:24 (God's attempted murder of Moses because Moses apparently was not circumcised), it is *Mastema*, according to the author of Jubilees, rather than God, who goes after Moses, intending to kill him (Jub 48:2–3).[23]

In the Enoch material, it is Azazel (or Semihazah) who is the rebel leader. The author of Jubilees assigns this function to Mastema (or, on occasion, Beliar), the angel of adversity, who commands a legion of subordinate, demonic spirits. These subordinates were, in a sense, allotted to Mastema by God. Whereas in Enoch these malignant spirits are bound hand and foot and tossed into a pit to await final judgment (1 En 10:4–7; 19:1–2), in Jubilees God acquiesces to Mastema's plea that he be allowed to retain a tenth of his gang of cosmic troublemakers (Jub 10:8–9):

O Lord, Creator, leave some of them [the evil Watchers] before me, and let them obey my voice. And let them do everything which I tell them, because

if some of them are not left for me, I will not be able to exercise the authority of my will among the children of men.[24] (Jub 10:8)

God's approval of this arrangement posed by Mastema leaves a corps of
fallen angels to bedevil humanity until the turning of the next eschatolog-
ical season. Why did not God simply destroy Mastema once and for all?
Although the question, a variation on the theme of theodicy ("divine justice"), is a legitimate one, we do not receive an answer. While it is significant that the author of Jubilees assigns the cause of evil and suffering to a
supernatural, evil being rather than to God, Jubilees fails to clarify whether
Mastema actually *causes* human suffering or if he is merely capitalizing on
the human inclination toward evil in the first place.[25]

Jubilees specifically refers to the Prince of Demons by the name "Satan"
on four occasions. Two of the references are in texts that promise believers
that Satan will no longer wield power in the next age.

And all of their days they will be complete
and live in peace and rejoicing,
and there shall be no Satan and no [one] who will destroy,
because all of their days will be days of blessing and healing.[26] (Jub 23:29)

And jubilees will pass, until Israel is purified from all the sin of fornication,
and defilement, and uncleanness, and sin and error. And they will dwell in
confidence in all the land. And then it will not have any Satan or any evil
[one.] And the land will be purified from that time and forever.[27] (Jub 50:5)

This somewhat idyllic vision of future restoration, when Satan will no
longer be a threat, is echoed in the New Testament (e.g., Mk 13:24–27) and
in other apocalyptic writings, such as the first-century Testament of
Moses.[28]

The third mention of Satan in Jubilees is a nostalgic look back at the
good old days, prior to Israel's enslavement in the land of Egypt, an act that
Jub 48:9 blames on Mastema. Prior to that, "there was no Satan or anything
evil all the days of the life of Joseph" (Jub 46:2).[29] The final mention of
Satan clearly indicates that he has replaced Mastema as the embodiment of
evil. In the passage, one of the members of the angelic posse who had
bound Mastema and the demons explains to Moses what happened:

And we acted in accord with all his words. All of the evil ones, who were cruel, we bound in the place of judgment, but a tenth of them we let remain so that they that they might be subject before Satan on the earth.[30] (Jub 10:11)

Here Satan is clearly identified as the name of the leader of evil beings, edging out Mastema. Although the Satan of Jubilees is not yet the Titan of Evil, he is nonetheless on his way.

Satan and the Dead Sea Scrolls

In 1947 ancient documents known as the Dead Sea Scrolls were first discovered in caves in the Judean wilderness. The writers of these documents were most likely the Essenes, the first-century B.C.E. inhabitants of the nearby community of Qumran. The Essenes were an austere, ultra-orthodox, secretive group who withdrew from society to form their own ascetic community. They were exclusively male, wore only white garments, and practiced celibacy.[31] For the purposes of our discussion, we assume an association between these documents and the Essenes, as most scholars do, though it is possible that the scrolls were hidden in the Dead Sea caves by a Jewish group other than the Essenes.

The Qumran literature makes it clear that the Essenes understood Satan to be an evil leader who commanded a legion of followers in heaven and on earth. They believed Satan was engaged in a cosmic battle with God, and they saw themselves as personally engaged in this battle alongside God. Moreover, according to Elaine Pagels, the Essenes believed that "the foreign occupation of Palestine—and the accommodation of the majority of Jews to that occupation"—was proof that Satan had "infiltrated and taken over God's own people, turning most of them into allies of the Evil One."[32] Finally, they believed they were living in the final days dominated by God's evil adversary (Satan), to whom others had fallen prey.[33]

This is dualism at its best: two conflicting spirits, one good (God), the other evil (Satan). The doctrine of two spirits, as described in that part of the Qumran documents known as the Damascus Covenant, has generated a great deal of controversy among scholars. It is likely that the influence of other religions, especially Persian dualism, with its focus on a good and loving god (Ahura Mazda) opposed to an evil, Satan-like being (Ahriman), is operative here, as Neil Forsyth points out: "What seems to have happened at Qumran . . . is . . . the combat terminology of many Old Testament passages, related as it was to several of the surrounding religions, has now become a radical apocalyptic myth . . . led by the spirit of light and the spirit of darkness. We may probably detect the influence of Iranian mythology."[34]

The Essenes called themselves the "sons of light," and those who did not agree with their orthodoxy (the vast majority of their Jewish brethren) were called the "sons of darkness."[35] According to the Community Rule (also known as the Manual of Discipline), another document from Qumran:

> From the God of knowledge comes all that is and shall be. . . . He has created man to govern the wicked and has appointed for him two spirits in which to walk until the end of time of his visitation: the spirits of truth and falsehood. Those born of truth spring from the fountain of light, but those born of falsehood spring from a source of darkness. All the children of righteousness are ruled by the Prince of Light and walk in the ways of light; but all the children of falsehood are ruled by the Angel of Darkness and walk in the ways of darkness. (Community Rule 3)[36]

Accordingly, the "sons of light" saw themselves as engaged in a war—a war that would ultimately result in a day of judgment when God and his army would sweep away the sons of darkness along with Israel's foreign oppressors.[37] This belief gave rise to messianic expectations within the Qumran community as they believed that "the Messiah would come at any moment and their salvation from the hands of Satan was imminent."[38] The followers of the Angel of Darkness (those who did not embrace the Essenes's orthodoxy), on the other hand, had been led astray by Satan (or Belial, "worthlessness").[39] The Damascus Covenant specifically mentions Satan and his involvement in this conflict: "During all those years Satan shall be unleashed against Israel."[40] The Qumran sect clearly despised Satan and viewed him as the root of all evil. Satan not only lured people away from God, but he also capitalized on the human inclination toward sin.[41]

According to the Essenes, it was God who created Satan in the first place as "an instrument of his vengeance against sinners."[42] This belief is problematic: If God created Satan, for whatever reasons, then God is ultimately responsible for evil and suffering in the world.[43] That God would ultimately destroy Satan's dominion was never in doubt, but theologically speaking, the Qumran sect came no closer to addressing the problem of theodicy than the authors of these intertestamental tracts or, for that matter, the savants of modern theology.

The Prince of Demons

Throughout the vast collection of intertestamental books, the Prince of Demons is known by many names. In Jubilees, the leader of the disembodied bastard children of the Watchers is known as Mastema while in 1 Enoch, the Prince of Demons is referred to as Satan. Linguistically, Mastema and Satan are cognate terms, both deriving from variant spellings of the same word, whose consonants are *ś-ṭ-n* or *m*." Forms of both words are found in the Hebrew Bible, but as adjectives, verbs, and common nouns (*the* satan, not Satan). But now, in second-century Jewish literature, the names "Mastema" and "Satan" appear for the first time as proper names for the Prince of Demons. But Satan and Mastema were not the only names used; we must open other scrolls to glimpse some of the Evil One's other names.

We have already mentioned the books of Enoch, Jubilees, the Testament of Moses, and the Damascus Covenant. Those are only a fraction of the fantastic and esoteric body of Jewish religious literature from around the turn of the common era. There are books of legends about prophets and sages, such as the first-century C.E. Lives of the Prophets, the Martyrdom of Isaiah, and the Testament of Solomon; deathbed revelations attributed to the patriarchs, such as the second-century B.C.E. Testimony of the Twelve Patriarchs; and mystical and cosmological explorations issued in the name of well-known (Apocalypse of Abraham) or obscure (1–3 Enoch) biblical figures. "Belial" and "Beliar" are names used for the Satan-figure in the Testimony of the Twelve Patriarchs, the Lives of the Prophets, and the so-called Damascus Covenant, which was among the Dead Sea Scrolls. "Sammael" ("the Blind God") is a name used for the Satan-figure in the Martyrdom of Isaiah (in 3 Enoch "Sammael" refers to one of Satan's assistants). "Azazel" (a name that may mean "the Strong God") appears in 1 Enoch as one of the

Watchers, but in the Apocalypse of Abraham, he is the prince of the rebel angels.[44]

To add to the complexity, the Prince of Demons is known as Beelzeboul in the Testament of Solomon. The meaning of that term is uncertain. It is assumed that its variant spellings Beelzebub/Baalzebub ("Lord of the Flies," i.e., "Lord of Putrefaction") are a pejorative alteration of Beelzeboul (or Baalzebul or Beelzebul) which could mean, "Prince Baal," an ancient Canaanite epithet, or "Lord of Heaven."[45] So the Devil goes by many names in this period: Satan, Mastema, Beelzebul, Belial, Sammael, and Azazel. Although the names may differ, the Prince of Demons' function remains the same. His role, regardless of the epithet preferred by a particular author, is a subversive one.

Legends of the Fall

As attested by the many names for the Prince of Demons in these texts, Satan, by whatever name, emerged as a potent character in the Jewish religious imagination during the Intertestamental Period. The narrative about the Watchers in 1 Enoch and Jubilees gives one version of how Satan fell: Satan was prince of the demonic spirits of the fallen giants sired by fallen angels known as the Watchers and born from the oh-so-fair daughters of men. We have referred to this particular story as the Watchers myth.

In addition to this myth, there are other versions of how the angels fell (or where Satan went wrong or why evil continues to plague the righteous) in literature.[46] Among these alternative "legends of the Fall" are tales that narrate what can be called the Lucifer myth. Many people mistakenly believe that "Lucifer" is simply another name for Satan from the Hebrew Bible. Who is Lucifer and how did his name come to be associated with the Devil? The Lucifer myth consists of two motifs: the Devil's fall from heaven, and his identification with the name "Lucifer."

This first motif appears in the Life of Adam and Eve, a first-century C.E. work that has been associated with the Pharisee movement, Satan is banished to the earth because he refused to genuflect before the newly created Adam. According to that work, Satan said: "I will not worship one inferior and subsequent to me. I am prior in creation; before [Adam] was made, I was already made. He ought to worship me" (Life of Adam and Eve 12:3). The Qur'an (2:34) also preserves this tradition, about how all the angels were commanded to worship "the image of the Lord God" (i.e., Adam, made in "the image of God"), but Satan refused.

It was as if this one son of God could not abide being displaced in the affections of the Divine Father by the creation of humans. Because of his jealous and proud refusal to kowtow to the new child, Satan was expelled from heaven to earth, where he now obsessively tortures the descendants of his rival, Adam. So whereas in the Watchers myth, sexual lust led the rebel angels to fall for human women, in this version, as in the biblical proverb, it is pride that cometh before the Fall (Prov 16:18).

A variation of this legend, about Satan's fatal sin of pride, also appears in 2 Enoch, and this version, indirectly, provides us with the motif of Lucifer. According to 2 Enoch, Satan, a high-ranking officer in the cosmic army, known in the Hebrew Bible as the *saba'ot* or the "[angelic] hosts," attempted a heavenly palace coup d'etat. When he failed, he was expelled from heaven and now flies through the air, "ceaselessly, above the Bottomless" (2 En 29:5–6).[47] This story of Satan falling from grace echoes several speeches from the prophets that mock the pretensions of ancient potentates and prophesy their eventual demise. For instance, Isaiah 14:3–23 taunts the king of Babylon:

> How the oppressor has ceased!
> How his insolence has ceased!
> The LORD has broken the staff of the wicked,
> the scepter of rulers. (Isa 14:4–5)

Later in this passage, Isaiah's exaggerated rhetoric about the first becoming last expands to cosmic proportions. Isaiah may be drawing upon the imagery of a Canaanite myth, for lore about the Day Star, or Morning Star, has been found among the texts unearthed from Ras Shamra in Syria. It could be, then, that Isaiah alludes to a lost Canaanite myth about a failed cosmic rebellion led by Morning Star in order to lend a mythic grandeur to the account of the Babylonian monarch's fall. For as Isaiah describes it, the king of Babylon does not merely fall from his elevated royal seat to the cold, hard ground; rather, he falls from celestial heights all the way to the innermost depths of the underworld:

How are you fallen from heaven,
O Day Star, son of Dawn! . . .
You are brought down to Sheol,
to the depths of the Pit. (Isa 14:12, 15)

This is where we get the name "Lucifer" for Satan, because the Greek translation of the Hebrew term translated above as "Day Star" is "Lucifer" ("Light-Bearer"). Postbiblical interpreters are responsible for connecting the dots between "Day Star"/Lucifer and Satan, an identification that was never made in the Hebrew Bible, however. Just as the obscure passage from Gen 6:1–4 led to legends about the Watchers, this passage from Isaiah serves as the backstory for a rival tale about how Lucifer and his rebel angels fell, and their coup having failed, found themselves consigned to the underworld.

The prophet Ezekiel, writing from Babylon in the early years of the Exile, addresses a series of speeches to the Lebanese city-state of Tyre and its ruler (Ezekiel 27–28). These speeches, like Isaiah's, borrow motifs from primeval lore known to his audience but which were not represented in the written biblical materials about creation in Genesis 1–11. The prince of Tyre, a proud and cultured figure whose demise, according to the Hebrew prophet, is imminent, is compared in Ezekiel 28:11–19 to a near-divine figure cast out of Paradise for the sin of pride. "Mortal," the oracle addressed by the LORD to Ezekiel begins, "raise a lamentation over the king of Tyre and say to him":

You [the king of Tyre] were . . . full of wisdom and perfect in beauty,
You were in Eden, the garden of God . . .
With an anointed cherub as guardian I placed you;
You were on the holy mountain of God. (Ezek 28:12–14)

Ezekiel is evidently referring to a legend about an Adam-like character who resided in an Edenic garden on the divine mountain in primordial times. This character, unlike the all-too-human characters in Genesis 2–3, is described as one "full of wisdom and perfect in beauty." Although the original Canaanite myth that tells this story has not been discovered, scholars assume that Ezekiel is referring to a creation legend that was known to his sixth-century B.C.E. audience.

Ezekiel's oracle contains even more hints about this lost myth: "In the abundance of your trade, you were filled with violence and you sinned" (Ezek 28:16a). In this line, the subject seems to be the king of Tyre in Ezekiel's day, here accused of controlling a vast seafaring economy and amassing untold wealth though rapacious violence. But in the very next line (Ezek 28:16b), the scene shifts again to mythic locations and primordial time: "So I cast you as a profane thing from the mountain of God, and the guardian cherub drove you out from among the stones of fire."

The end of the poem weaves together the ultimate fate of these two distinct characters, a sixth-century king of Tyre and a primeval demigod:

> Your [the primeval character's] heart was proud because of your beauty;
> You corrupted your wisdom for the sake of your splendor.
> I cast you to the ground;
> I exposed you [the Tyrian prince] before kings . . .
> By the multitude of your [this could refer to both characters'] iniquities,
> in the unrighteousness of your [the Tyrian prince's] trade . . .
> (Ezek 28:17–18)

As in Isaiah 14, Ezekiel 28 sets the rise and fall of an earthly monarch against the background of extrabiblical lore about the banishment of a celestial figure from the divine presence (in Ezekiel, for the sin of pride). Although, again, no such myth from Canaanite sources has yet been discovered, scholars have reconstructed an outline based on passages like these. So the Lucifer myth, the intertestamental legend about Satan's expulsion from the divine presence for some primordial sin—whether pride, envy, or rebellion—grew out of prophetic oracles that denounced earthly kings in these mythic terms. The Lucifer myth, in time, thanks largely to John Milton's reliance on it in *Paradise Lost*, would become the most popular legend of the Fall, the account of a failed primordial heavenly coup.

In addition to the Watchers myth and the Lucifer myth, there may also have been a third legend of the Fall. In a document entitled Third Enoch, which stems from the fifth and sixth centuries C.E., Satan is described as the head prosecutor in the heavenly court, similar to his role in Job and Zechariah (texts composed nearly a millennium before). This story does not detail Satan's fall from grace, but a much later (nineteenth-century)

Jewish tradition described in Louis Ginzberg's *Legends of the Jews* attributes Satan's demotion from the heavenly community to a punishment for his overzealous prosecution of Job.[48] This legend of the Fall might be more accurately called "The Story of the Prosecutor Who Went off the Deep End."

On one hand, there is no evidence that this legend has ancient roots. On the other hand, its existence is instructive because it reminds us that any number of stories about Satan's fall could have been (and surely were) constructed. The Watchers myth and the Lucifer myth were simply the most popular. The raw material for manufacturing such stories was the fund of biblical passages filled with obscure mythological allusions and unexplained narrative gaps. The Watchers myth, for example, came from the truncated story about the fallen angels in Gen 6:1–4; the Lucifer myth drew on prophetic allusions to Canaanite astral lore in Isaiah 14 and variant creation motifs preserved in Ezekiel 28.

The third legend of the Fall, the version that features Satan as an overly zealous prosecutor, grew out of the puzzling absence of *hassatan* from the final scenes of the book of Job. Who knows how many other legends about Satan's fall circulated in oral form or in lost scrolls? The Bible is filled with many other narrative holes into which imaginative interpreters could have ventured in order to mine new myths.

Satan's Role in the Intertestamental Literature

The diverse body of intertestamental writings reflects the myriad political, social, cultural, and religious changes taking place among Jews around the turn of the common era. In this literature God's adversary, who is known by a host of names, takes on more definition. The Satan figure in these texts acts independently, often commanding a loyal legion of demonic cohorts. Satan also becomes a concept, a way of defining one's enemies, whether earthy or spiritual. This is the essence of Satan's adversarial role. Satan represents opposing factions within Judaism, the foreign rulers, and the enemy within. These various representations—ranging from local demonic figures, to cosmic troublemakers, to earthy adversaries—eventually assimilate to become the Satan of the New Testament and beyond.

chapter 6

satan in
the new testament

The devil can cite scripture for his own purpose!
—William Shakespeare

here was a growing consensus about the existence of a supreme evil being in the Intertestamental Period, but the Prince of Demons had many names. Although these names resurface from time to time in the New Testament, one name emerges above the rest: Satan. It is this name, Satan, that will become the Prince of Demons' most popular designation, inducing fear and trembling at its mere mention for generations to come.

Satan assumes a more commanding role in the New Testament, and his demonic minions, in fact, abound in the New Testament (appearing some 568 times), cropping up in unlikely places and challenging the ultimate authority of Jesus. Even though Satan's character is more clearly defined in the New Testament than it had been in the Hebrew Bible (as we shall soon see, Satan is now the archnemesis of Jesus), his essential function in the Bible remains unchanged: He is still the troublemaker, the stumbling block, the Adversary. However, even as the figure of Satan grows more confident, more powerful, and more insidious—blatantly challenging Jesus' authority and even infiltrating the ranks of those close to him—he is not allowed to move about in the world unopposed. Indeed, Jesus, the hero of the New Testament, steps forward to confront the villain at every turn. Although the Devil may have a few tricks up his sleeve, the authors of the New Testament make it clear that Satan is no match for the obedient Son of God. Round after round hero and villain spar in a struggle for universal supremacy, but at the end of the struggle, God scores a knockout, throwing Satan into a "lake of fire and sulfur" (Rev 20:10).

As we have pointed out, belief in a demonic being called Satan evolved only over a long period of time. Several factors influenced this development, including the religious syncretism of the ancient Near East, the foreign domination of Palestine, the increased reflection about the origins of evil on behalf of Jews in the Second Temple period (538 B.C.E.–70 C.E.), and Jewish apocalyptic thinking. When the Babylonians razed the First Temple in Jerusalem in 587 B.C.E., they also unwittingly destroyed the efficacy of the Iron Age theology that equated punishment, measure for measure, with sin.

We need to keep in mind the precarious world into which Jesus of Nazareth is born. The destruction of Solomon's Temple (the First Temple) and the exile of many of Jerusalem's citizens, combined with the continued indignities of colonial life, inspired speculations about possible sources of evil that were more sinister and powerful than prophetic finger-pointing could account for. Evil seemed to be more than the inevitable consequences of human sin; it seemed to have a life of its own. Jesus' life is sandwiched between two important struggles for Judean independence: the successful Jewish rebellion against Antiochus IV (142 B.C.E.) and the unsuccessful Jewish rebellion against Rome that resulted in the destruction of Judea (66–73 C.E.). Following the Maccabean revolt (as recounted in the apocryphal books of 1–2 Maccabees), Judea experienced a period of autonomous Jewish rule under the ineffective Hasmonean dynasty. Dissension within various factions of Judaism, combined with corrupt leadership, led to the Roman occupation of Palestine and the puppet governments of the murderous and maniacal Herod and his disreputable sons. This dangerous and chaotic world is the world of Jesus. But it is also the world of the authors of the Gospels who narrate the events of Jesus' life. The Gospel accounts, then, must be read with an eye to their authors' current crises.

Satan in the Synoptics

Matthew, Mark, and Luke wrote for different audiences and sought to address specific issues within their respective communities. Taken as a whole, Matthew, Mark, and Luke are referred to as the Synoptic Gospels (*synoptic* is from the Greek, meaning "like-view") because these three Gospels contain similar material. We assume that Mark's Gospel was written between 65 and 70 C.E., Matthew's and Luke's between around 80 to 85 C.E.[1] Matthew and Luke used the Gospel of Mark, the earliest one written, as a primary source—along with another source scholars call "Q," a lost collection of Jesus' sayings unaccompanied by any stories—and to which each added additional unique material.[2] Before examining the common references to Satan in the Synoptics, it is important to discuss the background of each Gospel so that such references can be placed into their historical context.

Mark's Gospel was probably written during the last year of the Jewish war against Rome (64–70 C.E.).[3] The anonymous author (the identities of the authors of the four canonical Gospels remain a mystery, though religious traditions have attached names to each) seems to have this crisis in mind as he tells the story of Jesus' life. The entire Gospel has an apocalyptic tone, as if the author and his audience were living in the "last days." Mark understands Jesus' healing miracles and exorcisms as "breaking up the hold which Satan has on human beings."[4] So although Mark is anxious to impart this "good news," there is tension underneath the surface. Jesus' ministry and his inauguration of the reign of God are nothing short of a battle against the forces of evil embodied in Satan. According to biblical scholar Elaine Pagels: "Mark frames his narrative . . . with episodes in which Satan and his demonic forces retaliate against God by working to destroy Jesus."[5]

Matthew works within Mark's original framework, but updates events to reflect the concerns of his own time, a decade after Mark and after the cataclysmic events of the 70s. Matthew's Jesus is the long-awaited Messiah of the Hebrew Bible and the direct descendant of David predicted by the prophets. Matthew's Gospel is not only concerned with presenting Jesus as the Messiah, but also as the supreme teacher of both the Mosaic Law and of proper ethical behavior.[6] Matthew's rabbi-like Jesus, much as in the dualistic schemes of Zoroaster and the Essenes, offers his disciples the choice

between good or evil, light or darkness. The Jesus of Matthew's Gospel exhorts his followers to eschew an earthly kingdom in favor of a heavenly one:

> Do not store up for yourselves treasures on earth, where moth and rust con-
> sume and where thieves break in and steal; but store up for yourselves treasures
> in heaven, where neither moth nor rust consumes and where thieves do not
> break in and steal. For where your treasure is, there your heart will be also . . .
>
> No one can serve two masters; for a slave will either hate the one and love
> the other, or be devoted to the one and despise the other. You cannot serve
> God and wealth. (Mt 6:19–21, 24).

Matthew's community at this time is a marginalized group opposed by
the Pharisees, whom Matthew portrays as Jesus' opponents (Mt 12:34, 39,
45–46; 15:13; 16:1–12).[7] The Pharisees in Matthew's Gospel are cast in the
same role as the "sons of darkness" in the Qumran literature (see chapter 5).
The authors of the Dead Sea Scrolls and the author of Matthew all identify their sectarian religious rivals with Satan. In Matthew, Jesus' enemies
are identified with Satan; both the Pharisees and Satan oppose the Messiah
and seek to gain control over the Kingdom. The peculiarity of this development is that many New Testament scholars speculate that Jesus himself
may have been a Pharisee.

Jesus, like the Pharisees, came from "common stock," unlike the other
influential first-century Jewish group, the Sadducees, who came from
wealthier families. And Jesus, like the Pharisees, believed in the resurrection of the dead, an atypical belief among Jews in this period. Jesus'
staunch denunciation of the Pharisees in Matthew (and in the Gospels in
general) seems to reflect the kind of intimate knowledge of their beliefs
and practices that only a former insider might have. If Jesus parted ways
with the Pharisees, his condemnation of them—or at least the Gospel
writer's condemnation of them—might reflect this falling-out among former comrades.

Luke also emphasizes the connection between Jesus' enemies and Satan,
although in some ways, Luke is not as vitriolic as Matthew. For instance,
Luke does not condemn *all* Pharisees as enemies of Jesus but is more even-
handed, even featuring a group of Pharisees who warn Jesus to get out of
town because King Herod was intent on having him killed: "At that very

hour some Pharisees came and said to him, 'Get away from here, for Herod wants to kill you'" (Lk 13:31).[8] In other ways, however, Luke's Satan is more devious and insidious than the Satan of Mark and Matthew. Luke describes him as patiently waiting for the opportunity to strike.[9] An ominous warning that appears in a story early in the Gospel, following Jesus' first encounter with Satan (Lk 4:1–13), creates a tension that persists throughout the rest of Luke: "When the devil had finished every test, he departed from him until an opportune time" (Lk 4:13; Lk 22:1–3). Satan's role in Luke makes it clear that opportunistic evil forces are indeed active in the world and pose a threat to the Kingdom of God.

Satan (or the Devil) is a recurrent character in all three of the Synoptics, but each Gospel is different, and there are only four references to Satan (or the Devil) that at least two of the Synoptics have in common.[10] These common references warrant further investigation.

Jesus' Temptation in the Wilderness: Mk 1:12–13; Mt 4:1–11; Lk 4:1–13

In Mark, Matthew, and Luke Satan appears at the same point in the story, immediately after John the Baptist baptizes Jesus. Mark's account is the briefest:

> And the Spirit immediately drove him out into the wilderness. He was in the wilderness forty days, tempted by Satan; and he was with wild beasts; and the angels waited on him. (Mk 1:12–13)

Mark narrates that Jesus was immediately cast out into the desert, the traditional testing place in many ancient narratives, after his baptism.[11] This "casting out" foreshadows the casting out of demons, the exorcisms, that Jesus (and his apostles) subsequently perform:[12]

> And he cured many who were sick with various diseases, and cast out many demons; and he would not permit the demons to speak, because they knew him. (Mk 1:34)

> And he went throughout Galilee, proclaiming the message in their synagogues and casting out demons. (Mk 1:39)

And he appointed twelve, whom he also named apostles, to be with him, and to be sent out to proclaim the message, and to have authority to cast out demons. (Mk 3:14–15)

Jesus spends forty days in the wilderness, reminiscent of the Israelite's forty-year wilderness sojourn in Exodus. Although Mark does not yield any details about the actual temptations, we are told that Jesus is assisted by angels. Though they enter without fanfare, the arrival of the angels at the end of the temptation narrative in Mark brings us one step closer to completing the cast necessary for an apocalyptic drama. We now have Jesus, Satan, and Jesus' angelic militia. We lack only Satan's minions, the demons. They begin to appear in the very same chapter of Mark, as the texts we just mentioned indicate (e.g., Mk 1:34, 39). A war with many battles involving Jesus versus Satan, the angels versus the demons, and the spirit-filled versus the demon-possessed occupies the rest of Mark's Gospel.[13]

Matthew and Luke expand Mark's terse account of the temptation into a three-part dialogue between Satan and Jesus. In Matthew and Luke, Satan acts as the obstacle that deflects Jesus from his messianic role. Satan's temptations here have to do with power and address the nature and authenticity of Jesus' mission.[14]

The first temptation focuses on Jesus' physical needs. At the outset, we are told that Jesus had been fasting for forty days and was famished (Mt 4:2; Lk 4:2). The "tempter" (Mt 4:3), or "Devil" (Lk 4:3), takes advantage of Jesus' hunger to issue the first of his three challenges: "If you are the Son of God command these stones [Lk: 'this stone'] to become loaves [Lk: 'a loaf'] of bread" (Mt 4:3; cf. Lk 4:3). Jesus, whom Matthew portrays as the obedient Son of God, is not seduced by this challenge to gain mass popularity by instantly gratifying physical needs, even his own after a forty day fast. Jesus couches his response to the Devil with a quote from Deuteronomy (as he will in all three tests) that confirms the purpose of his mission, not as a worker of magic, but as the long-awaited Messiah. Jesus quotes Moses: "One does not live by bread alone, but by every word that comes from the mouth of God" (Mt 4:4; cf. Deut 8:3).[15]

In the Devil's second temptation in Matthew (in Luke, the third in the sequence), he dares Jesus to fling himself off the pinnacle of the Jerusalem temple. Since Jesus had volleyed scripture back to him in the earlier round, the Devil begins this set quoting scripture himself, Psalm 91:11–12:

Then the devil took him to the holy city and placed him on the pinnacle of the temple, saying to him, "If you are the Son of God, throw yourself down; for it is written, 'He will command his angels concerning you,' and 'On their hands they will bear you up, so that you will not dash your foot against a stone.'" (Mt 4:5–6)

This is another test of the nature of Jesus' brand of heroism—would he be a superman or a man of sorrows?—and Jesus counters with his own scriptural quotation: "Again it is written, 'Do not put the Lord your God to the test'" (Mt 4:7).

In the final temptation in Matthew (in Luke, the second), the Devil takes Jesus to a mountaintop and offers him worldly power in exchange for bowing down and worshipping him. Jesus reserves his strongest language for here: "Away with you, Satan! For it is written, 'Worship the Lord your God, and serve only him'" (Mt 4:10).

In this final scene, Jesus addresses his opponent as *Satan* for the first time. Satan acts as a stumbling block to Jesus' messianic mission, so the use of the term (which means "adversary") is fitting. The banishment of Satan at the end of the story demonstrates Jesus' power over evil, his messianic role, and the futility of Satan's plan.[16]

Although Luke's version of the temptation in the wilderness closely follows Matthew's version, there are differences. In Luke's second temptation, Jesus is offered power over all earthly kingdoms, as in Matthew: "Then the devil led him up and showed him in an instant all the kingdoms of the world" (Lk 4:5; cf. Mt 4:8). Then in a curious phrase unique to Luke, the Devil says to Jesus: "To you I will give their glory and all this authority; for it has been given over to me, and I give it to anyone I please" (Lk 4:6). The Devil's frightening assertion indicates that the world is in his power. This passage typifies the language of the combat myth motif so common in apocalyptic literature (especially as seen in Qumran).[17] Jesus stands on the verge of a cosmic battle with Satan, and Luke assumes that the present world is held hostage to the power of the Devil.[18] In the Acts of the Apostles, written by the same author who composed the Gospel of Luke, the words attributed to the apostle Paul allude to the same belief:

I am sending you to open their eyes so that they may turn from darkness to light and from the power of Satan to God. (Acts 26:18)

Jesus rejects the Devil's offer, again quoting from Deuteronomy (Lk 4:4; cf. Dt 6:13). The final temptation in Luke mirrors Matthew's version (of the second temptation), but instead of the scene ending with Jesus forcefully banishing the Devil, Luke ends the triptych on a much more foreboding note: "When the devil had finished every test, he departed from him until an opportune time" (Lk 4:13). Luke foreshadows a disquieting reality; there will be other tests to come: the Devil's return when he enters Judas (Lk 22:3), Jesus' anguished prayer on the Mount of Olives for relief from any more ordeals (Lk 22:40–46), and the physical and emotional torture that Jesus bears following his arrest (Lk 22:53ff).[19]

Jesus' temptation in the wilderness is a foundational Satan story. Though Jesus refuses to kowtow before the Prince of the Earth, countless stories would emerge in European and American folklore through the ages about magi and musicians who would gladly do business with the Devil. The best known form of the story is the European "Faust" legend about a learned man who sells his soul to the Devil in exchange for knowledge. But the motif remains productive. In twentieth-century Americana, it becomes one of the backstories in the mythology of rock-and-roll music, "the Devil's music." According to legend, the great Delta Blues musician Robert Johnson, the musical grandfather of every British bluesman, Anglo-American rockabilly, and African American soul-stirrer, met the Devil "hisself" down at "the crossroads," fell down on his knees, and made a pact: artistic brilliance in exchange for his soul. Robert Johnson died at 27 from alcohol poisoning, but generations of fans have mythologized the premature drug and alcohol-induced deaths of their musical heroes through recourse to this legend of a country-bluesman with "a hellhound on [his] trail," the latter the title of one of Johnson's own compositions.

Satan Casting out Satan

The first common Synoptic reference to Satan features Jesus in solo combat versus the Devil in the wilderness before Jesus begins his ministry. The second common Synoptic reference to Satan occurs as Jesus' healing ministry is under way, with the story of Jesus healing (i.e., casting out a demon from) a man with sensory disabilities:

Then they brought to him a demoniac who was blind and mute; and he cured him, so that the one who had been mute could speak and see. (Mt 12:22)

Now he was casting out a demon that was mute; when the demon had gone out, the one who had been mute spoke, and the crowds were amazed. (Lk 11:14)

After Jesus heals the man, his critics cite the miracle as more evidence that Jesus does not meet their messianic qualifications. They say, "He casts out demons by Beelzebul, the ruler of the demons" (Lk 11:15). Beelzebul is an alternative name for Satan in the Synoptic Gospels.[20] For his opponents, Jesus' ability to perform exorcisms reveals that Jesus is nothing more than another street magician armed with a kit bag of occult tricks. But Jesus, as keenly able and eager to debate these critics as he had the Devil in the wilderness, responds:

"Every kingdom divided against itself is laid waste, and no city or house divided against itself will stand. If Satan casts out Satan, he is divided against himself; how then will his kingdom stand? If I cast out demons by Beelzebul, by whom do your own exorcists cast them out?" (Mt 12:25–27)

This passage suggests that by the time of its writing in the late first century C.E., Matthew's audience would have assumed several things about Satan. Satan was the Prince of Demons, ruling an entire perverse kingdom dedicated to those forms of physical and mental illness that the ancients attributed to demon possession. Another implication is that Satan and his legions of demons were engaged in a conspiracy for world domination, for their Kingdom of Darkness to triumph over the Jesus' Kingdom of Light.

If we fast-forward a couple of millennia, we can make two observations about texts that portray Jesus in combat with demons. The history of the Christian practice of exorcism is based on this and similar New Testament texts. For the most part, the practice of exorcism is pre-modern and Roman Catholic, but it caught a wave in the 1970s through films such as *The Exorcist* and through an actual revival of the practice by Pentecostal and Charismatic Christians, perhaps as a reaction to the countercultural fascination with Satanic themes and the occult.[21] Furthermore, biblical accounts of Jesus casting out demons and combating the Devil are the inspiration for a library of stories and films, such as the 2005 movie *Constantine*. The film's protagonist John Constantine is a hybrid of a Christlike spiritual superhero Jesus and a film noir antihero. Both "JCs" have the ability to cast out demons and rescue souls. The character John Constantine even shoots demons dead with a crucifix-shaped gun. Cosmic Enemy Number One stalks both heroes, Jesus and Constantine, but in the end, according to the canons of both Holy Writ and Hollywood, the good guys triumph over the forces of evil.

Get Behind Me, Satan

Matthew and Mark locate the turning point of Jesus' ministry at Caesarea Philippi, for it is there that Jesus begins his journey to Jerusalem, to the cross (Mt 16:13–23; Mk 8:27–33). Luke includes the scene but does not identify its location (Lk 19:18–22). At Caesarea Philippi Jesus solicits opinions from his disciples regarding his true identity: "Who do people say that I am?" (Mk 8:27; cf. Mt 16:13; Lk 9:18). The disciples report the range of opinions they had heard regarding Jesus' identity: John the Baptist, Elijah, Jeremiah, a prophet (Mt 16:14; Mk 8:28; Lk 9:19).

Jesus then phrases the question in a personal way: "But who do you say that I am?" (Mk 8:29; cf. Mt 16:15; Lk 9:20). Peter, acting as spokesman for the twelve, confesses that Jesus is the Messiah (Mk 8:29; Mt 16:16; Lk 9:20). This passionate confession is followed, in Matthew's version, by Jesus' affirmation of Peter, whom Jesus also calls "Simon" or "Simon Peter":

> And Jesus answered him, "Blessed are you, Simon son of Jonah! For flesh and blood has not revealed this to you, but my Father in heaven. And I tell you, you are Peter, and on this rock I will build my church, and the gates of Hades will not prevail against it. I will give you the keys of the kingdom of heaven, and whatever you bind on earth will be bound in heaven, and whatever you loose on earth, will be loosed in heaven." (Mt 16:17–19)[22]

All three Synoptic Gospels report that Jesus enjoins his followers to keep his messianic identity a secret: "Then he sternly ordered the disciples not to tell anyone that he was the Messiah" (Mt 16:20; cf. Mk 8:30; Lk 9:21). Jesus then teaches about his true mission, a mission that involves suffering and death:

> From that time on, Jesus began to show his disciples that he must go to Jerusalem and undergo great suffering at the hands of the elders and chief priests and scribes, and be killed, and on the third day be raised. (Mt 16:21; cf. Mk 8:31; Lk 9:22)

Jesus' mission is difficult for the disciples to understand. Once he has had the fine-print of Christhood explained to him, a confused Peter admonishes Jesus: "And Peter took him aside and began to rebuke him, saying, 'God forbid it, Lord! This must never happen to you'" (Mt 16:22; cf. Mk 8:33). Jesus is certainly not the messiah Peter and the others had expected. What happens next is again omitted in Luke, but included by Matthew and Mark. This time is it Jesus who rebukes Peter:

> "Get behind me, Satan! You are a stumbling block to me; for you are setting your mind not on divine things but on human things." (Mt 16:23; cf. Mk 8:33)

The true meaning of the word "Satan" is revealed in the Matthew passage. Satan, in this case, is not meant to refer to the Devil per se, but is used in a generic sense to mean "obstacle." When he denies the element of suffering in Christ's mission, Peter becomes an impediment to Jesus' journey toward the cross.[23] Jesus' outburst, then, can be viewed a figure of speech and not taken to mean that Jesus believed Peter to be possessed by Satan. The use of the word "satan" here is similar to the usage in the Balaam story from the Hebrew Bible. The term "satan" is used in Num 22:22, 32 to refer to an angelic figure who blocks the path of Balaam's donkey. Of course, given the grim details presented to Peter and the other disciples concerning the nature of Jesus' mission—that it involves "taking up the cross" and "great suffering"—it seems only natural that Peter might register shock and dismay. Arrest, humiliation, and crucifixion were not part of the program that he and his fellow disciples had enrolled in when they left their fishing nets and families to follow their charismatic master.

The Parable of the Sower

The final mention of Satan common to all three Synoptic Gospels occurs in the context of the Parable of the Sower (Mt 13:1–9; Mk 4:1–9; Lk 8:4–8):

"Listen! A sower went out to sow. And as he sowed, some seeds fell on the path, and the birds came and ate them up. Other seeds fell on rocky ground, where they did not have much soil, and they sprang up quickly, since they had no depth of soil. But when the sun rose, they were scorched; and since they had no root, they withered away. Other seeds fell among thorns, and the thorns grew up and choked them. Other seeds fell on good soil and brought forth grain, some a hundredfold, some sixty, some thirty. Let anyone with ears listen!" (Mt 13:4–9)

This parable is included along with others that describe God's impending reign. Its message about how the righteous must be ever alert to seize the day is straightforward. But when the disciples fail to grasp its meaning, Jesus explains the parable to them (Mt 13:18–23; Mk 4:13–20; Lk 8:11–15). It is in Jesus' allegorical interpretation of this parable that we find the final reference to Satan common to all three Synoptic Gospels.[24]

Jesus is the sower, and the soil represents the types of people who hear his message. The roadway, the rocky soil, and the bramble-choked ground represent those who are either unable or unwilling to take advantage of life in the Kingdom of Light. The good soil stands for the faithful who hear the word and bear fruit. It is in Jesus' allegorical identification of the birds who eat the seed that fell on the pathway that we find the reference to Satan. In Mk 4:15, "Satan" is the name of the devourer who swallows up some seeds before they even sprout. In Mt 13:19, the birds are identified with "the evil one;" in Lk 8:12, with "the Devil." Satan in this parable is a strain of voracious antimatter that inhibits healthy life and productivity. This Satan impedes life before it gets off the ground, snatching possibilities before they have a chance to flourish.

Before moving past the Synoptic Gospels in our survey of Satan in the New Testament, we should note that these presentations of the Devil evolve from pre-existing ideas about Satan, either in the Hebrew Bible or in the intertestamental literature. For example, the Satan of the temptation stories is a descendant of the overzealous prosecutor in Job and Zechariah. In the Gospels, as in the prologue of Job, Satan tempts a righteous man, and the testing site is the wilderness (the setting for the dialogues of Job), the symbolic location for trials and rites of passage. Unlike in Job 1–2 and Zechariah 3, however, this tempter and auditor of virtue no longer seems to be in the divine employ, acts on his own, and is far more malevolently inventive than *hassatan* had been in postexilic biblical literature. Still, we cannot ignore the note in Mark, the earliest written Gospel, that it was "the Spirit [who] drove [Jesus] into the wilderness," as if even this ordeal is part of a divine plan, a necessary exercise or final exam, before Jesus begins his public ministry.

In the account in Mk 3:20–30 ("He has Beelzebul"; cf. Mt 12:22–32; Lk 11:14–26), Jesus defends himself against the charge that his uncanny powers are demonic. Here, Satan appears as the Prince of Demons, a motif we first saw in the Watchers myth from 1 Enoch and Jubilees. And in the account where Jesus refers to his trusted disciple and intimate friend Peter as Satan, the term has the same sense of "adversary" or "obstacle" that we saw in Numbers 22.

Satan in John

The Gospel of John tells the story of Jesus' life in terms of a cosmic battle between light and darkness, good and evil. Jesus is the cosmic redeemer who comes to earth to rescue the world from darkness and to cast out Satan, the "ruler of this world" (Jn 12:31; 14:30; 16:11).[25] This cosmic war is similar to Essene scenarios about a battle between the "sons of darkness" and "the sons of light." The situation of an embattled and fragile, post-resurrection (and post-Jewish War) community serves as the backdrop for the Fourth Gospel. Their community's struggle against an oppositional religious majority, the religious authorities who opposed their cause, is reflected in Jesus' struggles with the evil ruler of this world who seeks to undermine his mission.

The anonymous author of John was probably a convert to the Jesus movement who seems to share Luke's conviction that "those who reject Jesus accomplish Satan's work on earth."[26] John, like Luke, speaks of "the Jews" (John's catch-all name for Jesus' enemies) in unflattering terms.[27] Confrontations between Jesus and "the Jews" occur on nearly every page of John's Gospel. Jesus even accuses them of plotting to kill him: "Why are you looking for an opportunity to kill me?" (Jn 7:19), at which point his enemies accuse Jesus of paranoia, of being mentally ill, i.e., possessed by a demon: "The crowd answered, 'You have a demon! Who is trying to kill you?'" (Jn 7:20).

Much of John's rhetoric against the Jews reflects the dire situation of his community in 90 to 100 C.E.[28] This situation—which included a confrontation between John's community and the Jewish majority—would lead to the group's expulsion from synagogues, an action that apparently traumatized the Johannine community (who still very much considered themselves Jewish), as reflected in several passages in John that refer to the expulsion (Jn 9:22; 12:42; 16:2).[29]

We must pause here for a moment to comment on the strong language in John's Gospel for "the Jews" because, tragically, these ideas have served as fodder for anti-Semitism throughout Christian history. These texts emerge from inflamed rivalries between the Jesus movement, Jewish in origins, and its opponents within the first-century Jewish community. In John's day, this was still an intramural competition, and these were essentially estranged family members who were ardently arguing about who was to control their shared legacy. It is no surprise, then, that they reserved their most impassioned mud-slinging for each other.

John's Jesus has some rather strong opinions concerning the true identity of his opponents, going so far as to identify them as the children of the Devil:

> "You are from your father the devil, and you choose to do your father's desires. He was a murderer from the beginning and does not stand in the truth, because there is no truth in him. When he lies, he speaks according to his own nature, for he is a liar and the father of lies." (Jn 8:44)

Does this mean that Jesus understands the father of the Jews to be the Devil? Of course not. But it does mean that, for John, anyone who opposes Jesus' mission—whether the audience in the scene we just mentioned, or Judas (Jn 13:2), or even Peter himself (e.g., Mk 8:33)—is acting as a tool of Satan.

John does not depict Satan appearing as a freestanding supernatural being; rather, Satan appears in the guise of those people who oppose Jesus (and the Johannine community).[30] In his temptation episodes, John recasts the *people* in the role that Satan occupied in Matthew and Luke.[31] In the latter, for example, Satan had tempted Jesus with political authority over all the kingdoms of the world (Mt 4:8–9; Lk 4:5–6). By contrast, in John it is the people who tempt Jesus, drafting him to be their king: "When Jesus realized that they were about to come and take him by force to make him king, he withdrew again to the mountain by himself" (Jn 6:15). The temptation to turn stones into bread (Mt. 4:3; Lk 4:3) is transformed by John into an occasion when the people, rather than Satan, cite Scripture in an effort to coax Jesus into miraculously producing bread:

> So they said to him, "What sign are you going to give us then, so that we may see it and believe you? What work are you performing? Our ancestors ate the manna in the wilderness; as it is written, 'He gave them bread from heaven to eat.'" (Jn 6:30–31)

John's version of the temptation for Jesus to make a public display of his powers (Mt 4:5–6; Lk 4:9–12) has Jesus' own *brothers* tempting him to brazenly flaunt his powers in Jerusalem, in full view of his enemies:

> After this Jesus went about in Galilee. He did not wish to go about in Judea because the Jews were looking for an opportunity to kill him. Now the Jewish festival of Booths was near. So his brothers said to him, "Leave here and go to Judea so that your disciples also may see the works you are doing; for no one who wants to be widely known acts in secret. If you do these things, show yourself to the world." (For not even his brothers believed in him.) (Jn 7:1–5)[32]

Predictably, John's Jesus resists all the temptations and recognizes them as obstacles to his true mission (Jn 6:15; 32; 7:6–9).

The most chilling reference to the Evil One in John involves Jesus' betrayer, Judas Iscariot. Judas's betrayal is common to all four Gospels and his primary function—indeed his only function—is to fulfill his role as the one who would betray Christ. John's Jesus is quick to identify Judas as the Devil: "Did I not choose you, the twelve? Yet one of you is a devil?" (Jn 6:70), to which John adds the editorial aside: "He was speaking of Judas son of Simon Iscariot, for he, though one of the twelve, was going to betray him" (Jn 6:71). By revealing the identity of Jesus' betrayer so early in the story, John establishes an undercurrent of tension as the reader awaits the ultimate act of betrayal. Although money is cited as a motivation for Judas's betrayal of Jesus,

John (and Luke) indicates that money is not the sole motivation.[33] Judas's collaboration with the Jewish authorities who sought to put Jesus to death stems from a deeper, more frightening reality: the presence of Satan. John uses the Last Supper as the occasion for Satan's entrance into Judas (Jn 13:2, 27). John narrates that when the apostles ask about the identity of the betrayer (Jn 13:25), Jesus replies by confirming that the traitor is the one who receives the dipped bread: "It is the one to whom I give this piece of bread when I have dipped it in the dish" (Jn 13:26). Jesus then dips the bread and gives it to Judas; immediately "Satan entered into him" (John 13:27). It is almost as if Jesus' distribution of the bread to Judas is Satan's cue to step from the wings onto the stage.[34] John's Jesus, always directing the action, directs Judas to "do quickly what you are going to do" (Jn 13:27). As the betrayer departs, John's portentous observation, "And it was night" (John 13:30), reminds readers that the final showdown between the forces of darkness and the Son of Light is imminent.

Jesus knows he will be betrayed and by whom—that is never in question—but the fact that he, in effect, gives Satan permission to enter into the drama *does* raise some questions. Was it Judas who betrayed Jesus, or was it Satan, acting through Judas, who betrayed Jesus?[35] John's Satan only appears in the forms of his human agents. Satan, then, can be seen as an incarnate adversary who appears in Judas as well as within the other individuals and groups who oppose Jesus.[36] Understood in this way, Satan again fulfills his role as cosmic adversary and perennial obstacle.

John's Gospel follows the plot seen in some of the Qumran literature and in the Synoptics by depicting a redeemer figure who will rescue humanity from the grip of Satan. The battle is a familiar one: a struggle of good versus evil, expressed as a war of light against darkness. The struggles of the embattled Johannine community with fellow Jews late in the first-century are reflected in accounts of Jesus' struggles with those, including intimates such as members of his family and his disciples, who oppose and seek to destroy him. The Prince of Darkness works through human beings in insidious ways: through demonic possession, illness, and the corruption of hearts. John's Jesus assures us, however, that the powers of darkness will not prevail against the power of the Lord of Light. So, in effect, "Satan" is used in the Gospel of John as a personification of social rivals, as the rhetoric in the modern world casts a political enemy as "the Great Satan."

Satan in the Pauline Epistles

The earliest texts in the New Testament are the letters attributed to Paul. Written between 50 and 64 C.E., even before the earliest written Gospels, these letters were addressed to the fledgling churches that Paul had founded during his missionary journeys (mainly in Asia Minor and Greece). Paul, a former persecutor of followers of Jesus, exhibited the zeal of the converted and launched an aggressive missionary campaign that transformed Christianity from a sect within Judaism to a universal religion. In his own letters, Paul has this to say about his conversion:

> For I want you to know, brothers and sisters, that the gospel that was proclaimed by me is not of human origin; for I did not receive it from a human source, nor was I taught it, but I received it through a revelation of Jesus Christ. You have heard, no doubt, of my earlier life in Judaism. I was violently persecuting the church of God and was trying to destroy it. I advanced in Judaism beyond many among my people of the same age, for I was far more zealous for the traditions of my ancestors. But when God, who had set me apart before I was born and called me through his grace, was pleased to reveal his Son to me, so that I might proclaim him among the Gentiles, I did not confer with any human being, nor did I go up to Jerusalem to those who were already apostles before me, but I went away at once into Arabia, and afterwards I returned to Damascus. (Gal 1:11–17)

A more detailed (and, most scholars would argue, a more idealized) description is told by Luke in Acts (Acts 9:1–30; cf. 1 Cor 15:8–9).

In any case, Paul's writings indicate that he was a prolific writer, concerned pastor, and relentless proselytizer. Although thirteen letters in the New Testament are attributed to Paul, most biblical scholars agree that only Romans, 1–2 Corinthians, Galatians, Philippians, 1 Thessalonians, and Philemon are from his own hand.[37] In these seven letters, Satan appears sporadically, mentioned less than a dozen times in all seven epistles combined.

When Paul chooses to use the word "Satan" in his letters, he has one particular role in mind: Satan as obstructer. Specifically, Paul uses "Satan" to refer to those who hinder—usually through undermining Paul's teaching—the fully realized existence that the Christian religious experience offers.[38] A brief examination of Paul's references to Satan will help elucidate his particular use of the term.

Satan in Romans

Paul's letter to the church in Rome, known as Romans, was written around 56 or 57 C.E. Scholars have long questioned Paul's purpose(s) in writing to the Romans, and this particular issue remains the topic of debate. Some believe that Romans is a summation of Paul's theology; others contend that Paul wrote Romans as a way to expand his missionary base.[39] Whatever Paul's motives may have been, it is clear that Satan is *not* one of the apostle's central concerns. In fact, Satan is mentioned only once in Romans (Rom 16:20), during Paul's elaborate closing exhortation to the entire letter. Paul warns the Roman church to be careful of outsiders who might seek to cause dissention and scandal.[40] So, when Paul enjoins the Romans to "be wise in what is good and guileless in what is evil," because "the God of peace will shortly crush Satan under your feet" (Rom 16:20), Satan is understood to be symbolic of those who seek to disrupt and scandalize the Roman Christian community.[41]

This singular mention of Satan says much about Paul's Satan language.[42] His Satan language, similar to that in the Gospels, is deeply connected to the way in which evil disrupts and causes suffering to individuals and communities. Satan is at work through those who seek to disrupt Paul's missionary efforts and cause disharmony among his converts.

Satan in Paul's Corinthian Correspondence

Paul's first and second letters to the fledgling church in Corinth offer us the most extensive record of the development of the early Christian movement in the New Testament.[43] The development of the church in Corinth was a slow and painful process. According to Paul, the Corinthian community was racked with problems, including distortions of Paul's original teachings, factionalism, and a bizarre assortment of ethical problems.[44] It is likely that many of these problems arose as a result both of misunderstandings of Paul's message, and the persistent and, for Paul, pernicious influence of Hellenistic philosophy.[45]

A central teaching of Paul throughout his letters is the contrast he depicts between those who live in the *Spirit* and those who live in the *flesh*. Life in the Spirit, according to Paul, is a life governed by peace in Christ, while life in the flesh is dominated by sin and the satisfaction of the baser human needs:

> Now the works of the flesh are obvious: fornication, impurity, licentiousness, idolatry, sorcery, enmities, strife, jealousy, anger, quarrels, dissensions, factions, envy, drunkenness, carousing, and things like these. I am warning you, as I warned you before: those who do such things will not inherit the kingdom of God. (Gal 5:19–21)[46]

The Corinthians considered Paul's message about life in the Spirit liberating, but in a morally irresponsible way. They distorted Paul's message, emphasizing something Paul himself wrote to the church in Galatia, "If you are led by the Spirit, you are not subject to the law" (Gal 5:18). But the Corinthians had taken Paul's message out of context for, as Paul himself wrote earlier in the same passage, "Do not use your freedom [from Mosaic law] as an opportunity for self-indulgence" (Gal 5:13). No longer subjected to the ethical norms that governed others, the Corinthians shucked off the shackles of conventional morality and engaged in some flamboyantly irreligious behavior (1 Cor 5:1–13; 7:1–40). Paul felt he had to correct these misunderstandings without alienating the community altogether.

In 1 Corinthians 5, Paul deals with the issue of incest, admonishing the community for permitting a man to live with his stepmother (1 Cor 5:1)[47] Paul's suggested punishment for the man is severe: "You are to hand this man over to Satan for the destruction of the flesh, so that his spirit may be saved in the day of the Lord" (1 Cor 5:5). Although it is clear that Paul expects the man to be cast out of the community, we cannot gauge the full extent of the punishment that Paul envisions here. Still, whether the punishment was to be corporal or social, excommunication alone is a severe enough. The man in question "is denied all fellowship in the believing community and is left bereft of God as well."[48] According to Neil Forsyth, "Satanic opposition takes the form of opposition to Paul, so completely does Paul identify himself with the Christian message."[49] According to Paul, anyone who opposes him is satanic. When Paul calls for this sinner to be handed over to Satan, he intends that he be exiled from the church (i.e., the kingdom of Jesus) and, thus, delivered over to the domain of the Devil.

A similar passage speaks of confusion among the Corinthians concerning sexual relations in marriage (1 Corinthians 7). Although it is clear that Paul advocates a life of celibacy (1 Cor 7:1), he nonetheless acknowledges that for most people, marriage provides an acceptable outlet for the libido. For those who are married, Paul stresses the idea that each partner should take seriously the fulfillment of their mutual obligations, which include conjugal rights.[50]

> Do not deprive one another except perhaps by agreement for a set time, to devote yourselves to prayer, and then come together again, so that Satan may not tempt you because of your lack of self-control. (1 Cor 7:5)

Paul's mention of Satan in this passage is reminiscent of Satan's role as tempter in the wilderness stories from the Synoptic Gospels. The tempter in the Synoptics attacks Jesus at an opportune time, when he is weak and hungry from the wilderness ordeal, tempting him with worldly power and creature comforts (Mk 1:12–13; Mt 4:1–11; Lk 4:1–13). According to Paul, Satan might tempt sex-starved marriage partners with adultery, so "it is better to marry [and couple] than to be aflame with passion," vulnerable to the allure of illicit sex (1 Cor 7:9). This is the malevolent efficiency of Satan's attacks, to pounce when mortals are most vulnerable, to pick off those who stray from the path of righteousness. As Paul implies in 1 Cor 7:5 above, Satan can even lure believers into sexual indulgence, much like the Watcher angels did to the daughters of men in 1 Enoch.[51] Paul's central concern, as always, is the health of the entire community. Sexual immorality is dangerous not only for individuals, but also for the Corinthian church body through which this social disease threatens to spread.

There is no doubt that the church at Corinth is a challenging group for Paul. These challenges continue in the book of 2 Corinthians, a composite of several letters from Paul to the community that vacillate between anger, forgiveness, hope, and despair.[52] Satan is mentioned three times. The first mention (2 Corinthians 2) occurs as Paul recounts his painful initial visit to Corinth, and the fall-out from his chastisement of the community for their immorality. The specific problem that Paul is addressing in 2 Corinthians 2 is unclear, but it could be that the community was overzealous in its prosecution of the man accused of incest in 1 Cor 5:1–2. Paul urges the community to move past estrangement and to strive to restore a repentant member (2 Cor 2:5–11).[53] Paul's well-intentioned diagnosis of a sexual trespass that threatened the health of the Corinthian body inadvertently unleashed a different strain of sin, namely, the inhumane treatment of a sinner. For Paul, the sexual sin of a single member mutated into an epidemic of ill will among the entire Corinthian community and is evidence of a diabolic virus. The community, he exhorts, must forgive and reconcile with the offender, so that Satan does not triumph from misguided righteousness: "And we do this so that we may not be outwitted by Satan; for we are not ignorant of his designs" (2 Cor 2:11). Satan, it seems, never gives up finding ways to snatch victory from apparent defeat; here, beguiling the Corinthians into hating the sinner rather than the sin.

Paul's tone is conciliatory, but his mention of Satan's infiltration into the community is ominous. Paul obviously believes that Satan's designs include creating divisions within the Corinthian community. Paul understands that forgiveness—an amazing grace that he, a man with blood on his hands from the execution of Christians in his former life, had himself experienced—is a powerful weapon to be used against Satan's fractious designs.[54]

The second mention of Satan is in reference to Paul's detractors, the so-called "super-apostles" who seek to denigrate Paul's ministry:

> But I am afraid that as the serpent deceived Eve by its cunning, your thoughts will be led astray from a sincere and pure devotion to Christ. For if someone comes and proclaims another Jesus than the one we proclaimed, or if you receive a different spirit from the one you received, or a different gospel from the one you accepted, you submit to it readily enough. I think that I am not in the least inferior to these super-apostles. (2 Cor 11:3–5)

Although the identity of these detractors remains unclear, it is obvious they cause Paul a great deal of consternation.[55] So great is Paul's disdain for these rival apostles, in fact, that he accuses these ambassadors of Christ of being ministers of Satan:

> For such boasters are false apostles, deceitful workers, disguising themselves as apostles of Christ. And no wonder! Even Satan disguises himself as an

angel of light. So it is not strange if his ministers also disguise themselves as
ministers of righteousness. (2 Cor 11:13–15)

Here Satan is described as Paul's bitter opponent, reminiscent of the "enemies" we saw in John's Gospel, of Jesus' opponents who were identified as
"the children of the devil" (Jn 8:44).

Against these super-apostles Paul wages a verbal battle that culminates
in a kind of spiritual Olympics where the contestants compete to see who
has had the supreme ecstatic experience (2 Corinthians 12). He counters
the claims made by his opponents concerning their lofty visions and revelations with a little boasting about his own beatific vision:

> It is necessary to boast; nothing is to be gained by it, but I will go on to vi-
> sions and revelations of the Lord. I know a person in Christ who fourteen
> years ago was caught up to the third heaven—whether in the body or out of
> the body I do not know; God knows. And I know that such a person—
> whether in the body or out of the body I do not know; God knows—was
> caught up into Paradise and heard things that are not to be told, that no mor-
> tal is permitted to repeat. (2 Cor 12:1–4).

But just as Paul finds himself pulled into the game of spiritual one-up-
manship, he pulls back, steadies himself, and recalls the motif of suffering
so integral to the Christian message. Paul refers to a "thorn in his flesh,"
perhaps a painful (unspecified) physical disability: "Therefore, to keep me
from being too elated, a thorn was given me in the flesh, a messenger of
Satan to torment me" (2 Cor 12:7).[56] Paul presents a theologically complicated analysis of his inner self. On one hand, the unnamed malady Paul suffers is demonic, in the sense that illness is a result of sin's entrance into the
world and the Devil's machinations, according to the ancient view. On the
other hand, Paul recognizes that the thorn in his flesh acts like ballast to
ground him in the physical realm even as his ecstatic adventures seem to el-
evate him above the natural. So, as Paul says elsewhere, "All things work together for good for those who love God" (Rom 8:28). Even this "messenger
of Satan" can serve a divine purpose. The thorn helps to humble Paul and
is therefore a weapon against the satanic sin of pride.[57] In the end, we do
not know what Paul was referring to in this passage. The word "thorn"
might refer to one of Paul's opponents, for they, too, are "of Satan."[58] This

interpretation is more in keeping with Paul's use of the word Satan in the rest of his letters. Still, whether we interpret Paul's thorn as physical or social, the end of the matter for Paul is that, through the alchemy of divine grace, even the basest elements of life can be transformed by God into something useful, even precious.

Satan in 1 Thessalonians

The final mention of Satan in the undisputed Pauline epistles appears in 1 Thess 2:18–19. Composed in about 50 C.E., 1 Thessalonians is the earliest surviving letter of Paul. Since his correspondence predates the writing of the written Gospels, 1 Thessalonians constitutes the oldest surviving document in the Christian canon. It is criticism of Paul himself that evokes his letter to this community. Although the identity of these critics is debated, their destructive comments clearly have upset Paul (1 Thess 2:3–8). His detractors compare Paul to a fraudulent street preacher who bilks money from unsuspecting people and spreads a false gospel: "The critics are saying that Paul is an offensive, erroneous, unclean (in terms of the law), greedy trickster who is out for his personal glory."[59] These detractors seem to be a motivating factor in Paul's correspondence, but there are other problems in the Thessalonian church as well: questions emanating from the death of church members (1 Thess 4:13–18), concerns about sexual immorality (1 Thess 4:3–5), doubts about the return of Christ (1 Thess 5:1–11), and even challenges to Paul's personal integrity (1 Thess 2:3–8).

It is within the context of the latter issue, about whether Paul's attention to the church was guided by maternal (1 Thess 2:7) and paternal (1 Thess 2:11) concern or financial self-interest (cf. 1 Thess 2:5), that Paul mentions Satan in 1 Thessalonians 2. Paul uses the language of kinship throughout the chapter (addressing his audience as "brothers and sisters" in 1 Thess 2: 1, 9, 14, 17) to stress his longing to be with the Thessalonian church, but Paul claims that Satan has prevented the family reunion from taking place: "For we [Paul and his apostolic associates Silvanus and Timothy; cf. 1 Thess 1:1] wanted to come to you—certainly, I, Paul, wanted to again and again—but Satan blocked our way" (1 Thess 2:18–19). Here Satan is cited as the root cause of whatever unknown superficial factors led to Paul's prolonged absence.

Every mention of Satan in the Pauline corpus involves the Devil working through a human agent to thwart Paul's mission and prevent believers from attaining that quality of personal and social life, "life in the Spirit," that allegiance to Christ and membership in his body offers.[60] This continues the trend we saw in John, where Satan entered and inspired Jesus' opponents. The freestanding, wholly individuated Devil of the temptation stories in the Synoptics has faded from view. He is about to return in dramatic fashion.

Satan in the Book of Revelation

The fullest account of Satan in his starring role as the Titan of Evil appears in the final book of the Bible, the book of Revelation. We know the author only as "John," a man exiled to the island of Patmos for preaching the Christian message (Rev 1:19), though it should be understood that the author is not the same "John" who is credited with writing the fourth Gospel. Revelation is the supreme example of apocalyptic writing in the New Testament and in many ways typifies Jewish-Christian apocalyptic writing in general.

From the perspective of contemporary Western literature, we can also say this: though its writer and audience would neither recognize nor agree, Revelation can be considered the world's first horror story. Its cast includes the four horsemen of the apocalypse, two pale riders named Death and Hades, a seven-headed beast, and an entire battalion of demonic hybrids that grotesquely combine the features of insects, animals, and humans. Its locales include a bottomless pit, rivers of blood, and a lake of sulfur. Scenarios involve a red dragon pursuing a pregnant woman so that he might eat her child, a female prostitute drunk on the blood of martyrs, and every manner of catastrophe: hailstorms, firestorms, earthquakes, solar eclipses, and pitiless torture. Its portrayal of Jesus, the hero who leads the angelic hosts over the Devil and his armies, might shock those unacquainted with the book. Jesus is not the suffering Messiah who entered Jerusalem on the back of a donkey (Mt 21:1–9; Mk 11:1–11; Lk 19:28–38; Jn 12:12–15), a scene children reenact every Holy Week by waving palm branches. In Revelation, Jesus rides a white horse and wears a robe drenched in blood, fire issuing from his eyes and a scimitar from his mouth (Rev 19:11–16).[61]

Scholars refer to this kind of ancient story as "apocalyptic"; if written today, we would deem it a horror story or dark fantasy.

In keeping with the style of apocalyptic writing, the author of Revelation seeks to situate his current suffering within the context of a particular backstory.[62] This includes a cosmic battle between good and evil, and the current crisis serves as evidence that this battle is indeed under way.[63] Apocalypticism is, in essence, a cosmic conspiracy theory. Oppressive parties and ideological rivals in apocalyptic literature are "revealed" (the meaning of the Greek word *apocalypsis* is "a revelation") to be agents of cosmic forces working behind the scenes to destroy the righteous and conquer the world. Persecution, suffering, and great tribulation must be endured before God's final victory ushers in a new age for believers.[64]

It is important to remember that apocalyptic writing was a popular form of writing familiar to Jews and Christians during this time. In other words, the visions of John of Patmos would not seem as fantastical to his readers then as they are today. The particular Satan language of the Bible and the manner in which the author of Revelation uses such language is helpful in deciphering the various visions of John of Patmos. In Revelation (and in apocalypses in general), the opponents of God are often mentioned using Satan epithets.[65] The Roman Empire, for example, was understood as the embodiment of Satan and is a favorite Satan epithet of the author.

The Apocalypse of John of Patmos has the following pattern. It begins with visions and messages directed to the seven churches of Asia (Revelation 1–3), followed by visions that describe the present tribulation as the prelude to the end time (Revelation 4–18), and concludes with visions depicting God's triumphant victory over the forces of evil (Revelation 12–22).[66] Every Satan we have seen to this point—whether it be those cancerous cells in the body of Christ that Paul demonizes, the Satan who appears in embodied form to do solo combat with Jesus in the desert or the evil spirit who enters persons like Judas—will appear in Revelation. In Revelation, Satan is a culmination of his many roles in earlier biblical, apocryphal, and pseudepigraphical texts. Passages that refer to Satan "bring together most aspects of the combat myth, from the star-like angel to the accuser at the heavenly court and the *agent provocateur* who leads astray the whole world."[67] In sum, the Satan of Revelation is the malignant manifestation of all the evil in the world.

Addressed to persecuted churches in Asia Minor, Revelation was probably written between 81 and 96 C.E., during the reign of the Roman emperor Domitian.[68] These persecutions were a response to the refusal of Christians to publicly worship the emperor. Although there does not seem to be evidence that emperor veneration was ever strictly enforced throughout the Roman Empire, this does not preclude the possibility that, locally, such a practice was enforced.[69] It is in the context of such persecutions—and in anticipation of a reign of terror that the author felt was sure to come—that Revelation was written.[70]

Satan in the Visions Concerning the Seven Churches (Revelation 1–11)

The first mention of Satan appears in letters addressed to seven churches (Revelation 2–3): Ephesus, Smyrna, Pergamum, Thyatira, Sardis, Philadelphia, and Laodicea. The letters from a heavenly messenger that John saw in a vision are meant for the human communities to whom they are directed, but they are literally addressed to angels, e.g., "to the angel of the church in Ephesus" (Rev 2:1). Each letter describes a symbolic vision of a triumphant Christ and urges its audience to persevere under the persecution of evil forces, particularly the Roman Empire.[71] The entire premise of Revelation is fantastic—angels converse with angels and mortals overhear and then transcribe the conversations—but the pain of those addressed, who faced persecution and martyrdom, for whom a story set in the heavens provided their only hope, was wholly real.

Satan is first mentioned in the message intended for the Christian community at Smyrna. Smyrna was a beautiful city, active in trade and considered politically, religiously, and culturally developed.[72] In the message addressed to the Christians in Smyrna, John writes:

> I know the slander on the part of those who say they are Jews and are not, but are a synagogue of Satan. Do not fear what you are about to suffer. Beware, the devil is about to throw some of you into prison so that you may be tested. (Rev 2:9–10)

John speaks here of the persecution of Christians in Smyrna at the hands of the leaders of the Jewish synagogue (cf. Acts 13:50; 14:2, 5, 19; 17:5). It appears that these Jews felt, among other things, that the Christians were luring away potential converts to Judaism to the less rigorous demands of Christianity.[73] John the Revelator refers to these hostile Jews as agents of Satan, members not of the "assembly of the Lord" (i.e., synagogue) (Num 16:3; 20:4; cf. 31:16), but instead as members of the "synagogue of Satan."[74] New Testament scholar Pheme Perkins suggests that perhaps the passage refers to those Christians who, in order to avoid persecution, pretended to be Jewish.[75] In any case, the slanderous activities of these hostile individuals, John warns, may result in some Christian imprisonments that will lead to death. In the event of such a situation, Christians are encouraged to stand firm and promised that their perseverance will be rewarded.

> "[F]or ten days you will have affliction. Be faithful until death, and I will give you the crown of life." (Rev 2:10)

The "synagogue of Satan" is alluded to again in Rev 2:13:

> "I know where you are living, where Satan's throne is. Yet you are holding fast to my name, and you did not deny your faith in me even in the days of Antipas my witness, my faithful one, who was killed among you, where Satan lives."

It is explicitly mentioned in Rev 3:9:

> "I will make those of the synagogue of Satan who say that they are Jews and are not, but are lying—I will make them come and bow down before your feet, and they will learn that I have loved you."

In the message addressed to the church in Pergamum, John identifies the city as the "throne of Satan" (Rev 2:13). This designation may stem from his assumption that Pergamum is the center of the imperial cult.[76] Pergamum was one of the first cities in Asia in which the Roman cult was established, and a temple dedicated to Rome and Augustus was built there in 29 B.C.E.[77]

The letter addressed to Philadelphia echoes the earlier accusation directed to Smyrna (Rev 2:9), that those Jews who persecute Christians belong to a synagogue of Satan (Rev 3:9). Unlike the situation in Smyrna, however, there is some hope for the adversarial Jews in Philadelphia.[78] The hope is for their eventual conversion. Just as Isaiah envisioned a time when the Gentiles would pay homage to Israel:

> The descendants of those who oppressed you shall come bending low to you, and all who despised you shall bow down at your feet; they shall call you the City of the LORD, the Zion of the Holy One of Israel. (Isa 60:14)

now that hope is reversed: Jews will someday pay homage to the members of the Gentile church in Philadelphia.[79]

Looking back from the perspective of two millennia of Christian anti-Semitism, these New Testament texts that literally demonize Jews ("the synagogue of Satan") threaten to destroy the credibility of the entire movement. We must bear in mind, however, the blurry boundaries that separated the synagogue from the church in the late first-century C.E. We cannot say for certain whether John and the churches located themselves within the covenant with Israel. We could be eavesdropping on a desperate, hate-filled, name-calling battle between rival denominations of a single faith that had not yet differentiated into Jewish and Christian. That observation does little to ameliorate the atrocities that later Christian societies would visit upon their Jewish members, but it does help us understand the historical context that gave birth to these texts so that we can interpret them in healthy ways and gain some analytic control over scriptures that have been put to perverse uses throughout Christian history.

Revelation 12–14

In Revelation 1–11, "Satan" is a term used for the social opponents of the fragile, threatened early Christian communities whom the writer addresses. It is only in the remainder of the book of Revelation, from chapter 12 forward, that we encounter the Satan we know and loathe, the cosmic opponent of God, the raw and horrific red dragon (the latter symbol brought back to life in Thomas Harris's first novel about serial killer Hannibal Lecter, *Red Dragon*). Revelation 12–14 is preceded by several fantastic visions in which the seer is transported to heaven.

But as fantastic as these visions had been, they are as bland as Sunday school literature next to the vision in Rev 12:1–17. The vision begins with a woman in the throes of labor, who is "clothed with the sun, with the moon under her feet, and her head a crown of twelve stars" (Rev 12:1). The woman is traditionally associated with Mary, the mother of Jesus, but is more likely a symbol of the righteous who must persevere despite persecu-tion.[80] Then the villain arrives on stage:

> A great red dragon, with seven heads and ten horns, and seven diadems on
> his heads. His tail swept down a third of the stars of heaven and threw them
> to the earth. (Rev 12:3–4)

The dragon is red, symbolizing murder and bloodshed (cf. Rev 6:4), and his destruction of the stars reminds us of the beast described in Dan 8:9–10.[81] The many heads and diadems represent the vastness of Satan's earthly dominion.[82] This scenario of an astral rebellion is a variation on the Lucifer myth, and John is quick to identify the dragon as Satan: "The great dragon . . . that ancient serpent, who is called the Devil and Satan, the de-ceiver of the whole world" (Rev 12:9). Wilfrid J. Harrington notes: "In the Jewish tradition, the serpent or dragon symbolized the power of evil, the principle of all the suffering of Israel."[83] The imagery of the dragon, then, was probably quite familiar to John's readers. They would have recognized the "ancient serpent" as the liar who deceived Eve in Genesis 3 and the dragon as the "mythological monster of chaos which readily symbolizes the power of evil."[84] Such images abound in the Old Testament:[85]

> On that day the LORD with his cruel and great and strong sword will pun-
>   ish Leviathan the fleeting serpent, Leviathan the twisting serpent, and he
>   will kill the dragon that is in the sea. (Isa 27:1)

> You broke the heads of the dragons in the waters;
> You crushed the heads of Leviathan. (Ps 74:13–14)

> By his power he stilled the Sea;
> by his understanding he struck down Rahab. (Job 26:12)

Other images may have come to the audience's mind, including the ten-horned monster mentioned in Daniel 7, the Greco-Roman sea monster Hydra, and the legendary Canaanite sea monster Lotan.[86] The beast in Revelation 12, with its horns, tail, and red color, has influenced later de-scriptions of Satan's physical appearance.

The dragon stands before a woman (who symbolizes Israel) in labor (Rev 12:1–2).

The beast is intent on devouring her child as soon as it is born. The child born to the woman (i.e., Israel) transparently refers to the Messiah, who is quickly dispatched to the throne of God (Rev 12:5), thus slipping through the murderous clutches of Satan. In this brief passage, John summarizes the life, death, and resurrection of Christ.[87] The woman flees to the wilderness where she is protected by God (cf. Gen 21:14–21; Mt 4:11).

The rescue of the child unleashes a war in heaven. The forces of good are led by the guardian angel of Israel, Michael (Dan 10:13, 21; 12:1; Jude 9), and his heavenly troops war against the evil forces led by Satan and his demonic cohorts:

> And war broke out in heaven; Michael and his angels fought against the dragon. The dragon and his angels fought back, but they were defeated, and there was no longer any place for them in heaven. The great dragon was thrown down, that ancient serpent, who is called the Devil and Satan, the deceiver of the whole world—he was thrown down to the earth, and his angels were thrown down with him. (Rev 12:7–9)

Revelation 12:2–9 is strikingly similar to the stories about the Watcher angels in 1 Enoch and in the book of Jubilees (see chapter 5). Recall that, in Enoch an evil leader variously called Azazel, Semyaza, or Satan, was the commander of a group of unsavory comrades who fell to earth. As in Revelation, these malignant spirits were subdued, bound hand and foot and tossed into a pit to await final judgment (cf. Rev 20:10; 21:8–9; 1 En 10:12–15). In Jubilees, Mastema was the name of the commander of the legion of demonic spirits. But the defeat of Mastema by God is not as impressive in Jubilees as it is in Enoch. In Jubilees, God allows Mastema to retain a tenth of his army (Jub 10:7–9) which, in turn, continue to cause trouble for humans. This is the same sort of arrangement found in Revelation. That is, Satan and his minions are defeated in heaven, but they fall to the earth and therefore still pose a threat. In fact, the fall to earth so enrages Satan that he resumes his pursuit of the woman (now symbolizing the church) who gave birth to the Messiah.[88] Unable to destroy her, he turns toward her "children" and makes war on them:

> So when the dragon saw that he had been thrown down to the earth, he pursued the woman who had given birth to the male child. But the woman was given the two wings of the great eagle, so that she could fly from the serpent

into the wilderness, to her place where she is nourished for a time, and times, and half a time. Then from his mouth the serpent poured water like a river after the woman, to sweep her away with the flood. But the earth came to the help of the woman; it opened its mouth and swallowed the river that the dragon had poured from his mouth. Then the dragon was angry with the woman, and went off to make war on the rest of her children, those who keep the commandments of God and hold the testimony of Jesus. (Rev 12:13–17)

According to Wilfrid Harrington, the "children" here symbolize the faithful followers of the church "those who keep the commandments of God and hold the testimony of Jesus" (Rev 12:17).[89]

The persecution continues as the power of Satan is now symbolized in two additional hideous monsters. One rises out of the sea and is described as having ten horns and seven heads (Rev 13:1–8). The beast is intended to symbolize Rome: the seven heads may correspond to the seven hills of Rome, and the ten horns to Roman emperors (cf. Rev 17:9–10).[90] Connections to Daniel's fourth vision of a beast with ten horns are obvious, too (Dan 7:24).[91] As Myra Nagel maintains, "By John's time, Jews had often reinterpreted this beast [in Daniel 7] to signify the Roman Empire."[92] We can already see the flexibility of apocalyptic and satanic symbols. The legendary sea monster of the eastern Mediterranean, whether called Hydra, Lotan, or Leviathan, had been described with seven heads for centuries. Later interpreters likely viewed the above mentioned associations (the beast's seven heads and Rome's seven hills) as a conspiracy to torment them and as a missing piece to the cosmic puzzle. Apocalypticists and conspiracy theorists through the ages have followed in this train, connecting the vast assemblage of ancient symbols with features of their day, and proclaiming that these coincidences prove the veracity of their scenarios, that we are in the last days, that the contemporary Public Enemy Number One is none other than the Antichrist.

In Revelation 13, a second beast emerges, this time from the earth. This beast has two horns and attempts to enforce emperor worship, which, according to John, is equivalent to the worship of Satan (Rev 13:8).[93] This beast is associated with a false prophet who intentionally leads the faithful astray (Rev 16:13; 19:20; 20:10; cf. Mk 13:22; 2 Thess 2:9–12), and is identified cryptically by the number 666 (Rev 13:18).[94] The number 666 plays on the Hebrew numerological significance of seven; if seven signifies completion

and perfection and 777 is trebly perfect, then 666 symbolizes a hideously mutating outgrowth of imperfection (the beast so marked is an avatar of
Frankenstein's monster in Mary Shelley's Gothic classic).[95] The number 666
can also be related to the name of emperor Nero. In Hebrew, letters can be
used to represent numbers, and the numerical values of the Hebrew spelling
of the Greek title "Neron Caesar" add up to 666.[96] These satanic symbols
have their own curious afterlife. For example, the epithet "the Great Beast"
and the number 666 were embraced by the early twentieth-century British
occultist Aleister Crowley.

What follows in Revelation 14:1–20 are seven visions aimed at offering
reassurance and fortitude to the persecuted churches. Followers are to remain steadfast in their faith for the time of judgment is at hand:

> He said in a loud voice, "Fear God and give him glory, for the hour of his
> judgment has come; and worship him who made heaven and earth, the sea
> and the springs of water." (Rev 14:7)

Indeed, the evil empire is already as good as conquered and those who continue to worship (i.e., perform obeisance, prostrate themselves, or kowtow
before) the beast (i.e., Rome, the emperor) will suffer God's wrath (Rev
14:8), which is described in frightening detail:

> Those who worship the beast and its image, and receive a mark on their fore-
> heads or on their hands, they will also drink the wine of God's wrath, poured
> out unmixed in to the cup of his anger, and they will be tormented with fire
> and sulfur in the presence of the holy angels and in the presence of the Lamb.
> And the smoke of their torment goes up forever and ever. There is no rest day
> or night for those who worship the beast and its image. (Rev 14:9–11)

The image of this punishment by fire (Rev 19:20; 20:10; 21:8) is evoca-
tive of God's wrath unleashed on Sodom and Gomorrah, "Then the
LORD rained on Sodom and Gomorrah sulfur and fire from the LORD
out of heaven . . ." (Gen 19:24; cf. Ezek 38:22; Lk 17:29), and may have influenced the later Christian concept of hell as a place of flames and eternal
torment.[97] The purpose of the motif of the firestorm here, however, is to
emphasize the long-term consequences of worshipping the beast. The pas-

sage, Rev 14:10–11, serves as a warning to the faithful who might consider going astray.[98]

The account of the final battle between Christ (the Lamb) and Satan (the Beast) begins in Revelation 19. Christ enters the fray astride a white horse:

> He is clothed in a robe dipped in blood, and his name is called The Word of God. And the armies of heaven, wearing fine linen, white and pure, were following him on white horses. From his mouth comes a sharp sword with which to strike down the nations and he will rule them with a rod of iron; he will tread the wine press of the fury of the wrath of God the Almighty. (Rev 19:13–15; cf. Wis 18:14–16)

The significance of the crimson tunic is unclear, but many scholars believe that the blood-dipped robe can be understood in the context of judgment (e.g., Isa 63:1–3), since the sword and rod are instruments of judgment (Rev 1:16; 2:12, 27; cf. Ps 2:9; Isa 11:4; Hos 6:5; 2 Thess 2:8).[99] Christ is portrayed here not as Redeemer of the poor and virtuous, but as the one who renders ultimate judgment on the wicked (Rev 19:11–16).[100] Since John of Patmos often describes Christ in sacrificial terms (Rev 1:5; 5:9; 7:14; 12:11), it may be that the blood-soaked garment is symbolic of Jesus' sacrifice on the cross.

The opposition gathers and closes ranks as John's vision continues: "Then I saw the beast and the kings of the earth with their armies gathered to make war against the rider on the horse and his army" (Rev 19:19). The beast and his army are defeated, the commanders (the beast and false prophet mentioned in Rev 13:1–10) are thrown alive into a burning lake, and their followers are killed, their corpses picked over by birds:

> Then I saw an angel standing in the sun, and with a loud voice he called to all the birds that fly in midheaven, "Come, gather for the great supper of God, to eat the flesh of kings, the flesh of captains, the flesh of the mighty, the flesh of horses and their riders—flesh of all, both free and slave, both small and great." (Rev 19:17–18)

The agents of Satan are thus destroyed, and only the Devil himself remains at large:[101]

> Then I saw an angel coming down from heaven, holding in his hand the key
> to the bottomless pit and a great chain. He seized the dragon, that ancient
> serpent, who is the Devil and Satan, and bound him for a thousand years, and
> threw him into the pit, and locked and sealed it over him, so that he would
> deceive the nations no more, until the thousand years were ended. After that
> he must be let out for a little while. (Rev 20:1–3)

This angel, like the Greek god Hades, holds the keys to the underworld.
He casts Satan into the abyss for a millennium, during which time the martyrs brought to life reign in a world where the authorities are not seeking
to kill them:

> Then I saw thrones, and those seated on them were given authority to judge.
> I also saw the souls of those who had been beheaded for their testimony to
> Jesus and for the word of God. They had not worshiped the beast or its image
> and had not received its mark on their foreheads or their hands. They came
> to life and reigned with Christ a thousand years. (Rev 20:4)

But it is just like a matinee serial: the hero's victory over the villain
merely ends that episode, and is followed the next week by an initial scene
in which the villain escapes and the game is on again. The meandering direction of John's end-time road map continues with the release of Satan and
the final conflict: "When the thousand years are ended, Satan will be released from his prison and will come out to deceive the nations at the four
corners of the earth" (Rev 20:7–8). Satan incites the "nations" to join him
in the final battle against Christ and his church. Satan's legions are vast, "as
numerous as the sands of the sea" (Rev 20:8). But, despite their number,
Satan and his army are quickly defeated:

> And fire came down from heaven and consumed them. And the devil who
> had deceived them was thrown into the lake of fire and sulfur, where the
> beast and the false prophet were, and they will be tormented day and night
> forever and ever. (Rev 20:9–10)

The victory belongs to God alone, who brings about the end of the reign
of Satan and Satan's human agents (though Bible readers unnerved by the
twists and turns of the apocalyptic battle might rightfully worry that even

here, in the account of Satan's infernal incarceration on the next-to-last page of the Christian scriptures, the Devil is cagily plotting a jailbreak). Fire is God's weapon of destruction (cf. 1 En 18:11–15; Mt 3:10; 5:22; 13:40; 25:41; Mk 9:43; Lk 17:29–30), and is the tool of torture.[102] Eventually, Christian theology will democratize the Prince of Darkness's punishment in Revelation, extending it to all human sinners. Once Satan and his flock are defeated, the dead are resurrected (Rev 20:11–15) and a new age begins (Rev 21:1–27).

This new age ushers in the reign of cosmic peace. John's vision of Paradise includes a vision of God seated on a throne (Rev 21:1–3), proclaiming the new constitution:

> "See, the home of God is among mortals.
> He will dwell with them; they will be his peoples,
> and God himself will be with them;
> he will wipe every tear from their eyes.
> Death will be no more; mourning and crying and pain will be no more,
> for the first things have passed away." (Rev 21:3–4)

This new world is actually a return to the world as it was "in the beginning," in Genesis 1–2. There is the tree of life (Rev 22:2; cf. Gen 2:9), and the Edenic intimacy that Creator and creation shared (Rev 22:4; cf. Gen 3:8a) before the serpent led Adam and Eve to sin in Genesis 3. On the final page of the Bible we return to the age before Satan's corrupt reign began.

In sum, John of Patmos shares a series of visions in the apocalyptic book of Revelation that depict the conflict between good and evil. Intended for persecuted Christian communities in Asia Minor (Revelation 2–3), Revelation contains the fullest exposition of Satan in the Bible. Satan's many roles and symbols in Revelation become the fount for all his eruptions. In the visionary drama of Revelation 12–24, we see the fullest biblical expression of the stuff of nightmares. For "Satan" is not merely an epithet for social rivals, as in Revelation 1–11. Now Satan is the archvillain in command of an army of monsters and demons, pitted in a battle against God, the Lamb, the angels, and the saints. Moreover, this terrifying combat is truly cosmic in scope: the arena of his battle now includes the heavens, the earth, and the underworld.

The fiendish figure in Revelation presents Satan in his final biblical form: a terrifying monster who is far removed from his humble beginnings. Satan is more than simply a grown-up version of *hassatan*. He has become the apotheosis of evil, the dreaded demon that lurks around the corner, the antithesis of all that is good. This once-innocuous heavenly lackey gone bad will capture the imaginations of both saints and sinners throughout history and become the archetypal villain in prose, poetry, art, film, and, of course, religious imagination and practice. What happens to Satan beyond the pages of the Bible could be (and has been) the subject of several volumes. But our focus has remained steadfastly on the biblical Satan—what the *Bible* has to say about him. And now, as Satan comes of age, let us turn to a brief examination of his dwelling place, hell.

chapter 7

ḥell

Satan's Home

Which way I fly is Hell; myself am Hell.

— *Satan in Paradise Lost*

The book of Revelation concludes with a cosmic battle between the forces of good and evil that ends in the banishment of Satan and his demonic cohorts to the fiery depths of hell. The idea of hell, like the development of Satan, evolved over the course of centuries. Throughout hell's evolution, however, two essential elements are constant: hell is the postmortem torture chamber where the unrighteous are punished for their sins in this world, and hell is the residence of the Devil.

Although many of the ideas about "Satan's hell" have been influenced by popular culture, our central question is this: What does the Bible have to say about this cosmic polar opposite of heaven where the unrepentant are doomed to suffer? We begin our investigation with a brief overview of the biblical references to hell.

There is no hell in the Hebrew Bible. The proverbial pit of fire where sinners are tortured for all eternity is absent. All the dead, righteous and unrighteous, share a common destination, a subterranean world known as Sheol. The Hebrew Bible does have a heaven, imagined as being located above the dome of sky. But heaven was the abode of God and the angels, unavailable to mortals, except in special cases. Both Enoch (Gen 5:24) and Elijah (2 Kgs 2:11) bypassed death and Sheol, and went directly from mortal life to fellowship with God. In Jewish legend, Enoch and Elijah became mediator figures, moving between earth and heaven, since they did not have to spend eternity in the shadowlands of Sheol. Enoch makes periodic returns to earth in order to reveal cosmic secrets to seers, Elijah regularly visits earth in order to rescue the poor and share a Seder meal with Jewish families at Passover.

There was no vivid conception of the afterlife in the Israelite worldview, unlike the beliefs in neighboring Egypt which had an illustrated guidebook to the afterlife, the Book of the Dead. But the seeds of heaven and hell were scattered here and there: in the Enoch and Elijah legends, in the traditions about prophets who had been transported to the heavenly court (i.e., 1 Kgs 22:19–23), and in the widening chasm between the Judahites' experience and their theology. After centuries of unfulfilled hopes, Jewish thinkers in the Second Temple period began to consider the possibility that the day of judgment occurred not in this life but the next.

The idea of post-mortem judgment allowed Jews to maintain faith in divine justice without denying that, in this life, too often the wicked flourished while the virtuous languished. Once the awards banquet for life was postponed until the afterlife, Jewish thinkers had to find suitable locations, function rooms, to accommodate guests. The righteous would enter the heavenly precincts with God and the angels. But what to do with the unrighteous? There was no ready-made place in their current cosmology to incarcerate them. This required some new construction.

Inspired by a garbage dump outside Jerusalem where rites of child sacrifice had once been performed and fires burned incessantly, some Jewish thinkers in the Intertestamental Period began to identify that location, Gehenna ("Valley of Hinnom") as the place of judgment. Gehenna served as the portal to Sheol, which had been remodeled from a morgue into a torture chamber. Gehenna was the perfect location. It was a valley located at the base of the topographic trough on the perimeter of Jerusalem. At the apex of the incline rising from Gehenna was the Temple Mount. The topography of heaven and hell, then, was mirrored in the geologic profile of the Holy City. At its base lay the gates of death, at its height, the gate of heaven, the Holy of Holies in the Second Temple.

The idea of "hell" does not appear in the Bible until the New Testament. The actual word, however, never appears. "Hell" is a Germanic word, the name of an underworld goddess ("Hel"). The New Testament uses the terms "Gehenna" and "Hades" to refer to the places we know as hell.

Paul, the earliest Christian writer (writing between 50 and 64 C.E), does not mention hell at all. He has plenty to say about the fate of sinners, though, and even lists offenses that will exclude one from the Kingdom of God (which Paul views as an earthly reality):

Now the works of the flesh are obvious: fornication, impurity, licentiousness, idolatry, sorcery, enmities, strife, jealousy, anger, quarrels, dissensions, factions, envy, drunkenness, carousing, and things like these. I am warning you, as I warned you before: those who do such things will not inherit the kingdom of God. (Gal 5:19–21)

Do you not know that wrongdoers will not inherit the kingdom of God? Do not be deceived! Fornicators, idolaters, adulterers, male prostitutes, sodomites, thieves, the greedy, drunkards, revilers, robbers—none of these will inherit the kingdom of God. (1 Cor 6:9–10)

The good would live and the evil would die. As Paul writes elsewhere, "For the wages of sin is death, but the free gift of God is eternal life in Christ Jesus our Lord" (Rom 6:23). For Paul, those who received Christ would experience resurrection after death: "For since we believe that Jesus died and rose again, even so, through Jesus, God will bring with him those who have died" (1 Thess 4:14). Sinners and all those who rejected Christ would simply cease to exist (Gal 5:19–21; 1 Cor 6:9–10). "Sending sinners to hell" does not enter into Paul's theology.

The earliest reference we have to the idea of hell in the Bible is found in the Gospel of Mark, written around 70 C.E.:

"If your hand causes you to stumble, cut it off; it is better for you to enter life maimed than to have two hands and to go to hell [Gehenna], to the unquenchable fire. And if your foot causes you to stumble, cut it off; it is better for you to enter life lame than to have two feet and to be thrown into hell [Gehenna]. And if your eye causes you to stumble, tear it out; it is better for you to enter the kingdom of God with one eye than to have two eyes and to be thrown into hell [Gehenna], where their worm never dies, and the fire is never quenched." (Mk 9:43–48)

It is clear that at least by the time Mark pens his Gospel, hell is understood as a literal place for the punishment for sinners. And Mark's version of hell includes some very specific details: The unrepentant soul is not only tortured by fire, but also eaten by worms.

Luke refers to hell in the parable of the Rich Man and the Beggar (Lk 16:19–26). Luke condemns the actions of the rich man not because he lacked faith in Christ (also central concerns in both Paul and Mark) but because the rich man failed to help the poor man, Lazarus:

There was a rich man who was dressed in purple and fine linen and who feasted sumptuously every day. And at his gate lay a poor man named Lazarus, covered with sores, who longed to satisfy his hunger with what fell from the rich man's table; even the dogs would come and lick his sores. The poor man died and was carried away by the angels to be with Abraham. The rich man also died and was buried. In Hades, where he was being tormented, he looked up and saw Abraham far away with Lazarus by his side. He called out, "Father Abraham, have mercy on me, and send Lazarus to dip the tip of his finger in water and cool my tongue; for I am in agony in these flames." But Abraham said, "Child, remember that during your lifetime you received your good things, and Lazarus in like manner evil things; but now he is comforted here, and you are in agony. Besides all this, between you and us a great chasm has been fixed, so that those who might want to pass from here to you cannot do so, and no one can cross from there to us." (Lk 16:19–26)

The rich man's banishment to Hades, the name for the Greek underworld, and his ability to see the poor man comfortably situated in heaven reminds us of St. Thomas Aquinas' assertion that those who dwell in heaven are granted a bird's-eye view of the wretched souls languishing in hell. It is almost as if this heavenly window is a reward—a boon—for the select saved. This image of the righteous casting disapproving or fearful glances downward to their unlucky brethren suffering in the flaming pit is a common element in most artistic representations of hell. Luke's single mention of hell remains the most concrete portrayal of the after-death experience in the New Testament. Curiously absent in his description of hell, however, is Satan. Luke makes no mention of hell's dreaded caretaker.

Matthew (who wrote his Gospel in about 90 C.E.), however, turns up the flames under the pot. Not only does Matthew include a version of Mark's hellish story (cf. Mk 9:43–48 with Mt 5:29–30), but he also includes other references to hell. Matthew's Jesus makes a clear distinction between the righteous, who will be saved, and the evildoers, who will be remanded to hell. Not even so-called religious men can escape the coming wrath, as Jesus warns the Pharisees: "You snakes, you brood of vipers! How can you escape being sentenced to hell [Gehenna]?" (Mt 23:33).

Matthew depicts hell as a place of both annihilation and torture. The gnashing of teeth, weeping, and physical torment are persistent activities in his version of hell. Matthew also makes it clear that it is the Son of Man who separates the righteous from the unrighteous before assigning the appropriate rewards (heaven) or punishments (hell):

Do not fear those who kill the body but cannot kill the soul; rather fear him who can destroy both soul and body in hell [Gehenna]. (Mt 10:28)

Just as the weeds are collected and burned up with fire, so will it be at the end of the age. The Son of Man will send his angels, and they will collect out of his kingdom all causes of sin and all evildoers, and they will throw them into the furnace of fire, where there will be weeping and gnashing of teeth. Then the righteous will shine like the sun in the kingdom of their Father. Let anyone with ears listen! (Mt 13:40–43)

So it will be at the end of the age. The angels will come out and separate the evil from the righteous and throw them into the furnace of fire, where there will be weeping and gnashing of teeth. (Mt 13:49–50)

As for this worthless slave, throw him into the outer darkness, where there will be weeping and gnashing of teeth. (Mt 25:30)

Aside from the fact that Matthew mentions hell more times than the other Gospel writers, Matthew's contribution to our overall investigation of

Satan yields another important detail. In the previous references to hell, Satan (or the Devil) was never mentioned. Hell is a place of torment for sinners, but had not been identified with Satan in any way. Matthew makes it clear that Satan and his minions are indeed destined for hell:

> Then he will say to those at his left hand, "You that are accursed, depart from me into the eternal fire prepared for the devil and his angels." (Mt 25:41)

It would be unwise to draw too many conclusions from this handful of references to hell in the letters of Paul and the Gospels. We can, however, say this: hell was not a central element in the earliest Christian literature; in fact, the Gospel of John does not mention hell at all. But as with the development of Satan, hell's fullest exposition is found in the final book of the Bible, Revelation. We explore the Book of Revelation in some detail in chapter 6—with a particular eye to the development of Satan. Here we limit our discussion to Revelation's description of hell. More than any other book in the Bible, Revelation contributes most to our modern understanding of hell as a place of fire, damnation, and, of course, Satan.

> And the devil who had deceived them was thrown into the lake of fire and sulfur, where the beast and the false prophet were, and they will be tormented day and night forever and ever. (Rev 20:10)

In Revelation, we see echoes of Paul's "categories of sinners" who will suffer death, an idea that will capture the imaginations of two medieval poets, Dante Alighieri and John Milton, whose geographical maps of hell in their respective masterpieces, *The Divine Comedy* and *Paradise Lost,* will become the blueprint for our Western conception of the Devil's abode. Revelation also bears witness to Matthew's version of hell, whereby a judgment takes place and each individual is assigned to a particular postmortem fate (cf. Mt 13:40–43; 49–50; 25:41–46).

> But as for the cowardly, the faithless, the polluted, the murderers, the fornicators, the sorcerers, the idolaters, and all liars, their place will be in the lake that burns with fire and sulfur, which is the second death. (Rev 21:8)

> And I saw the dead, great and small, standing before the throne, and books
> were opened. Also another book was opened, the book of life. And the dead
> were judged according to their works, as recorded in the books. And the sea
> gave up the dead that were in it, Death and Hades gave up the dead that were
> in them, and all were judged according to what they had done. Then Death
> and Hades were thrown into the lake of fire. This is the second death, the
> lake of fire; and anyone whose name was not found written in the book of life
> was thrown into the lake of fire. (Rev 20:12–15)

In an even more disturbing scene, unfaithful Christians who bowed
down to the Roman emperor are singled out for a special punishment
consisting of constant torture. Moreover, reminiscent of the "watching
eyes from heaven" noted earlier (cf. Lk 16:19–26), this posthumous tor-
ture-fest will be witnessed by none other than Christ (the Lamb) and the
angels:

> Then another angel, a third, followed them, crying with a loud voice, "Those
> who worship the beast and its image, and receive a mark on their foreheads
> or on their hands, they will also drink the wine of God's wrath, poured un-
> mixed into the cup of his anger, and they will be tormented with fire and sul-
> fur in the presence of the holy angels and in the presence of the Lamb. And
> the smoke of their torment goes up forever and ever. There is no rest day or
> night for those who worship the beast and its image and for anyone who re-
> ceives the mark of its name." (Rev 14:9–11)

These terrifying, enduring images of hell will haunt God-fearing Christians for centuries and will become the linchpin of countless fire-and-
brimstone sermons designed to keep the faithful in line. Outside of the
canon, in early Christian literature, hell would take on even more definition as the apocalyptic imagination dreams up nightmarish new worlds.
The first few centuries of the common era gave birth to a vast array of
"apocalypses," including the Apocalypse of Peter, the Apocalypse of
Paul, and the Apocalypse of the Virgin, each featuring a guided tour of
hell.[1] In these tales, too numerous to describe here, hell becomes even
more terrifying. But it is the works of Dante and Milton that contribute
most to our modern understanding of hell, especially the physical aspects
of hell, which include the sinners who suffer there.

Dante Alighieri: *The Divine Comedy*

The Inferno, the first part of his three-part *Divine Comedy*, recounts a pilgrim's journey through a multilayered hell. Although Dante's work stands outside the biblical canon, it has had a tremendous impact on popular Christian thought, and many medieval (and even modern) Christians undoubtedly assumed that Dante's work was itself gospel truth. Dante proposes a wholly unique structure of hell and a surprising image of Satan, who dwells in hell's deepest hollow.

The protagonist of the *Inferno* is guided by the ghost of the Roman poet Virgil through the nine circles of hell.[2] As these adventurers make their circular way toward the center of the earth, the pilgrim hears the pitiable sounds of the accursed:

> Here sighs, with lamentations and loud moans,
> Resounded through the air pierced by no star,
> That e'en I wept at entering. Various tongues,
> Horrible languages, outcries of woe,
> Accents of anger, voices deep and hoarse,
> With hands together smote that swell'd the sounds,
> Made up a tumult, that forever whirls
> Round through that air with solid darkness satin'd,
> Like to the sand that in whirlwind flies. (Canto III, 21–29)

In Dante's scheme, these nine circles narrow, like a funnel, into the earth, and sinners are scattered among the rings, suffering punishments appropriate to their crimes. Dante paints a vivid picture of the different levels (or rings) of hell. Each ring is associated with specific transgressions that merit various forms of eternal damnation. The highest of the first four circles is Limbo (and above that, Purgatory), where Virgil himself lived and where no one is actually punished.[3] The second ring is for the lustful who must endure the infernal winds of desire for all eternity, while gluttons, who occupy the third circle, are condemned to live in a reeking garbage heap.

Those dwelling in the fourth ring, the misers and spendthrifts (many of whom, Dante notes, are priests) must struggle with one another while the angry and sullen occupants of the fifth ring are forced to languish in a loathsome swamp (choking on mud), part of the river Styx ("River of Hate") that separates upper hell from lower hell.[4]

It is in the lower rings of hell that we begin to find some striking similarities to many of the stories and myths discussed in previous chapters. Crossing the river Styx, Dante enters the City of Dis, the dwelling place of fallen angels (similar to the fiery pit in Revelation and also reminiscent of the Watchers myth and the fallen angels in that tale) and the housing project for the rest of hell. The Sixth Circle houses the heretics who must spend eternity burning in their graves. Oddly, the fire we commonly associate with hell is present only within the walls of lower hell. But it is this image of hell as a fiery pit that captures the imagination of the reader and becomes the staple for most subsequent stories about hell.

The seventh ring is home to murderers, thieves, and blasphemers; the eighth ring houses those guilty of fraudulence and malice (fortunetellers, flatterers, hypocrites, and the like). Finally, at the center of hell, in a place reserved for traitors, is a frozen lake with Satan immobilized in the center.

> . . . That Emperor, who sways
> The realm of sorrow, at mid breast from the ice
> Stood forth; and I in stature am more like
> A giant, than the giants are his arms.
> Mark now how great that whole must be, which suits
> With such a part. If he were beautiful
> As he is hideous now, and yet did dare
> To scowl upon his Maker, well from him
> May all our misery flow. Oh what a sight! (Canto XXXIV: 27–35)

Dante offers a unique description of a hell beyond hell, and his mention of the Prince of Demons is surprisingly brief. Satan, the frozen monster who weeps as he devours some of hell's more noteworthy occupants— namely, Judas Iscariot, Brutus, and Cassius—is not what we might imagine.[5] In Dante's vision, Satan appears as a somewhat pathetic creature, defeated, emasculated, and weak. We are almost tempted to feel sorry for him. Although Dante's Satan appears as a wretched creature who dwells in farthermost reaches of hell, Milton paints a different portrait of both the Devil and his underworld kingdom.

John Milton: *Paradise Lost*

John Milton's *Paradise Lost* offers a glimpse of another sort of hell. *Paradise Lost* depicts Satan at his devious best; some might even go so far as to say that Satan is the hero of Milton's poem.[6] Most of *Paradise Lost* focuses on the fall of humankind in the Garden of Eden, but the first two books focus on hell. Satan's roving activities on earth—his disruption of the paradisiacal world of Adam and Eve and his obsession with revenge—are all qualities we have come to know and fear in Satan.

In the story, following a failed rebellion against God, Satan and his followers are banished from heaven and cast into a fiery lake:

> Hurled headlong flaming from the ethereal sky,
> With hideous ruin and combustion, down
> To bottomless perdition, there to dwell
> In adamantine chains and penal fire,
> Who durst defy the Omnipotent to arms.
> Nine times the space that measures day and night
> To mortal men, he, with his horrid crew,
> Lay vanquished, rolling in the fiery gulf.
>
> (Book 1: 45–52; cf. Rev. 20:12–15; 21:8).

Satan makes several attempts to exact revenge against God by reinvading earth via a roadway that Satan's offspring, Sin and Death, had built. Milton follows the early Jewish and Christian identification of Satan with the snake of Genesis 3 who seduces Eve to sin, making him responsible for the fall of humankind:

Milton shows us a very different sort of hell than Dante had. Although it is, in contrast to heaven, dim (even the fires of hell cannot make it brighter) and somewhat formless, it is not the loathsome place described by Dante. Still, Milton's hell is a place of deep psychological and physical suffering:

> Confounded, though immortal. But his doom
> Reserved him to more wrath; for now the thought
> Both of lost happiness and lasting pain
> Torments him: round he throws his baleful eyes,
> That witnessed huge affliction and dismay,

Mixed with obdurate pride and steadfast hate.
At once, as far as Angels ken, he views
The dismal situation waste and wild.
A dungeon horrible, on all sides round,
As one great furnace flamed; yet from those flames
No light; but rather darkness visible
Served only to discover sights of woe,
Regions of sorrow, doleful shades, where peace
And rest can never dwell, hope never comes
That comes to all, but torture without end
Still urges, and a fiery deluge, fed
With ever-burning sulphur unconsumed.
Such place Eternal Justice has prepared
For those rebellious; here their prison ordained
In utter darkness, and their portion set,
As far removed from God and light of Heaven
As from the centre thrice to th' utmost pole.
Oh how unlike the place from whence they fell!
There the companions of his fall, o'erwhelmed
With floods and whirlwinds of tempestuous fire . . .   (Book 1: 53–77)

Not to be discouraged when they are banished from heaven, Satan and his demonic companions crawl out of the fire, and as they plot revenge, they build a palace named Pandemonium ("All Demons") on the side of a volcano.[7] The palace boasts a grand meeting hall where Satan and the other demons in hell gather to plot and scheme. Such cosmic meetings remind us of the meetings of the divine council in the Hebrew Bible.

In *Paradise Lost,* Satan makes the best of a bad situation. After his fall, instead of lamenting his fate, Satan musters his angelic exiles and builds a kingdom for himself. This is not the sort of hell we typically imagine when we think of Satan's underground dwelling, but Milton's description of Satan's world becomes part of our overall road map of the possibilities of hell. This is a hell that is organized, a hell that even the saints can admire for its fearful symmetry.

Milton's description of Satan as the winged demon who flies between hell and earth differs greatly from Dante's frozen Devil. In Milton we can sense a sort of glee in Satan's adventures, and the zeal with which he exacts revenge against God dispels any "heroic" notion we might have had about him, for this is evil in its purest and most basic form.

But the most important contributions of both *Paradise Lost* and *The Inferno* with regard to hell, come when they flow from their literary sources into the main current of Christian thought. The blending of these two poems with biblical texts, creeds, and systematic theologies creates a new vision of hell and of Satan that will endure for centuries. This vision of a terrifying, after-death torture is rendered even more frightening with the addition of a warden, Satan, the overseer of hell.

Now, as we move to the conclusion of our story, we reflect further on the blending of stories and traditions and how this process influenced the development of Satan. But perhaps most important, we discuss why Satan's story matters.

chapter 8

why satan matters

The world is richer for having a devil in it,
so long as we keep our foot upon his neck.
—*William James*

İn 1692 the citizens of Salem, Massachusetts, believed that the Devil had infiltrated their town. When several young girls fell ill with a mysterious illness—with symptoms consistent with demonic possession—Satan seemed the most likely culprit. The young women accused of practicing witchcraft and consorting with the Devil were imprisoned and brought to trial in an attempt to purge Satan and his agents from the community. In less than a year, twenty-five people were executed or died in prison. Did Satan stalk the streets of Salem, fulfilling his role throughout history as Adversary and Dreaded Demon? Or is there a more rational explanation for the apparent demonic possession of the Salem lasses who would later point accusing fingers at neighbors and friends, charging them with the forbidden practices of witchcraft and Satanism?

As it turns out, modern science may hold the key to unlocking one of the most baffling cases in American history. In an article first published in the journal *Science* in 1976, psychologist and researcher Linnda R. Caporael cites "convulsive ergotism" as "a physiological basis for the Salem witchcraft crisis in 1692."[1] Ergot, a fungus that typically infects grains like rye (the primary grain in Salem, and throughout Europe, used for making bread), produces LSD-like hallucinations and convulsing body spasms, much like the girls experienced. According to Caporael, the Salem girls' mysterious illness was likely due to the "ingestion of grain contaminated with ergot."[2]

Although the ergot theory makes sense, it is only a theory. There are some who maintain that Satan really did possess the Salem girls, while others reject the notion entirely, chalking up the whole terrible incident to nothing more than Puritan superstitions. Still others maintain another possibility: Maybe Satan *did* infiltrate Salem, but not in the way the townspeople and others believed. Perhaps Satan worked his evil magic through the infestation of the town's grain crop.

In this final chapter, we consider the varied functions of Satan; in particular, how Satan disrupts human activity, for this is Satan's recurrent role in both the Bible and beyond. We also consider the theological significance of Satan, that is, what we gain or lose when we edit Satan out of the theological triangle of God, humanity, and the Devil. In order to accomplish these final tasks, however, we return for a moment to Satan's beginnings and consider this question: If Satan emerges as the Prince of Demons during the Second Temple period, what factors contributed to his metamorphosis from a somewhat innocuous adversary in the Hebrew Bible to the Titan of Evil?

In addition, we pause here to make an observation. The character, Satan, and the genre of story that he appears in, apocalyptic, are of equal significance. Ever since his emergence in early Jewish and Christian literature, the Devil has functioned as the archvillain of world culture. The portraits of countless fictional criminals—Fydor Dostoevski's Grand Inquisitor, Sir Arthur Conan Doyle's Moriarity, J. R. R. Tolkien's Sauron, every evil comic book kingpin from Lex Luthor to Doctor Doom—are miniatures of Satan. When we add to this legacy the myriad variations throughout history on the ancient scenario of a universal, invisible evil conspiracy—originally consisting of the Devil and his hosts—we can see that the story of Satan and the accompanying apocalyptic narrative pattern that follows are among the most perennially popular story cycles that humans have ever created.

Key Components in the Development of Satan

The first component is something produced by every culture, namely, the countless local traditions about demons, ghosts, and things that go bump in the night. We can adapt the adage of Massachusetts politician Tip O'Neill about politics to our subject: "All *demonology* is local." That is to say, every village, every neighborhood, every region, every clan or tribe or social group has its own lore about forces, haunts, ghosts, spirits, bogeymen, and restless corpses in search of severed limbs. Every culture tells stories about the un-finished business of mortal lives that, assuming personified forms, haunts, seeks vengeance and casts palls over the living. Every culture and subcul-ture has its legends about demons and monsters, whether the sea serpent, for example, is named Tiamat and lives in the Indian Ocean, is named Lotan (or Leviathan or Hydra) and lives in the Mediterranean, is named Nessie from Loch Ness, or is even referred to as "Booger," the swamp thing of Walnut Creek, Alabama.[3]

From this ever-flowing fountain of folklore and superstition, all based on stories people told to each other, the avatars of our Satan began to emerge in written form during the second and first millennia B.C.E. Our Satan, the biblical Satan, the archvillain of Western literature, begins with the advent of writing, in Mesopotamian cuneiform, Egyptian hieroglyph-ics, and in the earliest alphabetic writings from Syria, Lebanon, Jordan, and Israel.

Two types of characters emerge in this literature that are essential in-gredients in all subsequent developments related to the Devil. The first are stories about opponents of the hero, whether divine or human, in combat myths. Earlier we mentioned Humbaba, the monstrous opponent of Gil-gamesh and Enkidu in the second-millennium Babylonian classic, The Epic of Gilgamesh, and the various opponents of El and Baal in the Syr-ian (Ugaritic) myths, such as Mot ("Death") and Yam ("Sea").[4] In this ocean of ancient pantheons and the vast library of ancient stories, a legion of cosmic opponents strove to disrupt health, stability, and productivity. The Jewish/Christian/Islamic Devil becomes the villain of the cosmic com-bat narrative that has dominated much of European and Middle Eastern culture in the common era.

The other important component in Satan's story that can be traced back to the earliest outpouring of Western literature is the character of "the chaos monster." Mesopotamian literature and art contains descriptions and images of misshapen, misbegotten monstrosities. These creatures can be identified from their composite physiques, a bewildering mix of fish and fowl, of aquatic and land forms, and of bestial and human features. The chaos monsters were hybrids: birdlike wings sprouted from the backs of human bodies that were capped with the heads of lions.

These characters, best seen in the Babylonian creation myth *Enuma Elish* as well as in depictions of many Canaanite demons, Egyptian sphinxes, and Hebrew cherubim, had an ambivalent function in narratives. Their mixed shapes testified to their chaotic personalities; these were creatures that defied all categories of classification and did not fit into any orderly scheme of creation or great chain of being. Their unstable personalities and ambivalent stance can best be seen in the plot of the *Enuma Elish*. There, in one of our earliest combat myths, they began as warriors in the service of Tiamat, the opponent of the gods of order. These scorpion-men, bull-men, and horned serpents were the mercenaries enlisted by Tiamat to defeat the forces of order led by Marduk, the god of Babylon.[5]

But when Marduk defeated Tiamat, ensuring routine, enacting normality, and chartering patterned, predictable reality, the divine hero did not destroy the chaos monsters. Instead Marduk caged them. Now they would serve the forces of order. Now their intimidating forms, in statuary, would guard temples and palaces. In the Bible, for instance, the cherubs (winged lions) would ward off trespassers into Eden and protect the invisible divine presence in the Holy of Holies of Solomon's Temple.

The chaos monsters, morphing into the gargoyles on medieval cathedrals and the mutant superheroes of modern comic books, have been powerful symbols ever since. In some cases, such as the Hunchback of Notre Dame cathedral who watches over the poor, the benevolent dinosaurs of children's literature, and Chewbacca of the *Star Wars* films, the chaos monsters remain on their leashes and protect culture from its enemies. In other narratives, these wolfmen and creatures from black lagoons escape from their cages and wreak havoc until a hero subdues them and brings them back under control. In either scenario, however, the most salient fact about the chaos monsters—anticipated by Marduk's experience with them—is that they are never wholly obliterated, at least before the Eschaton, the day of Kingdom Come. A profound logic at the heart of the stories about these monsters recognizes that chaos is essential to life. Chaos must be controlled, channeled, and restrained, but it must not and cannot be removed from the picture. Without chaos, there is no drama, no novelty, no surprise, and no evolution from the status quo.

We have discussed chaos monsters at length because they are an under-appreciated but foundational ingredient in the image of Satan. We elaborate on this idea when we discuss the functions of Satan. For now, it is sufficient to note that virtually all artistic portraits of Satan imagine his physiognomy as that of a chaos monster, a hybrid, a composite being. Satan has sat for many portraits, but in most he combines serpentine, humanoid, and animalistic features. Satan is horned, tailed, scaled, hoofed, and/or winged. These physical characteristics alone mark Satan as belonging to the phylum of chaos monsters. Later in this chapter we consider the next question this raises: whether Satan, like other chaos monsters, serves some essential purpose in the enterprise we know as life.

Four specific characters found in ancient Oriental and Mediterranean literature seemed to have left the most indelible impression in Satan's form. The profiles of the Canaanite demon Habayu, "the lord of horns and tail," and of the Greek deity Pan, half man and half goat, were assimilated into many of the images of Satan.[6] Satan inherits the thrones of the underworld deities of ancient eastern Mediterranean cultures, such as Syrian Mot and Greek Hades. Obviously, the character known in the Hebrew Bible as *hassatan*, "the Adversary," was a primary source for the character of Satan. From *hassatan*, Satan will get his name and one of his chief functions, that of tempter and tester, the devisor of dilemmas that reveal the true character of humans. The final character to make its way into the mix was the Persian deity Ahriman, the god of darkness in perennial opposition to Ahura Mazda, the god of light, in whatever form of Zoroastrianism the Jews in the eastern Diaspora encountered in the fifth through the third centuries B.C.E.[7]

Context

What was the cultural context in which these various components were forged into an enduring image? We have identified the era of Satan's birth as that of the Second Temple period in Jewish history, that is, between the fifth century B.C.E. and the first century C.E. Three conditioning factors influenced the development of the idea of Satan among the Jewish people in this period.

The first factor is the triumph of monotheism, as we discussed in the chapter 2. From the eighth to the sixth centuries B.C.E., a series of brilliant Hebrew religious thinkers, the prophets, isolated a rare and elusive element in their laboratories in the highlands of Judah and Ephraim and, during the Exile, on the steppes of Babylon. We know this idea as monotheism, a unified cosmic field theory. Amos rhetorically asked, "Does disaster befall a city unless the LORD has done it?" Two centuries later, during the Exile, Isaiah of Babylon answered Amos's question definitively. No, Isaiah wrote, speaking on behalf of the One, "I am the LORD. I create weal and woe."

But this austere prophetic view of God, regardless of its ultimate truth, was hard to handle. A God who was all-powerful, author of blessings and curses, good and evil, was not easy to get close to. Once this pure monotheism was exposed to real-life conditions outside the control of these prophets, it began to break down. Pure monotheism is theologically and existentially unstable. Although it is not impossible, it is extremely difficult to believe in the ultimate beneficence of a God who also bears ultimate responsibility for everything, including misfortune. In time, and it would take time, the idea of a cosmic force opposed to God, a shadowy anti-god who perversely, inversely reflected every virtue of the Creator, began to emerge. In other words, Satan might not have been the nominee of the party regulars and elite thinkers in Second Temple Judaism—his nomination came from the floor—but he swept the convention. It is as if the people demanded, "Give us a devil," just as in a text from 1 Samuel their ancestors had said, "Give us a king" (1 Sam 8:6).

Another conditioning factor in the development of Satan was the influence of the foreign cultures to which Jews were exposed in the Diaspora. Perhaps the most important of these, as mentioned earlier, was the dualistic system of Persian religion. As Jeffrey Burton Russell puts it, "Ahriman is the first real Devil in world religion."[8] Jewish communities were exposed to Ahriman during the Persian period, from 530 to 330 B.C.E. Satan as a divine opponent of the LORD and as author of evil does not appear until the second century B.C.E., by which time Jews in Babylon and Persia had been exposed to the dualism of Zoroastrianism and to its evil deity Ahriman for generations.

Without denying the significance of this and other foreign influences on evolving Jewish ideas about Satan, we must note that every ship bearing ideas about Canaanite demons, Greek underworlds or Iranian demiurges had to find a place to dock in the Jewish consciousness. These ideas had to fulfill a need, fit into a niche, and help to solve a problem, or they would not have been assimilated into the worldviews of the Jewish apocalypticists in the Second Temple period.

The existence of an evil deity opposed to the purposes of God eased (but did not finally solve) the tension between divine power and divine goodness. If there was a Devil, then God was not the author of evil; evil had its own independent source. Certainly this style of dualistic thinking touched on something that is apparently universal and thus applicable to ancient Jews: namely, the binary narrative frame that exists in the human mind, that separates reality into the opposing categories of Us and Them, Friend and Foe, Family and Stranger, and Hero and Villain. To put it simply, the Devil makes for a good story.

A final conditioning factor that caused the ingredients just mentioned to coalesce into the character of Satan was the increased amount of reflection on the origins of evil that occurred in the Second Temple period.[9] When the Babylonians sacked Jerusalem in 587 B.C.E., they not only destroyed the First Temple but they also destroyed the unchallenged efficacy of Iron Age theology. That theology, seen in the writings of the Former and Latter Prophets as well as in extrabiblical sources from the region such as the Moabite stela of King Mesha dated to the ninth century B.C.E., held that reality was governed by ethical cause and effect. Righteousness was rewarded and wickedness was punished, without exception. As the character of God complains in Robert Frost's satire about the book of Job, *A Masque of Reason,* "I *had to* prosper good and punish evil," as if even "Jehovah" himself felt straitjacketed by too strict a view of the covenant.[10] The jeremiads of the Hebrew prophets and the grand narratives of the Israelite authors of Joshua, Judges, Samuel, and Kings were all based on the principle that "whatsoever a man soweth, that [precisely, measure for measure] shall he reap" (Gal 6:7).

But the cataclysms of Jerusalem's destruction and the deportation of its elites, combined with the ongoing traumas of unfulfilled hopes during the Diaspora, led to new ideas about the issues of suffering and evil, in short, of theodicy. There had to be more going on in reality than simple cause and effect could explain. The enormity of misfortune experienced by the Jews seemed immeasurably greater than their errors.

This Iron Age theology did not die. The principle of ethical cause and effect still works—for all of the people some of the time and for some charmed individuals all (or most) of the time. Only the extremely dishonest, chronically disorganized, or radically cynical would deny that virtue bears fruits, that industry is rewarded, or that investments, in good deeds or fiduciary trusts, reap benefits. But this idea, as foundational as it was and ever shall be, is never fully sufficient because it does not explain random tragedy, undeserved misfortune, and disproportionate punishment.

This escalation of concerns about theodicy and about the origins of evil spurred Second Temple biblical writers to new insights (although in folktales like Esther and the stories about Daniel and his companions, the old theology still reigned). Isaiah of Babylon, in a series of amazing poems that have deeply influenced Christian theology, suggested that some suffering might have a redemptive purpose:

> He [the LORD's servant] was despised and rejected by others;
> a man of suffering and acquainted with infirmity.
> Surely he has borne our infirmities and carried our diseases;
> yet we accounted him stricken,
> struck down by God, and afflicted.
> But he was wounded for our transgressions,
> crushed for our iniquities;
> upon him was the punishment that made us whole,
> and by his bruises we are healed. (Isa 53:3–5)

The author of Job took his readers for a magic carpet ride on the divine whirlwind so that they could view reality from a God's-eye view. In Job 38–41, the author sketched the wheels-within-wheels complexity of human and animal life and of meteorological and astronomical networks, as if to say to humanity: Life is exquisitely complicated and there are some things that only God understands.

> Then the LORD answered Job out of the whirlwind:
> "Gird up your loins like a man;
> I will question you, and you shall declare to me.
> Where were you when I laid the foundation of the earth?
> Have you entered into the springs of the sea?

Where is the way to the dwelling of light?
Have you entered the storehouses of snow?
Can you bind the chains of the Pleiades?
Do you know when the mountain goats give birth?
Do you observe the calving of the deer?
(Job 38:1, 3, 4, 16, 129, 21, 32; 39:1)

One biblical author, identified as Ecclesiastes or, in Hebrew, Qohelet, wrote a series of world-weary essays that admitted, "Yes, life is unfair, random events do happen. Go figure!" For Ecclesiastes, it was all vanity; it was all vaporous, and misty.[11] The meanings behind events were opaque.

For this study's purposes, however, the most relevant product of the escalating concern for an answer to the theodicy question was the rise of apocalyptic literature during the Second Temple period. For these writers, the meanings behind events were far from opaque, as they had been to the author of Ecclesiastes. The apocalyptic scenarists had seen the Plan. They knew the times and seasons. And as we have pointed out, this literary genre is crucial to the birth of Satan. As the biblical scholar Stephen Cook has noted, apocalyptic literature takes the deepest, foundational stories of a culture, its myths, and imposes them on the surface of history.[12] In the case of biblical apocalyptic literature, this meant that features from creation stories and ancient combat myths would be used as a lens through which to view the events of the day. For instance, in the book of Daniel the oppressive ancient empires of Babylon, Media, Persia, and Greece are personified as winged lions, bears with three tusks, bird-leopards, and a multihorned beast with iron teeth (Dan 7:1–7). Daniel is superimposing features from before time, such as in the Babylonian creation story with its chaos monsters, onto his interpretation of the events of his day.

As we said in earlier chapters, apocalyptic is essentially a cosmic conspiracy theory. The real meaning of history is not apparent, it can only be revealed, and under the surface of everyday life lays a vast nefarious network, a murderous, invisible, universal, and ageless conspiracy dedicated to thwarting happiness and fouling the wellsprings of kindness, to sowing discord and conquering the universe in the name of Death. Satan (or Mastema or Belial) is the name given to the mastermind behind all this in Jewish apocalyptic literature.

We have also noted that the apocalyptic style of thinking is not only ancient. It persists, even thrives, in pockets of contemporary culture. Modern sociologists use the term "subversion theory" to describe the patterns of thought that collect the discarded pearls of medieval heretics and secret societies, and rites and symbols from pre-Christian European, ancient Mediterranean, Near Eastern, and Indo-Aryan religions, and arrange them along the thinnest strings of logic in order to fashion the jewelry of folk belief.

If the subversion theory is advanced by communities or individuals suspicious of the government, its Satan and demons are an international network of elites who purportedly control the powers that *seem to* be. The identity of this cabal of elites varies according to the social prejudices of the theory's adherents. Anti-Semites suspect an international Jewish conspiracy. This, by the way, is the cruelest irony: that a narrative pattern invented by ancient Jews would be reversed to make its original composers into the enemy. Right-wingers suspect a Communist or atheistic conspiracy while left-wingers fear a military-industrial complex. Protestant John Birchers fear the Vatican, and hysterical Roman Catholics fear the Freemasons. Some middle-class Americans coping with the enormous economic and cultural changes of the late twentieth-century have imagined that a network of Satanists and sexual deviants seek to abduct their children from shopping malls or violate their children in day care centers. Many Westerners see an international Islamic conspiracy dedicated to destroying Jewish and Christian culture, while some Muslims fear the reverse. There is and will always be enough evidence of human chicanery from all these alleged perpetrators to keep such theories afloat. There are also the U.F.O. enthusiasts who warn us about the advance corps of aliens that have already begun to infiltrate our atmosphere. The "thickest" subversion theories manage to combine two or more of these stocks into a hearty stew of paranormal paranoia, such as in the *X-Files* movie where the aliens are in league with a government elite.

This book has concentrated on a single historical question: How did Satan emerge in Jewish and Christian literature up until the end of the biblical period? As we near the end of our story, we broaden our perspective to think about Satan in light of the two millennia that have followed the biblical period. The history of Satan, the immense task of accounting not only for Satan's birth but his adulthood too, has been chronicled in five volumes by Jeffrey Burton Russell.[13] Satan has had many adventures: his combats with desert hermits, Protestant Reformers, and Roman Catholic exorcists; the hysterias he has inspired among late-medieval churchmen, New World Puritans, and small-town Americans.

The story of Satan dominates the biggest stories constructed in Western culture, in official Christian theologies and, to a far lesser but still significant degree, in Jewish legends, and in epic literature such as Dante's *Inferno*, Milton's *Paradise Lost*, and Goethe's *Faust*, literary works that the biblically illiterate masses swallowed hook, line, and sinker as gospel truth. We briefly mentioned the work of the medieval Italian poet Dante Alighieri in chapter 7 during our discussion of hell. Dante chronicles his journey to hell and encounter with the Prince of Demons in the first part of his three-part *Divine Comedy* aptly entitled *The Inferno*. Dante refers to the concierge of hell, whose relentlessly beating wings fan the pitiable inhabitants with an icy wind, by a variety of names: Satan, Lucifer, and Beelzebub. Much like its Greek counterpart, Dante's hell is divided into various levels where sinners, whether hypocrites or gluttons, heretics or cowards, suffer punishments appropriate to their sins. But the most vivid and enduring treatment of Satan in Western literature would come from an epic poet inspired by Dante, England's John Milton.

In *Paradise Lost*, Milton offers the systematic theology of Satan that curious biblical audiences had been seeking for almost two millennia. Milton adopts the Lucifer myth of Satan's origins (Satan had led a heavenly rebellion of angels and was banished to the lower realms), ensuring its triumph over the Watchers myth (that Satan was the scion of the angels who mated with human women) in Christian tradition. Milton organizes all the Christian lore that existed about Satan, about his physical form, about his demonic ranks, about the architecture of his netherworldly palace "Pandemonium," and about the landscape of hell into its "canonical" form. Milton's Satan reprises his biblical role of adversary, first disrupting heavenly order and then corrupting human beings.

Johann Wolfgang von Goethe's *Faust* is a pessimistic tale about a man whose desire for knowledge and power leads him to sell his soul to the Devil, called here Mephistopheles. All three of these works have inspired artists, playwrights, and filmmakers, but it is their impact on the popular image of Satan among ordinary people that is of central importance here. For within a relatively short period of time, these literary works (and countless more) actually became part of the Christian story of Satan, blurring the biblical portrait of Satan with their own refinements and embroiderings. And so the faithful and faithless alike have inevitably garnered most of their impressions about Satan not from the pages of the Bible but rather from a sloppy amalgamation of postbiblical lore.

Indeed, the imprint of these classical literary portraits has been deep and enduring, but it pales next to the thousands of images inked, etched, painted, and tiled that depict Satan, let alone the impact of satanic portraits in recent popular culture. The impact of the lurid Devils in 1950s comic books and in third-millennium graphic novels, and the satanic antiheroes of horror writers and filmmakers such as Edgar Allen Poe, H. P. Lovecraft, Roger Corman, Stephen King, and Clive Barker are as vital in satanic lore as the literary masterworks. These artists tap into popular veins outside the canon where Satan has always been most vividly alive.

We cannot tell the story of Satan's adulthood here.[14] Suffice it to say that the Devil has made an amazing comeback from the assaults of the Enlightenment, the scientific revolution, and the advent of modern psychology. These cultural changes had reduced Satan to a character of primitive folklore or to some undigested scrap of moral guilt. But a full account of Satan's rebirth in modern culture is simply too overwhelming. We will instead attempt something far more modest: to offer some impressionistic comments on the functions Satan plays in narratives and to reflect on the theological significance of the Devil, for this is at the very heart of why Satan's story matters.

Satan's Functions

First seen in the Watchers myth from the Intertestamental Period, Satan is the Prince of Demons, the organized leader of the great conspiracy to make all things work together for evil. But Satan has many other roles as well.

The Tempter

Satan always held on to the portfolio of the Hebrew *hassatan*, whose task was to conduct audits of human virtue. It is fascinating to watch the way this necessary function—separating the wheat from the chaff, the pious from the pompous, the faithful from the phonies—gets passed around from character to character in the Bible and early Jewish literature. In the well-known story about the (near) sacrifice of Isaac written in the First Temple period, it is God who administers the exams: "After these things God tested Abraham" (Gen 22:1). In the early Second Temple period, in the initial chapters of the book of Job, a certain angel, *hassatan,* has been deputized to test humans, although under divine supervision. By the second century B.C.E., in the pseudepigraphical book Jubilees, when the story of Abraham and Isaac is retold, it is "Prince Mastema," not God, who initiates this test to see whether Abraham loves his child more than he loves God (Jub 17:15–18).

The psychological import of this development is clear: Satan has relieved God of a very unpleasant task. There are now layers of deniability protecting God from legal action for breach of contract. Satan performs this same kind of testing in the Gospel narratives about Jesus' temptations. These kinds of stories take on a life of their own, and in them Satan hones his malevolent inventiveness in devising traps to ensnare the morally weak.

The Father of Lies

The image of Satan as the author of heresies and animator of paganisms is clearly present in the New Testament period, as the quote from John 8:44–45, "The devil . . . is the father of lies," demonstrates. In the Intertestamental Period, we see evidence of this satanic function in the epithet, Sammael, "the Blind God," from the Martyrdom of Isaiah, and in the Watchers myth from 1 Enoch, where the rebel angels instruct humans in esoteric and occult arts. From a sociological perspective, it seems clear that this is a way that ancient religious writers demonized their sectarian rivals, by accusing them not merely of being in error, but of being seduced by the Devil into false beliefs. This satanic function grows along with Satan himself through history. This is the Islamic *shaitan* who tampers with the Qur'an, inserting "satanic verses" that lead the weak from the path of sound doctrine. This is the Mephistophelean character of European stories, the high priest of the occult arts, who initiates seekers into the esoteric realms of "black" magic.[15]

The Dungeon Master and King of Hell

Satan is the punisher of the wicked in the afterlife. This idea does not appear in the biblical period, but it has roots in the stories about the underworld gods of Canaanite and Greek mythologies whose thrones Satan inherits. Whether it is called hell or Hades or Gehenna, whether it is conceived of as muddy, frozen, fiery, musty, or arid, Satan is king of the chthonic terrain.

In this function Satan, who develops into an ingenious sadist, plays an essential role in many eschatologies by balancing the cosmic books. Heavenly justice requires that the prosperous wicked receive a punishment in hell commensurate with their undeserved pleasures on earth. This is the Satan to whom we commend our enemies when we curse them with "Go to hell." This is another essential chore of the divine administration from which Satan, perhaps too energetically, relieves God.

The Kingpin of the Underground Economy

This Satan presides over a back-alley bazaar, a black market, where everything is for sale, but there are no bargains. Every ware has the same price: a human soul. This image of Satan is at the heart of the Faust legend in all its variant forms, all those stories about people making deals with the Devil. This function is hinted at in the Gospel accounts of Jesus' temptation. "All the kingdoms of the world" are offered to one who agrees to bow down to Satan. This Satan, the lender of last resort, the last-minute financial rescuer of and investor in doomed schemes, practices extreme loan-sharking, and he always collects. The Devil always gets his due.

Chaos Monster

As we noted earlier, Satan never loses his connection to the ancient category of monstrous hybrid creatures. Like the chaos monsters, Satan is constitutionally destructive, leading his gang of demons in their gleeful vandalism of stable structures and in their unbinding of the wise restraints that make men free. As the ultimate chaos monster, Satan serves as the cosmic renderer, processing the carcass of matter in a lake of fire.

This Satan inspires rebellion and the flaunting of conventional morality. This Satan offers artistic and hedonistic freedom untethered from covenant, from concern for the morning after, or from concern for neighbor. This is Satan at his most attractive, because sometimes chaos works like a balm on chafed wrists bound by the laws and customs of community and order.

It is Satan as chaos monster that appeals to alienated groups who adopt satanic imagery. Bikers, Goths, heavy metalists: for them satanic emblems function as markers of contrariness, emblems of anarchy, and of their identity as agents of chaos. This may also be the stylish Satan of the Romantic poets and artists of the late eighteenth century, who saw the Devil as a champion of political and artistic freedom, a figure who reappears two centuries later as Mick Jagger's "man of wealth and taste."[16]

The irony is that the Satan championed by the counter-culture is only powerful when he is juxtaposed with religious orthodoxy and mainstream values. The occult needs a (mainstream) cult, the magus needs the priest. The *grimoires* of Neo-Pagans are dangerous and fashionable only if they are opposed by the grammars of traditional faith. Every diabolic symbol is a twisted version, the evil twin, of some orthodox sibling. The pentagram is a reorientation of the Star of David, 666 is an unstable derivative of 777, the Satanic Black Mass is a Eucharist without the poetic transubstantiation of symbolism (actual blood instead of wine, sexual intercourse instead of spiritual communion). To this extent, then, the faithful should take heart. The Satanists need them just as much as the traditionally religious need their Devil. The Satan story is just one more way in which these ancient partners, chaos and order, continue their uneasy but necessary dance to the music of time.

Our Ancient Foe

The phrase, "our ancient foe," borrows from Martin Luther's great hymn, "A Mighty Fortress Is Our God":

> For still our ancient foe
> Doth seek to work us woe;
> His craft and pow'r are great,
> And, armed with cruel hate,
> On earth is not his equal.

This is Satan as the opponent of God. "History," in the words of the contemporary philosopher Fredric Jameson, "is what hurts."[17] If that is so, then Satan, the King of Pain, is necessary for the drama of history. "No sand, no pearl." Satan must also be part of the plan.

Satan is the ancient foe, but his opposition forces God, the angels, and the saints to bring their best game, summoning from them greater virtue. Without Satan's opposition, would we strive? It is as if even after he was banished from heaven, Satan would always be part of the divine government, although on a special, secret mission, under the deepest, deepest cover, like one of John le Carré's or Len Deighton's master spies. Satan— lost yet essential, doomed yet necessary—was assigned the dirty work that makes history possible.

Satan's Virtues

Satan is a crucial part of the relationship triad that includes God, humans, and the Devil. In such a relationship, we might fail to recognize that the Prince of Demons plays an important role in keeping this relationship afloat. Virtually all of the just-mentioned functions of Satan, at a distance, at a safe remove from their immediate effects, serve necessary purposes in the divine government: testing mortals, punishing the wicked, chaotically upsetting convention and destabilizing the status quo so that new forms can emerge, and creating the morally competitive environment that forces infantile self-interest to grow into mature love.

Theologically, Satan's greatest virtue is to serve as the cosmic scapegoat, saving God from blame for evil. Satan is indispensable for certain popular Christian views of God. Because the first followers of Jesus were so much a part of the culture of Second Temple Jewish apocalypticism, they easily adopted Satan into their worldview. This allowed for a far sunnier view of God to dawn in the New Testament than had in the Hebrew Bible. The God of the Hebrew Bible tested Abraham (Gen 22) and sent an evil spirit into Saul (1 Sam 16:14). *Satan* does these kinds of things in the New Testament, not the triune Christian God. By assuming all the unpleasant tasks of the divine government and accepting responsibility for evil, Satan freed Christians from the tensions of the family arguments between children and their heavenly father that Judaism prizes. Satan, indirectly, allowed for the pieties of "Fairest Lord Jesus" and "the Holy Spirit who is our Comforter."

We saw this trend at work even before Satan fully emerged, in the way that the rewritten history of the Chronicler overwrote its source in 2 Samuel, making "Satan," not "the anger of the LORD," the instigator of David's ill-founded census (cf. 1 Chr 21:1 with 2 Sam 24:1). We saw this in the way that the author of Jubilees, late in the Second Temple period, distanced God from responsibility and blamed Mastema/Satan for testing Abraham (Jub 17:15–16) and ambushing Moses (Jub 48:1–3). The psychology of all this scapegoating is clear: Satan is a theological coping mechanism, the screen onto which repellent traits about God are projected. In Satan all the dry bones of disquieting doubts and disfiguring experiences with the divine massed, grew sinew, organs and circulatory systems, and were finally animated by an evil spirit. And up from the grave he arose. Elaine Pagels makes this point well: Satan represents the ultimate embodiment, in Jewish and, especially, Christian culture, of the Other, the enemy, the foreigner.[18]

Another virtue of the story of Satan is that it provides a parallel narrative to orthodoxy. Satan fell, and so did Adam. Satan abused his moral freedom by rebelling against the divine will; such rebellions are humanity's favorite leisure activity. In the Watchers myth, it was the desire for illicit love, the angels' amorous interest in the forbidden fruit of mortal women, that led to their fall from grace. Similarly, religious traditions urge their congregants to marry within the tribe. In the Lucifer myth, it was the vaunting pride of the rebel angels that led to their fall; as John Milton had Satan say, "Better to reign in hell than serve in heav'n" (*Paradise Lost* 1:264). Similarly, as the author of Proverbs warned, "Pride goeth before a fall" (Prov 16:18). Thus, Satan is a useful teaching tool, the ultimate bad example in religious instruction; living proof, if indeed he can be said to "live," of what happens when freedom is not wedded to responsibility.

It is as if Satan is an allegorical representative of the human race. Perhaps this is another reason why Satan remains such an attractive figure in Western culture and why his story matters to us. As strange as it may sound, we might actually feel a degree of kinship with the Devil. Indeed, this truth is buried deep within the lore of Satan, in the core tradition of the Watchers myth. For all his horrific personas, Satan is, in many respects, our half-sibling. As the Watchers myth tells it, Satan's father may have been one of the rebel angels, but his mother was one of the daughters of men. Satan may be our evil older brother, but he is our brother nonetheless. And, through the ingenious machinations of his temptations and traps, we recognize that Satan knows us better than we know ourselves.

Postscript: Is Satan Real?

All Jewish, Christian, and Muslim theologies that feature Satan inadvertently give themselves away as false. In the creation story, on the first day, Satan was not present; rather, Satan had to fall. Furthermore, on the last day, Satan will not stand.

In short, Satan was provisional, Satan was ad hoc. Satan was a convenience and a contrivance, an incomplete idea, an insufficient response to a child's question about where evil came from, although the story was told so well that it often forestalled its logical follow-up, "But why did and does God allow Satan to rebel and operate and torment?" In the end, the patronizing answers—"Satan is the source of evil," "The Devil made me do it"—never answer the question of the origins of evil. Because if God is initially, fully, and finally God, the Alpha and the Omega, then Satan is merely the Beta and the Psi. Satan may have emerged before time, but not before God, and on the next to last day, Satan will be defeated.

In the mid-twentieth century, the German theologian Paul Tillich formulated the phrase "the God above (or beyond) God."[19] Tillich's words remind believers that in Jewish terms, at the heart of monotheistic faith is the enigma of "I am who I am," that in Christian terms, "we see through a glass darkly," and that in Muslim terms, even the ninety-nine names for Allah do not suffice. The God of the cosmos, a universe eons old and light-years big, is only hinted at in human theologies, however accurately. But human beings are storytellers and pattern makers, and the philosophic formulations of scholars like Tillich lack the detail and color necessary to sustain virtue and give order to our lives. We need stories. So, provisionally, with fingers crossed, people of faith walk in the light of their traditional stories, happy for the truth and light, the consolations and motivations, they have received.

This detour to a paradox posed by a theologian is intended to lure sophisticated readers into an unfamiliar place in their thinking and to inspire in them a greater tolerance for the storytelling and pattern making about Satan in Jewish, Christian, and Muslim traditions. We have hoped to convince them of the value of traditional conceptions of God in the monotheistic faiths—that they may contain truth if not the whole truth—and of the necessity for these penultimate expressions, of names for God in human languages, of personalizing characterizations for God, of storytelling about God, because these names, personifications, and stories have a kind of energy—the power to inspire courage, tenderness, justice, and hope—that cosmological and philosophic abstractions cannot match.

If "God," then, is the term we use, for convenience, to refer to this nameless or infinitely named source of cosmic harmony and meaning, for the ultimate hospitality of the universe toward life, for this heavenly host, as it were, then it is hardly surprising that many monotheists have constructed the embodiment, in stories and art and imaginings, of the energy and forces in life that seem inhospitable, disorderly, and fractious. This is the character we know as Satan, whose origins are the subject of this book. We cannot know, or at least we do not, whether there is a Satan beyond this Satan. But even if what we know of Lucifer, "the Light-Bearer," is a mere reflection of some mysterious cosmic process, a trick of light, this character who has shadowed humanity now for over two millennium is worthy of our respectful consideration.

Given so, what are we to do with this information? How can Satan's story help us as we grapple with the evil in our own lives and in the world in general?

First, the stories about Satan teach us that evil can be deceptive. For, like Satan himself, evil assumes many forms: the earnest-sounding accountant who defrauds his clients; the smiling young woman who gives away free samples of cocaine to her friends until they are addicted; the pedophile priest disguised as God's servant.[20] Understanding Satan's forms and functions can help us to recognize that evil enters our own lives in many different shapes and sizes. And, consequently, we may also recognize our own deceptive behavior as destructive, which offers the opportunity for change.

Second, one of the most salient features of the various "Satan stories" is the fact that Satan never moves about in the world unopposed. In every instance, there is someone who steps into the fray to take on the Adversary. There is a certain nobility in these skirmishes because of the courage involved in stepping onto the battlefield against such a formidable opponent. And, perhaps more important, stories about wrestling with Satan mirror our own struggles against temptation and injustice.[21] Satan's defeat in these stories offers us hope that we can overcome the evil that sometimes overshadows our own lives, teaching us to take responsibility for our own actions and to turn to others for help in our struggles.[22]

Finally, we return to the perennial question: Is Satan real? The theological and scriptural arguments for and against the existence of Satan are as vast and as formidable as are the variations in personal beliefs concerning Satan. Yet whether Satan is to be taken as a metaphor, as a symbolic, or literal being, Satan is real in the sense that evil is real. Indeed, the fearsome red demon who pursued so many of us in our childhood nightmares pales in comparison to the real and palpable evil at work in the world today in the form of murderous regimes, maniacal serial killers, and suicide bombers.

When we dismiss the biblical Satan as a primitive or outdated concept, when we effectively edit him out of the theological equation and ignore the truths of the stories about him, we run the risk of missing the great lessons the biblical writers were trying to impart. They did not try to explain away evil, for evil was then, and is now, a reality that cannot be denied. And yet, in the final analysis, the Bible reassures us that God is on our side, that the Devil can be resisted, that love wins out in the end.

notes

Preface

1. Jodi Matthews. "Devil Alive and Well in U.S. Polls." *Daily Ethics.com,* April 23, 2003. <http://www.baptists4ethics.com/article_detail.cfm?AID=2468>. See also Jennifer Robinson. "The Devil and the Demographic Details," *The Gallup Organization,* February 25, 2003, July 27, 2004, <http://www.gallup.com/content/login.aspx?ci=7858>.

Introduction

1. Neil Forsyth, *The Old Enemy: Satan and the Combat Myth* (Princeton, N.J.: Princeton University Press, 1987), 4. The Hebrew word *śṭn* and the Greek word *diabolos* both contain the same root meaning: "opponent." Forsyth notes that in Greek the name can also mean "slanderer" as in a prosecutor/accuser, which is the same function of *hassatan* in the Old Testament. According to Dianne Bergant, "the word 'satan' appears with an article indicating that here the word is a title or description and not a proper name" (*Job, Ecclesiastes.* Old Testament Message 18 [Wilmington, Del.: Michael Glazier, 1982], 27).
2. Elaine Pagels, *The Origin of Satan* (New York: Vintage, 1995), xv.
3. Apocalyptic is a highly symbolic style of literature that deals with the "end time." From the Greek *apokalyptein,* it means "to uncover, unveil, or reveal." See Bernhard W. Anderson and Katheryn Pfisterer Darr, *Understanding the Old Testament,* 4th ed. (Englewood Cliffs, N.J.: Prentice-Hall, 1998), 559.
4. Pagels, *The Origin of Satan,* xvii.
5. According to Jeffrey Burton Russell, Hellenistic thought, "which assigned ontological existence and moral perfection to the One, and denied evil ontological existence or attributed it to the lowest level of being," is combined with Judaism, "which had separated the good from the evil element in God . . . demoting the evil aspect . . . to the status of an inferior being or angel" (*The Devil: Perceptions of Evil from Antiquity to Primitive Christianity* [Ithaca, N.Y.: Cornell University Press, 1977], 222).
6. For "orthodox" Satanism, see Anton Szandor LaVey, *The Satanic Bible* (New York: Avon Books, 1986), 99–105.

Chapter 1

1. Although *The Birth of Satan* is intended to stand alone as a resource to help readers understand the emergence of the biblical Satan, some might find it helpful to

use the Bible in conjunction with this book. There are many fine English translations of the Bible, but we recommend *The New Oxford Annotated Bible* (with Apocrypha). This particular Bible, which includes the New Revised Standard Version
translation, also has scholarly commentary about each section, detailed footnotes,
maps, and other helpful study materials intended to appeal to a diverse (ecumeni-
cal) audience. Unless otherwise noted, this particular translation is used when citing biblical passages throughout this book. See Michael D. Coogan, ed., *The New
Oxford Annotated Bible*, 3rd ed. (New York: Oxford University Press, 2001).

2. Readers interested in apocryphal writings should see James Charlesworth's *Old
Testament Pseudepigrapha*, 2 vols. (New York: Doubleday, 1983, 1985) and Wilhelm Schneemelcher's *New Testament Apocrypha*, 2 vols. (Louisville, Ky.: Westminster John Knox, 1991).

3. Another difference between the order of books in the Jewish Bible and the Christian Old Testament is that the book of Lamentations, traditionally associated with
the prophet Jeremiah, immediately follows the latter book in Christian Bibles.

4. Why is the idiom for immigration to the Holy Land "a going-up," "an ascent,"
aliyya? Because, symbolically, the site of the Temple, and by extension Jerusalem
and the entire region around it, is the spiritual apex of the planet.

5. For an introduction to the literature of the New Testament from a modern scholarly perspective, see Bart D. Ehrman, *A Brief Introduction to the New Testament*
(New York: Oxford University Press, 2004).

6. These letters include Ephesians, 1–2 Timothy, Titus, Hebrews, 2 Thessalonians,
and Colossians. Although most scholars agree that these six letters were not written by Paul, some assert that both 2 Thessalonians and Colossians are authentically
Pauline. See Marcus J. Borg, *Reading the Bible Again for The First Time: Taking the
Bible Seriously but Not Literally* (San Francisco: Harper Collins, 2001), 228–29.

7. Ehrman suggests the following dates for the composition of the Gospels: Mark
between 65 and 70 C.E., Luke and Matthew between 80 and 85 C.E., and John
between 90 and 95 C.E. (*A Brief Introduction to the New Testament*, xxvi–xxvii).

8. We refer throughout this chapter to the religion of ancient Israel and of the ancient Jewish people as "Judaism." A more precise term might be "Judahism," the
faith of persons indigenous to ancient Judah. (Generally speaking, the geographical designation "Judah is used to refer to the region before Roman conquest in 63
B.C.E., and "Judea," the Roman name of the province, afterwards.) Scholars argue
about when Judahism, the parent religion of Judaism and Christianity, gave birth
to Judaism. Some would say that Judaism, or rabbinic Judaism, does not exist until
after the destruction of the Temple in 70 C.E., and the reorganization of religious
practices around themes other than temple sacrifice. See Donald Harman Akenson, *Surpassing Wonder: The Invention of the Bible and the Talmuds* (Chicago: University of Chicago Press, 1998).

9. Jeffrey Burton Russell, *The Prince of Darkness: Radical Evil and the Power of Good
in History* (Ithaca, N.Y.: Cornell University Press, 1988), 280–81.

10. Russell, *The Prince of Darkness*, 112.

11. Russell, *Lucifer: The Devil in the Middle Ages* (Ithaca, N.Y.: Cornell University
Press, 1984), 248–50.

12. Russell, *The Prince of Darkness*, 8.

Chapter 2

1. The best sustained treatment of biblical theology, one that never loses its respect
for or fails to express its bewilderment at the dynamic character of Yhwh, is Wal-

ter Brueggemann's *Theology of the Old Testament: Testimony, Dispute, Advocacy* (Minneapolis: Fortress Press, 1997). Consider this representative line: "tension, oddness, incongruity, contradiction, and lack of settlement are to be understood . . . as the central data of the character of Yahweh" (82).

2. We have borrowed the idea of "testimony" as the best term to describe the affirmations about God in the Bible from Brueggemann, *Theology of the Old Testament*, 117–44.

3. The phrase "Hebrew religious geniuses" is from Donald Harman Akenson, *Surpassing Wonder: The Invention of the Bible and the Talmuds* (Chicago: University of Chicago Press, 1998), 98. It is embedded in a longer passage that deserves repeating here: "Yahweh personifies . . . ultimate reality exactly. Life is bounteous, so too is Yahweh; life is unfair, so too is Yahweh (just ask Job). Yahweh is the name for reality invented by Hebrew religious geniuses who paid attention to the way the world works."

4. "Assur" was the national god of the Assyrian empire, whose capital was ancient Nineveh.

5. "The Valley of (the son of) Hinnom," criticized by Jeremiah in this passage as the site of illicit rites, would come to be an important place in the history of hell. Its Hebrew name is *ge* ("valley of") *hinnom*, which came to be known as *Gehenna* (Hebrew *ge hinnom*, Aramaic *gehinnam*, Greek *geenna*, Latin *gehenna*). The valley, located near Jerusalem, was the site of rites of child sacrifice in the Iron Age. By the time of the New Testament, "Gehenna" had become "divorced from . . . its geographical location . . . [and] had become hell itself." Duane Watson, "Gehenna, *Anchor Bible Dictionary* (New York: Doubleday, 1994), 2:927. Several factors may have led to Gehenna's evolution from a feature in the geographic landscape to one in the cosmic landscape. There were the traditions about child sacrifice rites there, and its ongoing use as refuse dump (for corpses; Jer 7:29–34) with "continually burning fires" (Watson, "Gehenna," 2:927). The stinking pyres of Gehenna came to symbolize, for Judahites around the turn of the common era, the sulfurous lake to which all wicked would ultimately be condemned.

6. Jack Miles, *God: A Biography* (New York: Vintage, 1995), 29.

7. We will not consider in this book another interesting question about pre-exilic Israelite monotheism, namely how widespread was veneration of Asherah as Yhwh's consort, as the supreme Israelite goddess? The biblical evidence would deny that Yhwh had a wife. The archeological evidence is a conditional yes; prayers to "Yhwh and his Asherah" inscribed on potsherds have been discovered at sites of rural shrines. For more on the question, see N. Wyatt, "Asherah," in *Dictionaries of Deities and Demons in the Bible*, rev. edited by K. van der Toorn, B. Becking, and P. W. van der Horst, eds. (Leiden: Brill: Eerdmans, 1999), 99–105. But if the worship of Asherah was widespread, it is curious that archeologists have uncovered so few examples of ancient Israelite names that include references to her. Jeffrey Tigay, *You Shall Have No Other Gods: Israelite Religion in the Light of Hebrew Inscriptions* (Atlanta: Scholars Press, 1986).

8. For the meaning of the name Yhwh, see Frank Moore Cross, *Canaanite Myth and Hebrew Epic: Essays in the History of the Religion of Israel* (Cambridge, Mass.: Harvard University Press, 1973), 60–75.

9. According to Jewish tradition, the *Torah* came in two forms: the written *Torah* known in scripture and the "Oral *Torah*," the authoritative interpretation of the written *Torah* that emerged in later rabbinic literature. This oral *Torah* was also granted authoritative status in Jewish tradition, on the basis that it was not novel but had been handed down through the generations and ultimately stemmed from Moses himself.

10. Variations of this formula are in Ex 20:5–6; Num 14:18; Neh 9:17; Ps 86:15, 145:8; Joel 2:13; Jonah 4:2; and Nah 1:3.

11. David Schloen, *The House of the Father as Fact and Symbol: Patrimonialism in Ugarit and the Ancient Near East* (Winona Lake, Ind.: Eisenbrauns, 2001).

12. The feminine metaphors for God in Isaiah are in 42:14; 45:9–11; 46:3–4; and 49:15.

13. For the deity who leads clans into battle, see, for instance, Judges 5 and Psalm 18. For the deity who punishes those who are inattentive to ritual detail or lack respect for Yhwh's holiness, see Num 25:1–9 and 2 Sam 6:11.

14. In traditional religious discourse, these were called pagan gods, but we should remain suspicious of the term "pagan." The word "pagan" came to us from Latin and means "country-dweller." So "pagan" carries with it, at best, a tone of condescension and, at worst, an oppressive arrogance from urban elites and ordained, deputized, religious professionals about the supposed backward beliefs and practices of the "primitives" who live in rural areas.

15. The Authorized (King James) Version preserves the traditional reading of Dt 32:8b, which is based on the Masoretic Text, the traditional Jewish authority: "[God] set the bounds of the people according to the number of the children of Israel." The difference between the New Revised Standard Version and the King James Version is that the former (following the texts of the Greek Septuagint and one of the Dead Sea Scrolls) is a translation of an original "according to the number of *the sons of God,*" while the latter, based on the Masoretic Text, translates the phrase "according to *the sons of Israel.*" As Bernard Levinson writes, "The unintelligible reading the of the MT [Masoretic Text] represents a 'correction' of the original text (where God presides over other gods) to make it conform to the later standard of pure monotheism." *The Jewish Study Bible* (New York: Oxford University Press, 2004), 441.

16. According to Jeffrey Burton Russell, "Satan is the personification of the dark side of the God, that element within Yahweh which obstructs the good" (*The Devil: Perceptions of Evil from Antiquity to Primitive Christianity* [Ithaca, N.Y.: Cornell University Press, 1977], 176–77).

17. As Job laments, "How then can I answer [God]? . . . I must appeal for mercy to my accuser" (Job 9:14–15).

18. Miles, *God: A Biography,* 29.

19. To get a sense of the density of allusions in the Bible to divine beings other than the LORD, see the over 600 listings in *Dictionaries of Deities and Demons in the Bible.*

20. Passages that mention or allude to a divine council include Gen 1:26, 3:22, 11:7; 1 Kgs 22:19–22; Job 1:6, 15:8; Ps 82:1–7, 89:8; Isa 6:1–11; Jer 23:18–22; Zech 3:1–10; and Revelation 4–5.

21. Gen 1:26 (cf. Gen 3:22, 11:7), Jer 23:18–22.

22. Although in this verse (Isa 6:8), it is not the angels but the lowly mortal, Isaiah, who eagerly volunteers for duty with these words.

23. Ps 78:49, in Hebrew, refers to *mal'akim raim,* that is, "evil" or "harmful messengers" sent from God.

24. The word for "mark" in the Hebrew of Ezek 9:4 is *tav,* the ancestor of our (Roman) *t.* But in the Hebrew alphabet of Ezekiel's day, the letter *tav* was similar in form to the *x* of the Roman alphabet.

25. The contingent of divine agents of punishment in Ezekiel 9 totals seven: a clerical type who carries a writing instrument and marks the foreheads of those to be

spared and the squad of six executioners. The idea of a team of seven agents of punishment is also found in Mesopotamian literature (see "Erra and Ishum" in Stephanie Dalley, *Myths from Mesopotamia* [Oxford: Oxford University Press, 1989), and may be a distant relation of other adventure narratives about teams of seven, including Aeschylus' fifth-century B.C.E. play *Seven Against Thebes* and Akira Kurosawa's Japanese film classic *The Seven Samurai.*

26. The Destroyer in Ex 12:23 is programmed to notice only a single datum: Does this door have a mark of blood on it or not? The destroying agents in Ezekiel 9 note marks on foreheads. The monstrous locusts of Revelation 9 in the New Testament are also narrowly programmed. These locusts, whose king is named "Destruction" (Rev 9:11), torture everyone they encounter, sparing only those with "the seal of God" on their foreheads (Rev 9:4).

27. I.e., Gen 16:7–13, 21:15–21, 22:11–12, 31:11–13. For more cites and a fuller discussion of biblical angels, see Carol Newsom, "Angels," *Anchor Bible Dictionary* 1:250.

28. Rivkah Schärf Klüger, *Satan in the Old Testament* (Evanston, Ill.: Northwestern University Press, 1967), 59.

29. See these articles in *Dictionary of Deities and Demons in the Bible:* H. Huffmon, "Name," 610–12; J. E. Fossum, "Glory," 348–52; and C. L. Seow's comments on the idea of the "the Presence"/*Shekinah,* in the article entitled "Face," 322–25.

30. From our perspective, the most distressing aspects of early portraits of Yhwh in the Bible are these two: child sacrifice and the ritual slaughter of enemies after battle. The specter of child sacrifice haunts certain biblical passages. Clearly, the practice is condemned in the Bible and did not become normative in Israelite religion, but the taint remains: Was child sacrifice, the supreme act of devotion, a feature of Yhwh worship in its earliest centuries? The logic of child sacrifice, though not its practice, endures into the Christian Bible, in the formulation of John 3:16: "For God so loved the world that he gave his only begotten son." See Jon Levenson, *The Death and Resurrection of the Beloved Son: The Transformation of Child Sacrifice in Judaism and Christianity* (New Haven, Conn.: Yale University Press, 1993). The other element of ancient Israelite religion that seems most at odds with the ethical sensibilities of the religions that grew from the Bible was the ritual slaughter of enemies following battle. This practice—called the *cherem*—was thought to fulfill the demands of Yhwh but was eventually discarded.

31. Israel had received "double" punishment for its sins, but according to Isa 40:2, the twin punishments (the destruction of Jerusalem and the Exile) had been too much. Later in Second Isaiah (Isa 54:7), the LORD seems to admit that the above catastrophes had been over the top, "In overflowing wrath for a moment I hid my face from you." See Brueggemann, *Theology of the Old Testament* (384), for his comment about the implications of this verse.

32. For this perspective on Yhwh, see Mark Smith, *The Early History of God: Yahweh and the Other Deities in Ancient Israel,* 2nd ed. (Grand Rapids, Mich.: Eerdmans, 2002).

Chapter 3

1. Peggy L. Day, *An Adversary in Heaven: Satan in the Hebrew Bible* (Atlanta: Scholars Press, 1988), 25.

2. Day, *An Adversary in Heaven,* 26.

3. Edom, often called *Seir* in the Bible, was the region located southeast of the Dead Sea.

4. Rivkah Schärf Klüger notes that these passages presage the concept of a celestial Satan: "Here one already senses the fateful, metaphysical background behind the adversary who still appears here as a human being." *Satan in the Old Testament* (Evanston, Ill.: Northwestern University Press, 1967), 35.

5. Day, *An Adversary in Heaven*, 31.

6. Day, *An Adversary in Heaven*, 45.

7. The text that refers to "Balaam, the son of Beor" is from Deir Alla, Jordan, and was discovered in 1960 and dated to the eighth-century B.C.E. For more on this text, see Klaas A. D. Smelik, *Writings from Ancient Israel: A Handbook of Historical and Religious Documents* (Louisville, Ky.: Westminster John Knox, 1991), 79–92.

8. As Walter Brueggemann puts it, the book of Job raises two questions: "Job asks, 'Is God reliable?' [and God] asks, 'Is Job serious?'" *Theology of the Old Testament: Testimony, Dispute, Advocacy* (Minneapolis: Fortress, 1997), 387.

9. For Job as a "dissident," see William Safire, *The First Dissident: The Book of Job in Today's Politics* (New York: Random House, 1992).

10. Regarding Job as "the Jordanian Abraham": According to Job 1:1, Job is from the land of Uz, either in the region of southern Jordan or northern Arabia. In Jewish folklore, Job is one of three great Gentile (i.e., non-Israelite), wise men from antiquity, along with Balaam (Numbers 22–24) and Reuel/Jethro, Moses' Kenite father-in-law (Exodus 18). For the trio in Jewish folklore, see Louis Ginzberg, *Legends of the Jews* (Baltimore: Johns Hopkins University Press, 1998), 2: 254–55. By referring to Job as "the Jordanian Abraham," we are suggesting that the figure of Job was a well-known character in ancient Israel, a legendary wise man from a neighboring culture. As such, "Job" was the perfect model for a hypothetical story about a righteous man who underwent undeserved suffering, because Jewish readers would have recognized his sagacity but would have, at the same time, remained at an emotional distance from him. The use of Job by this ancient Hebrew writer would be analogous to a European or American author telling a story about Confucius.

11. *Hassatan* means "the Adversary." Norman Habel, *The Book of Job: A Commentary* (London: Cambridge University Press, 1975), 17; Dianne Bergant, *Job, Ecclesiastes* (Wilmington, Del.: Michael Glazier, 1982) 27. It also means "the Accuser." Carol Newsom, "The Book of Job," *The New Interpreter's Bible*, vol. 4 (Nashville, Tenn.: Abingdon Press, 1996), 347–48.

12. Job 1:6; cf. Gen 6:2; 1 Kgs 22:19–23; Ps 29:1; 82; 89:5–8; Isa 6:1–8; Dan 7:7–9; 14.

13. According to Bergant, "Nowhere is it even suggested that he [*hassatan*] is the actual cause of evil" (*Job, Ecclesiastes*, 27). John E. Hartley links the activity of *hassatan* to Persian court spies who scope out possible disloyalty to the king. *The Book of Job* (Grand Rapids, Mich.: Eerdmans, 1988), 73. Habel associates *hassatan's* roaming activities with espionage and compares Job 1:7c with Zech 1:10–11 (*The Book of Job*, 17).

14. God's designation of Job as his "servant" immediately sets Job apart from other humans and elevates him to a preferred status. Hartley notes that this designation is used in these biblical contexts: of Abraham (Ps 105:6, 42); Jacob/Israel (Isa 41:8); Moses (Ex 14:31); Joshua (Josh 24:29); David, (2 Sam 7:5, 8); Isaiah (Isa 20:3); and the prophets, (2 Kgs 9:7; Amos 3:7). Hartley, *The Book of Job*, 73. Bergant asserts that this "term of endearment" precedes Job's name whenever God refers to him (cf. Job 2:3; 42:7–8). Bergant, *Job, Ecclesiastes*, 73.

15. According to Bergant, (*Job, Ecclesiastes*, 28), "It is easy to be loyal to God when things are going right and one is happy with life." Habel concurs, and remarks that

according to *hassatan*, "Job's good conduct has been motivated by self-interest not deep conviction." Habel, *The Book of Job*, 18.

16. Newsom asserts that the word "hedge" (the New Revised Standard Version renders this word as "fence") denotes a particular kind of protection (cf. Ps 80:8–13; Isa 5:1–7) that, in Job's case, includes his person, his family, and his possessions. Newsom, "*The Book of Job*," 349. In fact, so efficacious is God's protection it is easy to concur with *hassatan's* suggestion that Job's piety is motivated by self-interest.

17. For an analysis of Job's fences, see J. Gerald Janzen, *Job*, Interpretation (Atlanta: John Knox, 1985), 45–47.

18. There seems to be something akin to sibling rivalry here, reminiscent of Cain and Abel (Gen 4:2–16), Jacob and Esau (Gen 25:22–34; 27; 28:1–9; 32–33), and Joseph and his brothers (Genesis 37; 39–50). Hartley connects Job's fear that one of his children may have inadvertently "cursed God in their hearts" (Job 1:5) with *hassatan's* challenge intended to provoke Job to curse God to his face (Job 1:11). Hartley, *The Book of Job*, 73.

19. Hartley, *The Book of Job*, 77. In the face of grief, Job takes comfort in ritual and in the platitudes of biblical Wisdom literature (cf. Job 1:21; Pss 104:27–30; 113:2). He does not blame God for his ruin, but sees his misfortune as God's right (cf. Job 1:21; Eccl 5:15; Sir 40:1). Newsom, *The Book of Job*, 352.

20. The use of "rounds" to describe the tests that the LORD inflicts on Job is borrowed from Stephen Mitchell in *The Book of Job* (New York: Harper Perennial, 1987), although he uses the terms when describing later events in the book, the three cycles of conversation among Job and his friends in chapters 3 to 27.

21. In Job 2:4–5, according to Newsom, *hassatan* plays on Job's own "bodily" words (Job 1:21). Newsom, *The Book of Job*, 354. Hartley notes that the bones were "considered the seat of illness (Lam 1:3)." Hartley, *The Book of Job*, 81.

22. Janzen, *Job*, 46–47.

23. Job's next test is designed to press him to the limits of human endurance. Interestingly, this is the third "fence" the LORD will place around Job (cf. Job 1:12; 2:6), and although it seems of small consequence, given the extent of Job's suffering, it is nonetheless indicative of God's love of Job and God's confidence that Job will pass yet another test of faith.

24. Hartley proposes that Job's illness was the result of boils, considered to be evidence of God's wrath (Ex 9:8–12; Deut 28:35). Hartley, *The Book of Job*, 82–83.

25. See Genesis 22, the account of the "testing" of Abraham, and Genesis 19, the account of the punishment of Sodom.

26. According to Day (*An Adversary in Heaven*, 107–9), Zechariah envisioned a Jerusalem ruled by priest and king, from the House of David. "Thus, Joshua and Zerubbabel, priest and scion of David, would preside over a reconstituted community with the temple at its center, ushering in an age of peace and prosperity."

27. For the image of "a brand plucked from the fire," see Am 4:11.

28. Neil Forsyth, *The Old Enemy: Satan and the Combat Myth* (Princeton; N.J.: Princeton University Press, 1987), 118.

29. Ex 30:11–16 describes census taking as against the divine will. "The census is by nature directed against the power of God because is serves human interests, the power of an earthly king." Klüger, *Satan in the Old Testament*, 151; cf. Forsyth, *The Old Enemy*, 120.

30. Most scholars assign the book of Chronicles to a date between 520 and 400 B.C.E., some 30 to 130 years after the composition of the material in 2 Samuel 24. Day, *An Adversary in Heaven*, 127–32.

31. Forsyth, *The Old Enemy*, 119.
32. Forsyth, *The Old Enemy*, 120.
33. Day, *An Adversary in Heaven*, 142.
34. Day, *An Adversary in Heaven*, 127; Klüger, *Satan in the Old Testament*, 155; Forsyth, *The Old Enemy*, 121; C. Breytenbach and P. L. Day, "Satan," in *Dictionary of Demons and Deities in the Bible*, rev. ed. by K. van der Toorn, B. Becking and P. W. van der Horst, eds. (Leiden: Brill, 1999), 729.
35. Klüger, *Satan in the Old Testament*, 155; Forsyth, *The Old Enemy*, 121. Day disagrees with the suggestion that *satan* is being used as a proper noun here, and instead recognizes this figure as one of two "celestial accusers" (the second being the *mal'ak Yhwh*, who expresses God's anger). Day, *Adversary in Heaven*, 144–45.
36. According to Klüger, *Satan in the Old Testament*, 155: "Satan is divested of his character as a divine function. He no longer appears, as in the book of Job, as part of the divine court; he is an independent figure, apparently separated from God, who no longer stands in dialectic confrontation with God or his angel, as in Job and Zechariah."
37. Klüger, *Satan in the Old Testament*, 155.
38. Klüger, *Satan in the Old Testament*, 155.
39. For the text of the Life of Adam and Eve, see the translation of M. D. Johnson in *Old Testament Pseudepigrapha* 2, edited by James Charlesworth (New York: Doubleday, 1985), 249–95. For a review of intertestamental literature that associates the serpent with Satan, see James L. Kugel, *The Bible As It Was* (Cambridge, Mass.: Belknap Press, 1997), 72–75.
40. For a summary of the scholarly debate about the nature of the Molech ritual, see G. C. Heider, "Molech," *Dictionary of Deities and Demons in the Bible*, 581–85.
41. Jeffrey Burton Russell, *Lucifer: The Devil in the Middle Ages* (Ithaca, N.Y.: Cornell University Press, 1984), 248–49.

Chapter 4

1. James B. Pritchard, *Ancient Near Eastern Texts Relating to the Old Testament*, 3rd ed. (Princeton, N.J.: Princeton University Press, 1969), 72–73.
2. Neil Forsyth, *The Old Enemy: Satan and the Combat Myth* (Princeton, N.J.: Princeton University Press, 1987), 22.
3. Pritchard, *Ancient Near Eastern Texts*, 79.
4. Andrew George, *The Epic of Gilgamesh: A New Translation* (New York: Barnes & Noble, 1999), 91.
5. Forsyth, *The Old Enemy*, 22.
6. Pritchard, *Ancient Near Eastern Texts*, 129. See also Niels Peter Lemche, *Prelude to Israel's Past: Background and Beginnings of Israelite History and Identity* (Peabody, Mass.: Hendrickson, 1998), 172. Most of the Ugaritic texts date to the reign of Niqmaddu II, 1370–1335 B.C.E.
7. Neal H. Walls refers to Anat as a "tomboy" in *The Goddess Anat in Ugaritic Myth* (Atlanta: Scholars Press, 1992), 218.
8. See Pritchard, *Ancient Near Eastern Texts*, 128–142, and William Foxwell Albright, *Yahweh and the Gods of Canaan: An Historical Analysis of Two Contrasting Faiths* (Winona Lake, Ind.: Eisenbrauns, 1990), 130–32. Jeffrey Burton Russell notes: "In one of his [Baal's] forms, Baal-Qarnaïm, Baal possessed two horns and a tail." *The Devil: Perceptions of Evil from Antiquity to Primitive Christianity* (Ithaca, N.Y.: Cornell University Press, 1977), 94.

9. Simon Parker, ed., *Ugaritic Narrative Poetry* (Atlanta: Scholars Press, 1997), 138, 208

10. Pritchard, *Ancient Near Eastern Texts*, 140.

11. Forsyth contends that Baal's death and resurrection "gave rise to the hypothesis of a 'dying and rising god' archetype" (*The Old Enemy*, 60).

12. P. Xella, "Haby," in *Dictionary of Demons and Deities in the Bible*, edited by K. van der Toorn, B. Becking, and P. W. van der Horst; rev. ed. (Leiden: Brill: 1999), 377.

13. Xella, "Haby," in *Dictionary of Deities and Demons in the Bible*, 377.

14. Russell, *The Devil*, 76.

15. Russell, *The Devil*, 77.

16. David Adams Leeming, *Mythology: The Voyage of the Hero*, 3rd ed. (Oxford: Oxford University Press, 1998), 161–64. See also Joseph Campbell, with Bill Moyers, *The Power of Myth* (New York: Doubleday, 1988), 220–23.

17. This synopsis is based on the retellings of Leeming (*Mythology*, 161–64) and Campbell (*The Power of Myth*, 220–23).

18. C. Scott Littleton, ed., *Mythology: The Illustrated Anthology of World Myth & Storytelling* (London: Duncan Baird Publishers, 2002), 72–75.

19. The color green seems to be associated with death. See Rev 6:8 for a description of a green horse that represents "death and Hades."

20. Stephen Von Wyrick, "Gehenna," *Eerdmans Dictionary of the Bible* (Grand Rapids, Mich.: Eerdmans, 2000), 489.

21. For this description of the punishment of the wicked in Egyptian religion, see Leonard H. Lesko, "Death and the Afterlife in Ancient Egyptian Thought," in *Civilizations of the Ancient Near East 3*, edited by Jack Sasson (Peabody, Mass.: Hendrickson, 2000), 1768–69.

22. Russell, *The Devil*, 79–80.

23. See Bill Ellis, *Raising the Devil: Satanism, New Religions, and the Media* (Lexington, Ky.: University Press of Kentucky, 2000), 120–42.

24. For the Temple of Set, see Joe Adams, "Temple of Set," *The Religious Movements Homepage Project,* December 8, 2000. http://religiousmovements.lib.virginia.edu/nrms/satanism/tempset.html.

25. Keith Crim, *The Perennial Dictionary of World Religions* (San Francisco: Harper San Francisco, 1989), 827–28. We will not enter the debate about whether Zarathustra was a historical figure; see Paul Carus, *The History of the Devil and the Idea of Evil* (New York: Gramercy Books, 1996), 50–52.

26. Lewis M. Hopfe and Mark R. Woodward, *Religions of the World*, 9th ed. (Upper Saddle River, N.J.: Prentice Hall, 2005), 225–26.

27. Hopfe and Woodward, *Religions of the World*, 221.

28. Carus, *The History of the Devil*, 55. Like Yhwh (Isa 45:7; 54:14), Ahura Mazda creates both light and darkness. Cf. Anthony E. Smith, "Angra Mainyu," *Encyclopedia Mythica*, 20 August 2003, <http://www.pantheon.org/articles/a/angra_mainyu.html>.

29. Philip Davies, *Scribes and Schools: The Canonization of the Hebrew Scriptures* (Louisville, Ky.: Westminster John Knox, 1998), 89–125.

30. Carus, *The History of the Devil*, 53.

31. Carus, *The History of the Devil*, 53. Some sources state that Ahura Mazda and Ahriman were created by the one creator God and endowed with God's goodness. Ahura Mazda remained true and sought to promote goodness, while Ahriman rebelled and became evil. See Thomas Bulfinch and Richard P. Martin, *Bulfinch's Mythology* (New York: Harper Collins, 1991), 278–79.

32.   Carus, *The History of the Devil*, 53. For an online version of this *yasna* and for a complete translation of the Avesta (the sacred scriptures that contain the Gathas), see: Avesta.org, "The Gathas (Hymns) of Zarathustra," 15 September 2003 <http://www.avesta.org/gathas.htm>.

33.   Hopfe and Woodward, *Religions of the World*, 226–27.

34.   Hopfe and Woodward, *Religions of the World*, 227.

35.   Hopfe and Woodward, *Religions of the World*, 228–29.

36.   Hopfe and Woodward, *Religions of the World*, 228–29.

37.   Alan F. Segal, *Life after Death: A History of the Afterlife in Western Religion* (New York: Doubleday, 2004), 195–96.

38.   Hopfe and Woodward, *Religions of the World*, 228–29; Joseph Campbell, *The Masks of God: Occidental Mythology* (New York: Viking, 1964), 198–199.

39.   Carus, *The History of the Devil*, 58.

40.   Carus, *The History of the Devil*, 58.

41.   Hopfe and Woodward, *Religions of the World*, 232–33.

42.   Hopfe and Woodward, *Religions of the World*, 233–34.

43.   Russell, *The Devil*, 139.

44.   W.K. Freiert, "Orpheus: A Fugue on the Polis," in *Myth and the Polis*, edited by D. C. Pozzi and J. M. Wickersham (Ithaca, N.Y.: Cornell University Press, 1991), 32–48.

45.   Russell notes that, in Greece, "there is no one principle of evil (*The Devil*, 123).

46.   Russell, *The Devil*, 123.

47.   Littleton, *Mythology*, 188–89, 191.

48.   Russell, *The Devil*, 126.

49.   Littleton, *Mythology*, 161. These three goddesses are Tisiphone, Megaera, and Alecto, i.e., the Furies.

Chapter 5

1.   Donald Harman Akenson writes that "the culture of Palestine [in this period] . . . was analogous to a teeming pool in which all sorts of religious life-forms evolved, interacted, and mutated." Akenson, *Surpassing Wonder: The Invention of the Bible and the Talmuds* (Chicago: University of Chicago Press, 1998), 112.

2.   The best single source for translations of and commentary about many of these documents are the two volumes edited by James H. Charlesworth, *The Old Testament Pseudepigrapha* (Garden City, N.Y.: Doubleday, 1983, 1985).

3.   Elaine Pagels, *The Origin of Satan* (New York: Vintage Books, 1996), 55–56.

4.   Jeffrey Burton Russell, *The Devil: Perceptions of Evil from Antiquity to Primitive Christianity* (Ithaca, N.Y.: Cornell University Press, 1977), 186. The Jewish book Ben Sira (or Sirach or Ecclesiasticus), dated to around 200 B.C.E., found in the Protestant Apocrypha and in Roman Catholic and Orthodox canons, also alludes to the myth of Watchers (Ben Sira 16:7).

5.   Pagels, *Origin of Satan*, 50. According to Gen 5: 24, Enoch, a seventh-generation descendant of Adam and the father of Methuselah, never died. Like Elijah (2 Kgs 2:1–12), Enoch disappears from earth: "Enoch walked with God; then he was no more, because God took him" (Gen 5:24). Enoch's mysterious exit from the Bible allowed him to be brought back on stage for countless performances as the source for esoteric and end-time revelations.

6.   Pagels, *Origin of Satan*, 50.

7.   Pagels, *Origin of Satan*, 50. According to Russell, the Watchers "do not fall" to earth, but descend there purposely, to carry out their evil intentions (*The Devil*, 191).

8. Pagels, *Origin of Satan*, 50.

9. Neil Forsyth, *The Old Enemy: Satan and the Combat Myth* (Princeton, N.J.: Princeton University Press, 1987), 163.

10. Pagels observes the manner in which this story reflects the sociopolitical realities of its day. She poses the rhetorical question: "Are Jews who thus embellish the story of angels that mate with human beings covertly ridiculing the pretensions of their Hellenistic rulers?" Pagels, *Origin of Satan*, 50–51. These "pretensions" include the Greek belief that "Greek kings had claimed to be descended from gods, and that the heroic demigods had divine parentage. The story could also reflect a conflict within the Jewish community about intermarriage.

11. Forsyth, *The Old Enemy*, 161. Azael is mentioned in Leviticus 16 when the high priest offers two goats as sin-offerings for the people and is directed to choose, by casting lots, one goat for the LORD and one for Azazel (Lev 16:8). The goat chosen for Azazel is to be sent into the wilderness as the community scapegoat. Myra Nagel, *Deliver Us from Evil: What the Bible Says about Satan* (Cleveland: United Church Press, 1999), 18. Russell cites 1 En 54:6 as naming Satan as the leader of the rebel angels (*The Devil*, 192).

12. Russell, *The Devil*, 191; Bernd Janowski, "Azazel," in *Dictionary of Demons and Deities in the Bible*, edited by K. van der Toorn, B. Becking, P. W. van der Horst (rev. ed.; Leiden: Brill, 1999),131; Greg J. Riley, "Devil," in *Dictionary of Demons and Deities in the Bible*, 246. For primary texts that refer to Azael, see 1 En 8:1, 9:6; 69:2.

13. Pagels, *Origin of Satan*, 52–53.

14. Russell, *The Devil*, 207.

15. Russell, *The Devil*, 206.

16. Russell, *The Devil*, 188.

17. Russell, *The Devil*, 187–88.

18. For an analysis of these types of accounts, see Bill Ellis, *Raising the Devil: Satanism, New Religions, and the Media* (Lexington, Ky.: University Press of Kentucky, 2000), especially chapter 7, "Hippie Commune Witchcraft Blood Rites," 167–201.

19. O. S. Wintermute, "Jubilees," *The Old Testament Pseudepigrapha* 2 (Garden City, N.Y.: Doubleday, 1985), 44.

20. There is much debate concerning the dating of Jubilees. Pagels maintains a date of 160 B.C.E. (*Origin of Satan*, 53); Russell states that the book was written by a Pharisee between 135 and 105 B.C.E. (*The Devil*, 92).

21. Forsyth, *The Old Enemy*, 182. Mastema is the term most often used in Jubilees for the Satan-figure, or "prince of the hostile angels." Mastema means "hateful one," or "animosity" in Hebrew (Riley, "Devil," in *Dictionary of Deities and Demons in the Bible*, 246).

22. Pagels, *Origin of Satan*, 54.

23. Russell, *The Devil*, 204. Cf. Jub 17:15–18:12 with Gen 22:1–19, and Jub 48:1–3 with Ex 4:24.

24. Translation by Wintermute, "Jubilees," 276.

25. The author of Jubilees neither explains the origin of Mastema nor does he clarify why God allows him to continue his evil work, as Forsyth notes (*The Old Enemy*, 190).

26. Translation by Wintermute, "Jubilees," 102.

27. Translation by Wintermute, "Jubilees," 142.

28. Forsyth, *The Old Enemy*, 250.

29. Translation by Wintermute, "Jubilees," 137. According to Forsyth, it is not un-common in apocalyptic literature to find the Golden Age and the Future Age linked together in this way (*The Old Enemy*, 189).

30. Translation by Wintermute, "Jubilees," 76.

31. Pagels, *Origin of Satan*, 56–57.

32. Pagels, *Origin of Satan*, 57.

33. Forsyth, *The Old Enemy*, 200.

34. Forsyth notes that "the Jews had been subject for two centuries to the authority of the Persian Empire. A cosmic struggle between light and darkness was already implied in such myths as Baal's battle with Mot . . . but it was in the Zoroastrian tradition that this kind of narrative came to be seen as all-encompassing" (*The Old Enemy*, 199).

35. Pagels, *Origin of Satan*, 58.

36. Russell, *The Devil*, 212. The Qumran reading is based on Geza Vermes, *The Dead Sea Scrolls in English* (2nd. ed.; Harmondsworth, U.K.: Penguin, 1970), 75–76.

37. Pagels, *Origin of Satan*, 58.

38. Russell, *The Devil*, 214.

39. Russell, *The Devil*, 213.

40. Russell, *The Devil*, 214.

41. Russell, *The Devil*, 214.

42. Russell, *The Devil*, 214.

43. Russell, *The Devil*, 214.

44. Cf. the reference in Mt 12:22–29 to the Devil as "the strong man."

45. Theodore J. Lewis, "Beelzebul," *Anchor Bible Dictionary*, edited by D. N. Freedman (New York: Doubleday, 1992), 1:638–40.

46. For a similar summary of the Watchers myth and the Lucifer myth, as well as further discussion of the idea of the biblical Devil, see Riley, "Devil," in *Dictionary of Deities and Demons in the Bible*, 246.

47. Translation by F. I. Andersen, *Old Testament Pseudepigrapha* 1:148.

48. Louis Ginzberg, *The Legends of the Jews*, trans. Henrietta Szold; 7 vols. (Baltimore: Johns Hopkins University Press, 1998), 2:242; 5:389–90.

Chapter 6

1. We follow here Bart D. Ehrman, *A Brief Introduction to the New Testament* (New York: Oxford University Press, 2004), xxvi–xxvii.

2. "Q" is from the German word *Quelle*, meaning "source."

3. Elaine Pagels uses texts such as Mk 13:1–17 to date the composition of Mark to a time during the Jewish War (66 to 70 C.E.) before the destruction of the Temple in 70 C.E. *The Origin of Satan* (New York: Vintage Books, 1995), 6.

4. Pheme Perkins notes, "The destruction of the power of evil is one of the signs of the coming of God's messiah (Mk 3:22–27)." Perkins, *Reading the New Testament: An Introduction*, 2nd ed. (New York: Paulist Press, 1988), 208.

5. Perkins, *Reading the New Testament*, 11.

6. Stephen L. Harris, *The New Testament: A Student's Introduction* 2nd ed. (Mountain View, Cal.: Mayfield, 1995), 112.

7. Pagels. *The Origin of Satan*, 61.

8. Pagels, *The Origin of Satan*, 91.

9. Pagels, *The Origin of Satan*, 90.

10. Myra Nagel, *Deliver Us from Evil: What the Bible Says about Satan* (Cleveland: United Church Press, 1999), 31.

11. Neil Forsyth notes that Jesus' time in the wilderness is a typical literary motif, "the testing of the hero before his main encounter with the enemy." Forsyth, *The Old Enemy: Satan and the Combat Myth* (Princeton, N.J.: Princeton University Press, 1987), 289.

12. Edward J. Mally, "The Gospel According to Mark," *The Jerome Biblical Commentary* (Englewood Cliffs, N. J.: Prentice-Hall, 1968), 25 (NT).

13. The literature of Qumran "portrays angels as an army fighting on God's side against evil spirits," according to Mally, "Mark," 25 (NT).

14. John McKenzie, "The Gospel According to Matthew," *Jerome Biblical Commentary*, 68–69 (NT). Stephen Harris notes that the Devil uses the phrase "If you are the Son of God" to qualify his first two temptations, perhaps as a way to create doubts in Jesus concerning his mission as God's agent (*The New Testament*, 119).

15. Jesus will later perform the very feat that the Devil dares him to do, that is, bread multiplication (Mt 15:33–39).

16. McKenzie, "Matthew," 69 (NT).

17. Forsyth, *The Old Enemy*, 289–290.

18. Carroll Stuhlmueller, "The Gospel According to Luke," *Jerome Biblical Commentary*, 130 (NT).

19. William S. Kurz, *Reading Luke-Acts: Dynamics of Biblical Narrative* (Louisville, Westminster John Knox 1993), 20.

20. Greg J. Riley, "Devil," in *Dictionary of Demons and Deities in the Bible*, edited by K. van der Toorn, B. Becking, P. van W. van der Horst, rev. ed. (Leiden: Brill, 1999), 247.

21. For a folklorist's analysis of the "deliverance" (i.e., exorcism) ministries in American Pentecostal groups, see Bill Ellis, *Raising the Devil: Satanism, New Religions, and the Media* (Lexington, Ky.: University Press of Kentucky, 2000).

22. McKenzie, "Matthew," 92 (NT). The Greek play on words (*Petros:* "Peter" and *petra:* "rock") are obvious. Forsyth notes the paradox of Jesus, in one breath, proclaiming Peter as the rock upon which the church will be built and then, in the next, calling Peter "Satan." "Indeed, the ambivalence of the idea of a church itself—its dependence on heresy or opposition—was to be one of the principal reasons for Satan's continued power in the Christian tradition" (*The Old Enemy*, 288).

23. Forsyth, *The Old Enemy*, 288.

24. Following the Parable of the Sower, Matthew's Jesus launches into the Parable of the Weeds (Mt 13:36–43) in which the weeds (i.e., Jesus' enemies) are said to be the children of the "evil one," the Devil (cf. John 8:44–45; Rev 2:9; 3:9). See Pagels, *The Origin of Satan*, 83.

25. Forsyth, *The Old Enemy*, 316.

26. Pagels, *The Origin of Satan*, 98.

27. For an analysis of John's repeated use of the term "the Jews," see Pagels, *The Origin of Satan*, 103–05.

28. Pagels, *The Origin of Satan*, 103–05.

29. Perkins, *Reading the New Testament*, 248–49.

30. Pagels, *The Origin of Satan*, 101.

31. Pagels, *The Origin of Satan*, 101.

32. Pagels, *The Origin of Satan*, 101–2; See also Robert Kysar, *John*, Augsburg Commentary on the New Testament (Minneapolis: Augsburg, 1986), 93–100.

33. Forsyth, *The Old Enemy*, 315–16. Unlike the Synoptic versions, John omits the monetary aspect of Judas's betrayal, although Judas is acknowledged as the one who kept the "money purse" for the group (Jn 13:29).

34.   Forsyth, *The Old Enemy*, 314.

35.   There is another interpretive possibility, one exploited by Bob Dylan in the song "With God on Our Side" (from his 1964 recording "The Times They Are A-Changin'"), namely, that Judas unwittingly played a necessary role in the Passion drama, that he needed to betray Jesus as part of a divine plan that would bring Jesus to the cross, and ultimately humanity to redemption. Dylan sings, "In a many dark hour I've been thinkin' about this/That Jesus Christ was betrayed by a kiss./ But I can't think for you. You'll have to decide/Whether Judas Iscariot had God on his side."

36.   Pagels, *The Origin of Satan*, 111.

37.   Ehrman, *Brief Introduction to the New Testament*, 197.

38.   Forsyth, *The Old Enemy*, 260.

39.   Marion Soards outlines many of the current scholarly positions on this subject in *The Apostle Paul: An Introduction to His Writings and Teaching* (New York: Paulist Press, 1987), 100–1.

40.   Joseph A. Fitzmeyer, "The Letter to the Romans," *Jerome Biblical Commentary*, 330 (NT).

41.   Fitzmeyer, "Romans," 330–31 (NT).

42.   Nagel, *Deliver Us from Evil*, 30.

43.   Charles B. Puskas dates 1 and 2 Corinthians to the spring and fall of 57 C.E., respectively. *The Letters of Paul: An Introduction* (Collegeville, Minn.: Liturgical Press, 1979), 47.

44.   Mary Ann Getty, "1 Corinthians," *The Collegeville Bible Commentary* (Collegeville, Minn.: Liturgical Press, 1988), 1100–1104.

45.   Puskas, *The Letters of Paul*, 47–50.

46.   Nagel, *Deliver Us from Evil*, 66–67.

47.   According to Leander Keck, the action of the man in 1 Corinthians 5 is "contrary to both Jewish and Roman law." Keck, *Paul and His Letters* (Philadelphia: Fortress, 1988), 106.

48.   According to Harris, the outcast nonetheless remains a candidate for salvation upon Christ's victorious return in glory. *Understanding the Bible*, 6th ed. (Boston: McGraw-Hill, 2003), 256.

49.   Forsyth, *The Old Enemy*, 260.

50.   Forsyth, *The Old Enemy*, 260.

51.   Forsyth, *The Old Enemy*, 267.

52.   Ehrman, *Brief Introduction to the New Testament*, 237–39.

53.   Getty, "2 Corinthians," 1138.

54.   Getty, "2 Corinthians," 1138.

55.   John J. O'Rourke, "The Second Letter to the Corinthians," *Jerome Biblical Commentary*, 289 (NT).

56.   Getty, "2 Corinthians," 1149.

57.   Getty, "2 Corinthians," 1149.

58.   O'Rourke, "Second Corinthians," 289.

59.   Soards, *The Apostle Paul*, 49.

60.   Forsyth, *The Old Enemy*, 260.

61.   The contrast between the depictions of these "two riders," both Christ, although in radically different modes, was pointed out to us by church historian Mark Burrows.

62.   Nagel, *Deliver Us from Evil*, 78.

63.   Nagel, *Deliver Us from Evil*, 78.

64.   Nagel, *Deliver Us from Evil*, 78.

65. Pheme Perkins, "Revelation," *Collegeville Bible Commentary*, 1275.

66. Nagel, *Deliver Us from Evil*, 78.

67. Forsyth, *The Old Enemy*, 304.

68. Domitian preferred to be addressed as "Lord and God," which caused problems for Christians. Although it is unclear whether this issue alone was the cause of the persecution of Christians that lies in the background of Revelation, it very likely played a part. See Nagel, *Deliver Us from Evil*, 76; Perkins, "Revelation," 1268–69.

69. Perkins, "Revelation," 1267–68.

70. Nagel, *Deliver Us from Evil*, 76–77.

71. Perkins, *Reading the New Testament*, 311–16. The "angels" of these churches are the direct recipients of the visions although it is clear that the visions are intended for all persecuted Christians. The role of the angels is consistent with the Second Temple Jewish understanding that God assigned angelic guardians to the various nations on earth. Perkins, "Revelation," 1272–73.

72. William Barclay, *The Revelation of John*, vol. 1 (Philadelphia: Westminster, 1976), 75.

73. Barclay, *The Revelation of John*, vol. 1, 76.

74. Barclay, *The Revelation of John*, vol. 1, 80.

75. See Perkins, "Revelation," 1267. Forsyth contends that the "Christians" during the time of John of Patmos still thought of themselves as Jews. Taken a step further, these Jewish Christians thought of themselves as the only *real* Jews; all others were considered part of the worldly opposition, members of the "synagogue of Satan." Forsyth, *The Old Enemy*, 314.

76. Wilfrid J. Harrington, *Understanding the Apocalypse* (Washington, D.C.: Corpus Books, 1969), 88.

77. Harrington, *Understanding the Apocalypse*, 88.

78. Harrington, *Understanding the Apocalypse*, 98.

79. Harrington, *Understanding the Apocalypse*, 97; Barclay, *The Revelation of John*, vol. 1, 113.

80. Perkins, "Revelation," 1285. For Harrington, "the woman symbolizes the people of God which brings forth the messianic age." *Understanding the Apocalypse*, 166.

81. Jean-Louis D'Aragon, "The Apocalypse," *Jerome Biblical Commentary*, 482 (NT). The color red is associated with death and destruction. Recall the Egyptian connection between the evil god, Set, and the color red. In Revelation 6:4, the red horse symbolizes Satan, the destroyer of peace and initiator of war.

82. D'Aragon, "The Apocalypse," 482.

83. Harrington, *Understanding the Apocalypse*, 166.

84. Harrington, *Understanding the Apocalypse*, 166.

85. Cf. Ps 89:10; Isa 51:9; 1En 60:7–8; 2 Bar 29:4.

86. Nagel, *Deliver Us from Evil*, 80.

87. Harrington, *Understanding the Apocalypse*, 168; Nagel, *Deliver Us From Evil*, 81.

88. Harrington, *Understanding the Apocalypse*, 173.

89. Harrington, *Understanding the Apocalypse*, 173.

90. Nagel, *Deliver Us from Evil*, 83. One of the heads is described as having a mortal wound that healed. According to Nagel, this may refer to rumors circulating at this time about the suicide death of Nero. According to the rumor, Nero would be resurrected and bring about the downfall of the Roman Empire.

91. D'Aragon, "The Apocalypse," 483. Daniel's beast (Dan 7:7) had ten horns that represented Greek emperors, one of whom was the despised Antiochus Epiphanes IV.

92. Nagel, *Deliver Us from Evil*, 83.

93. Harris, *Understanding the New Testament*, 332; Harrington, *Understanding the Apocalypse*, 179.
94. Harrington, *Understanding the Apocalypse*, 182.
95. Nagel, *Deliver Us from Evil*, 84.
96. According to Harrington, the numerical value of the Greek, *Neron Kaisar*, transliterated into Hebrew script (*nrwn qsr*) was 666 (*Understanding the Apocalypse*, 183).
97. The Essenes believed in a judgment of fire for the wicked. Robert H. Mounce, *The Book of Revelation* (Grand Rapids, Mich.: Eerdmans, 1977), 275.
98. Mounce, *The Book of Revelation*, 277–78.
99. Harrington, *Understanding the Apocalypse*, 229–30.
100. Harrington, *Understanding the Apocalypse*, 229–30.
101. Nagel, *Deliver Us from Evil*, 92.
102. Nagel, *Deliver Us from Evil*, 95.

Chapter 7

1. Alice K. Turner, *The History of Hell* (New York: Harcourt Brace & Company, 1993), 83.
2. See chapter 4.
3. This ring is reminiscent of the Greek Elysian Fields, the land of dead heroes. See chapter 4.
4. Turner, *The History of Hell*, 136–37.
5. Turner, *The History of Hell*, 140–141.
6. Paul Carus, *The History of the Devil and the Idea of Evil* (New York: Gramercy Books, 1996), 352–53.
7. Turner, *The History of Hell*, 180–81.

Chapter 8

1. Linnda R. Caporael, "Ergotism: The Satan Loosed in Salem?" *Science* 192 (2 April 1976).
2. Caporael, "Ergotism: The Satan Loosed in Salem?"
3. For "Booger" and a host of miscellaneous "swamp things," see John A. Keel, *The Complete Guide to Mysterious Beings* (New York: TOR, 2002), 101.
4. Neil Forsyth, *The Old Enemy: Satan and the Combat Myth* (Princeton, N.J.: Princeton University Press, 1987).
5. For an English translation of Enuma Elish, see Stephanie Dalley, *Myths from Mesopotamia* (Oxford: Oxford University Press, 1989).
6. For Habayu, see P. Xella, "Haby," in *Dictionary of Deities and Demons in the Bible*, edited by K. van der Toorn, B. Becking, P. W. van der Horst, rev. ed. (Leiden: Brill, 1999), 377.
7. For the influence of ideas about Ahriman on the emergence of the Jewish Satan, see Jeffrey Burton Russell, *The Devil: Perceptions of Evil from Antiquity to Primitive Christianity* (Ithaca, N.Y.: Cornell University Press, 1977), 104–21.
8. Russell, *The Prince of Darkness: Radical Evil and the Power of Good in History* (Ithaca, N.Y.: Cornell University Press, 1988), 19.
9. James H. Charlesworth, "Introduction for the General Reader," *The Old Testament Pseudepigrapha* 1, ed. J. H. Charlesworth (New York: Doubleday, 1983), xxx–xxxi.
10. Robert Frost, *A Masque of Reason* (New York: Holt, 1945), 5.

11. As the biblical scholar Choon-Leong Seow points out, the meaning of the Hebrew word *hebel* in Ecclesiastes, commonly rendered in English translations as "vanity," is "vapor" or "shadow," that which is ungraspable. Seow, *Ecclesiastes*, Anchor Bible 18C, (New York: Doubleday, 1997), 101–2.

12. Stephen L. Cook writes about how apocalyptic seers "seize upon the ancient myths of [a] group and integrate them into a linear view of world history." Cook, *Prophecy and Apocalypticism: The Postexilic Social Setting* (Minneapolis: Fortress Press, 1995) 49.

13. Russell has devoted five volumes to the story of Satan: *The Devil: Perceptions of Evil from Antiquity to Primitive Christianity* (1977); *Satan: The Early Christian Tradition* (Ithaca, N.Y.: Cornell University Press, 1981); *Lucifer: The Devil in the Middle Ages* (Ithaca, N.Y.: Cornell University Press, 1984); *Mephistopheles: The Devil in the Modern World* (Ithaca, N.Y.: Cornell University Press, 1986); and a condensed and revised version of the entire sequence, *The Prince of Darkness: Rational Evil and the Power of Good in History* (1988).

14. Readers curious about Satan's history are encouraged to see the works of Russell cited in note 13.

15. See Russell, *Lucifer*, 293–301.

16. For the Romantic Satan, see Russell, *Mephistopheles*, 168–213. "Mick Jagger's 'man of wealth and taste'" is a reference to the song "Sympathy for the Devil" by the Rolling Stones (from the 1968 recording, *Beggars Banquet*).

17. Fredric Jameson, *The Political Unconscious: Narrative as a Socially Symbolic Act* (Ithaca, N.Y.: Cornell University Press, 1981), 102.

18. Elaine Pagels, *The Origin of Satan* (New York: Vintage Books, 1996).

19. Paul Tillich, *The Courage to Be* (New Haven, Conn.: Yale University Press, 1952), 182.

20. Myra Nagel, *Deliver Us from Evil: What the Bible Says about Satan* (Cleveland: United Church Press, 1999), 36–37.

21. Nagel, *Deliver Us from Evil*, 36–37.

22. Nagel, *Deliver Us from Evil*, 36–37.

resources

Achtemeir, Paul J. *Harper Collins Bible Dictionary*. San Francisco: Harper San Francisco, 1996.

_____ . "Hell." *Harper's Bible Dictionary*. San Francisco: Harper & Row, 1985. p. 382.

Akenson, Donald Harman. *Surpassing Wonder: The Invention of the Bible and the Talmuds*. Chicago: University of Chicago Press, 1998.

Albright, William Foxwell. *Archaeology and the Religion of Israel*. 5th ed. Garden City, N.Y.: Doubleday, 1968.

_____ . *Yahweh and the Gods of Canaan: An Historical Analysis of Two Contrasting Faiths*. Winona Lake, Ind.: Eisenbrauns, 1990.

Alighieri, Dante. *The Divine Comedy: Inferno*. Translated by Mark Musa. New York: Penguin Books, 2002.

Alter, Robert. *The Art of Biblical Narrative*. New York: Basic Books, 1981.

Anderson, Bernhard W., and Katheryn Pfisterer Darr. *Understanding the Old Testament*. 4th ed. Englewood Cliffs, N.J.: Prentice-Hall, 1998.

Armstrong, Karen. *A History of God*. New York: Knopf, 1993.

Bamberger, Bernard J. *Fallen Angels*. Philadelphia: Jewish Publication Society of America, 1952.

Barclay, William. *The Revelation of John*. Vol. 1. Philadelphia: Westminster, 1976.

Beasley-Murray, G. R. "The Interpretation of Daniel 7." *Catholic Bible Quarterly* 45 (1983): 44–58.

Bergant, Dianne. *Job, Ecclesiastes*. Old Testament Message 18. Wilmington, Del.: Michael Glazier, 1982.

Berlin, Adele, and Marc Zvi Brettler, eds. *The Jewish Study Bible*. New York: Oxford University Press, 2004.

Blatty, Peter. *The Exorcist*. San Francisco: Harper Collins, 1971.

Blumenthal, David R. *Facing the Abusing God*. Louisville, Ky.: Westminster John Knox, 1993.

Boadt, Lawrence. *Reading the Old Testament: An Introduction*. New York: Paulist Press, 1984.

Boling, Robert G., and G. Ernest Wright. *Joshua*. Anchor Bible 6. New York: Doubleday, 1982.

Breytenbach, C., and P. L. Day. "Satan." *Dictionary of Deities and Demons in the Bible*. See van der Toorn, et al. pp. 726–32.

Bright, John. *The Kingdom of God*. Nashville, Tenn.: Abingdon Press, 1953.

Broderick, Robert C., ed. *The Catholic Encyclopedia*. Nashville, Tenn.: Thomas Nelson, 1987.

Brown, Raymond E. *The Gospel According to John*. Anchor Bible 29A. Garden City, N.Y.: Doubleday, 1970.

Brown, Raymond E., Joseph Fitzmyer, and Roland E. Murphy, eds. *The Jerome Biblical Commentary*. Englewood Cliffs, N.J.: Prentice-Hall, 1968.

Brueggemann, Walter. *Theology of the Old Testament: Testimony, Dispute, Advocacy.* Minneapolis: Fortress Press, 1997.

Bulfinch, Thomas with Richard P. Martin. *Bulfinch's Mythology.* New York: Harper Collins, 1991.

Bury, J. B., S. A. Cook, and F. E. Adcock, eds. *The Cambridge Ancient History: The Persian Empire.* Vol. 4. Cambridge: Cambridge University Press, 1964.

Campbell, Joseph with Bill Moyers. *The Power of Myth.* New York: Doubleday, 1988.

Carus, Paul. *The History of the Devil and the Idea of Evil.* New York: Gramercy Books, 1996.

Charles, R. H. *The Book of Jubilees or Little Genesis.* New York: Macmillan, 1917.

Charlesworth, James H., ed. *The Old Testament Pseudepigrapha.* 2 vols. New York: Doubleday, 1983 and 1985.

Coogan, Michael David, ed. *The New Oxford Annotated Bible with the Apocryphal/Deuterocanonical Books.* 3rd ed. New York: Oxford University Press, 2001.

Cook, Stephen L. *Prophecy and Apocalypticism: The Postexilic Social Setting.* Minneapolis: Fortress Press, 1995.

Crim, Keith. *The Perennial Dictionary of World Religions.* San Francisco: Harper & Row, 1989.

Cross, Frank Moore. *Canaanite Myth and Hebrew Epic: Essays in the History of the Religion of Israel.* Cambridge, Mass.: Harvard University Press, 1973.

D'Aragon, Jean-Louis. "The Apocalypse." *The Jerome Biblical Commentary.* See Brown, et al. pp. 467–93 (NT).

Dalley, Stephanie. *Myths from Mesopotamia.* Oxford: Oxford University Press, 1989.

Davies, Philip. *Scribes and Schools: The Canonization of the Hebrew Scriptures.* Louisville, Ky.: Westminster John Knox, 1998.

Day, Peggy L. *An Adversary in Heaven: "Satan" in the Hebrew Bible.* Atlanta: Scholars Press, 1988.

Dresden, Michael J. *Mythology of Ancient Iran.* Mythologies of the Ancient World, Samuel N. Kramer, ed. New York: Doubleday Anchor, 1961.

Driver, G. R. *Canaanite Myths and Legends.* Edinburgh: T & T Clark, 1956.

Eisenman, R., and M. Wise. *The Dead Sea Scrolls Uncovered.* New York: Barnes & Noble, 1992.

Finkelstein, Israel, and Neil Asher Silberman. *The Bible Unearthed: Archaeology's New Vision of Ancient Israel and the Origin of Its Sacred Texts.* New York: Simon & Schuster, 2002.

Fitzmeyer, Joseph A. "The Letter to the Romans." *The Jerome Biblical Commentary.* See Brown, et al. pp. 291–331 (NT).

Forsyth, Neil. *The Old Enemy: Satan and the Combat Myth.* Princeton, N.J.: Princeton University Press, 1987.

Fossum, J. E. "Glory." *Dictionary of Deities and Demons in the Bible.* See van der Toorn, et al. pp. 348–52.

Freedman, David Noel, ed. *Anchor Bible Dictionary.* 6 vols. New York: Doubleday, 1992.

Freiert, W. K. "Orpheus: A Fugue on the Polis." *Myth and the Polis.* Edited by D.C. Pozzi and J.M. Wickersham. Ithaca, N.Y.: Cornell University Press, 1991.

Frost, Robert. *A Masque of Reason.* New York: Henry Holt, 1945.

Garbini, Giovanni. *History and Ideology in Ancient Israel.* Translated by John Bowden. New York: Crossroad, 1988.

George, Andrew. *The Epic of Gilgamesh: A New Translation.* New York: Barnes & Noble, 1999.

Getty, Mary Ann. "1 Corinthians." *Collegeville Bible Commentary.* See Karris. pp. 1100–33.

———. "2 Corinthians." *Collegeville Bible Commentary.* pp. 1134–50.

Gibson, J. C. *Language and Imagery in the Old Testament.* Peabody, Mass.: Hendrickson, 1998.

Ginzberg, Louis. *The Legends of the Jews.* Translated by Henrietta Szold. 7 vols. Baltimore: Johns Hopkins University Press, 1998.

Godolpin, F. R. B., ed. *Great Classical Myths.* New York: Random House, 1964.

Gunkel, Hermann. *Genesis.* Macon, Ga: Mercer University Press, 1997.

Habel, Norman. *The Book of Job: A Commentary.* London: Cambridge University Press, 1975.

Hanson, Paul D. *Isaiah 40–66.* Interpretation. Louisville, Ky.: John Knox, 1989.

Harrington, Wilfrid J. *Understanding the Apocalypse.* Washington, D. C.: Corpus Books, 1969.

Harris, Stephen L. *The New Testament: A Student's Introduction.* 2nd ed. Mountain View, Calif.: Mayfield, 1995.

_____ . *Understanding the Bible.* 6th ed. Boston: McGraw-Hill, 2003.

Hartley, John E. *The Book of Job.* Grand Rapids, Mich.: Eerdmans, 1988.

Havener, Ivan. "1 Thessalonians." *Collegeville Bible Commentary.* See Karris. pp. 1151–1159.

Heider, G. C. "Molech." *Dictionary of Deities and Demons in the Bible.* See van der Toorn, et al. pp. 581–85.

Hodell, Jerome. "Luke." *Collegeville Bible Commentary.* See Karris. pp. 936–80.

Hopfe, Lewis M., and Mark R. Woodward. *Religions of the World.* 9th ed. Upper Saddle River, N.J.: Prentice Hall, 2005.

Huesman, John E. "Exodus." *The Jerome Biblical Commentary.* See Brown, et al. pp. 47–66 (OT).

Huffmon, Herbert. "Name." *Dictionary of Deities and Demons in the Bible.* See van der Toorn, et al. pp. 610–12; J. E.

Jameson, Fredric. *The Political Unconscious: Narrative as a Socially Symbolic Act.* Ithaca, N.Y.: Cornell University Press, 1981.

Janzen, Gerald J. *Job.* Interpretation. Atlanta, Ga.: John Knox, 1985.

Janowski, B. "Azazel." *Dictionary of Deities and Demons in the Bible.* See van der Toorn, et al. pp. 128–31.

Johnson, M. D. "Life of Adam and Eve." *Old Testament Pseudepigrapha* 2. See Charles Worth pp. 249–95.

Josephus, Flavius. *The Complete Works of Josephus.* Translated by W. Whiston. Grand Rapids, Mich.: Kregel, 1981.

Karris, Robert J., ed. *The Collegeville Bible Commentary.* Collegeville, Minn: Liturgical Press, 1988.

Keck, Leander E. *Paul and His Letters.* Philadelphia: Fortress, 1988.

Keller, Werner. *The Bible as History.* New York: William Morrow and Co., 1981.

Klüger, Rivkah Schärf. *Satan in the Old Testament.* Evanston, Ill.: Northwestern University Press, 1967.

Knight, George A. F. *Deutero-Isaiah: A Theological Commentary on Isaiah 40–55.* New York: Abingdon Press, 1965.

Kreeft, Peter. *Three Philosophies of Life: Ecclesiastes, Life as Vanity Job, Life as Suffering Song of Songs, Life as Love.* San Francisco: Ignatius Press, 1989.

Kugel, James L. *The Bible as It Was.* Cambridge, Mass.: Belknap Press, 1997.

Kurz, William S. *Reading Luke-Acts: Dynamics of Biblical Narrative.* Louisville, Ky.: Westminster John Knox, 1993.

Kushner, Harold S. *When Bad Things Happen to Good People.* New York: Avon Books, 1981.

Kysar, Robert. *John.* Augsburg Commentary on the New Testament. Minneapolis: Augsburg, 1986.

Lattimore, Richard. *Hesiod: The Works and Days, Theogony, the Shield of Herakles.* Ann Arbor, Mich.: University of Michigan Press, 1965.

LaVey, Anton Szandor. *The Satanic Bible.* New York: Avon Books, 1986.

Leeming, David Adams. *Mythology: The Voyage of the Hero.* 3rd ed. Oxford: Oxford University Press, 1998.

Lemche, Niels Peter. *Prelude to Israel's Past: Background and Beginnings of Israelite History and Identity.* Peabody, Mass.: Hendrickson, 1998.

Lesko, Leonard H. "Death and the Afterlife in Ancient Egyptian Thought." *Civilizations of the Ancient Near East.* Edited by Jack Sasson. 2 vols. Peabody, Mass.: Hendrickson, 2000. pp. 1763–74.

Levenson, Jon D. *Creation and the Persistence of Evil: The Jewish Drama of Divine Omnipotence.* San Francisco: Harper & Row, 1988.

———. *The Death and Resurrection of the Beloved Son: The Transformation of Child Sacrifice in Judaism and Christianity.* New Haven, Conn.: Yale University Press, 1993.

Littleton, C. Scott, ed. *Mythology: The Illustrated Anthology of World Myth & Storytelling.* London: Duncan Baird, 2002.

MacQueen, James G. *Babylon.* New York: Frederick A. Praeger, 1964.

Mally, Edward J. "The Gospel According to Mark." *The Jerome Biblical Commentary.* See Brown, et al. pp. 21–61 (NT).

Mason, Rex. *The Books of Haggai, Zechariah, and Malachi.* Cambridge Bible Commentary. Cambridge: Cambridge University Press, 1977.

McCann, J. Clinton, Jr., "The Book of Psalms." *The New Interpreter's Bible.* Vol. 4. Nashville, Tenn.: Abingdon, 1996. pp. 639–1280.

McKenzie, John. "The Gospel According to Matthew." *The Jerome Biblical Commentary.* See Brown, et al. pp. 62–114 (NT).

Meier, S. A. "Destroyer." *Dictionary of Deities and Demons in the Bible.* See van der Toorn, et al. pp. 240–44.

Miles, Jack. *God: A Biography.* New York: Vintage, 1995.

Milgrom, Jacob. *Numbers.* JPS Torah Commentary. Philadelphia: Jewish Publication Society, 1990.

Milton, John. *Paradise Lost.* Edited by Stephen Orgel and Jonathan Goldberg. New York: Oxford University Press, 2004.

Mitchell, Stephen. *The Book of Job.* New York: Harper Perennial, 1987.

Mobley, Gregory. "The Wild Man in the Bible and the Ancient Near East." *Journal of Biblical Literature* 116 (1997): 217–33.

Moriarty, Frederick L. "Numbers." *The Jerome Biblical Commentary.* See Brown, et al. pp. 86–100 (OT).

Mounce, Robert H. *The Book of Revelation.* Grand Rapids, Mich.: Eerdmans, 1977.

Nagel, Myra B. *Deliver Us from Evil: What the Bible Says About Satan.* Cleveland: United Church Press, 1999.

Newsom, Carol A. "The Book of Job." *The New Interpreter's Bible.* Vol. 4. Nashville, Tenn.: Abingdon, 1996. pp. 317–637.

———. "Angels." *Anchor Bible Dictionary* 1:248–53.

Newsom, Carol A., and Sharon H. Ringe, eds. *The Women's Bible Commentary.* Louisville, Ky.: Westminster John Knox, 1992.

Olmo Lete, G. del. "Deber." *Dictionary of Deities and Demons in the Bible.* See van der Toorn, et al. pp. 31–32.

O'Rourke, John J. "The Second Letter to the Corinthians." *The Jerome Biblical Commentary.* See Brown, et al. pp. 276–290.

Pagels, Elaine. *The Origin of Satan.* New York: Vintage Books, 1996.

Pardee, Dennis. *Ritual and Cult at Ugarit.* Atlanta: Scholars Press, 2002.

Parker, Simon. *Ugaritic Narrative Poetry.* Atlanta: Scholars Press, 1997.

Perkins, Pheme. *Reading the New Testament: An Introduction.* 2nd ed. New York: Paulist Press, 1988.

_____ . "Revelation." *Collegeville Bible Commentary.* See Karris. pp. 1265–1300.

Pregeant, Russell. *Engaging the New Testament: An Interdisciplinary Introduction.* Minneapolis: Fortress, 1995.

Pritchard, James B. *Ancient Near Eastern Texts Relating to the Old Testament.* 3rd ed. Princeton, N.J.: Princeton University Press, 1969.

Propp, Vladimir. *Morphology of the Folktale.* Austin: University of Texas Press, 1968.

Puskas, Charles B Jr., *The Letters of Paul: An Introduction.* Collegeville, Minn.: Liturgical Press, 1979.

Rad, Gerhard von. *The Message of the Prophets.* San Francisco: HarperCollins, 1967.

Russell, Jeffrey Burton. *The Devil: Perceptions of Evil from Antiquity to Primitive Christianity.* Ithaca, N.Y.: Cornell University Press, 1977.

_____ . *Satan: The Early Christian Tradition.* Ithaca, N.Y.: Cornell University Press, 1981.

_____ . *Lucifer: The Devil in the Middle Ages.* Ithaca, N.Y.: Cornell University Press, 1984.

_____ . *Mephistopheles: The Devil in the Modern World.* Ithaca, N.Y.: Cornell University Press, 1986.

_____ . *The Prince of Darkness: Radical Evil and the Power of Good in History.* Ithaca, N.Y. York: Cornell University Press, 1988.

Safire, William. *The First Dissident: The Book of Job in Today's Politics.* New York: Random House, 1992.

Schloen, David. *The House of the Father as Fact and Symbol: Patrimonialism in Ugarit and the Ancient Near East.* Winona Lake, Ind.: Eisenbrauns, 2001.

Schneemelcher, Wilhelm. *New Testament Apocrypha.* 2 vols. Louisville, Ky.: Westminster John Knox, 1991.

Schulz, Regine, and Matthias Seidel, eds. *Egypt: The World of the Pharaohs.* Köln: Könemann, 2002.

Segal, Alan F. *Life after Death: A History of the Afterlife in Western Religion.* New York: Doubleday, 2004.

Seow, Choon-Leong. *Ecclesiastes.* Anchor Bible 18C. New York: Doubleday, 1997.

_____ . "Face." *Dictionary of Deities and Demons in the Bible.* See van der Toorn, et al. pp. 322–25.

Smelik, Klaas A. D. *Writings from Ancient Israel: A Handbook of Historical and Religious Documents.* Louisville, Ky.: Westminster John Knox, 1991.

Smith, Mark. *The Early History of God: Yahweh and the Other Deities in Ancient Israel.* 2nd ed. Grand Rapids, Mich.: Eerdmans, 2002.

Soards, Marion L. *The Apostle Paul: An Introduction to His Writings and Teaching.* New York: Paulist Press, 1987.

Sperling, S. D. "Belial." *Dictionary of Deities and Demons in the Bible.* See van der Toorn, et al. pp. 169–70.

Stanley, D. M. "Balaam's Ass, or a Problem in New Testament Hermeneutics." *Catholic Bible Quarterly* 20 (1958): 50–56.

Stuhlmueller, Carroll. "Deutero-Isaiah." *The Jerome Biblical Commentary.* See Brown, et al. pp. 366–86 (OT).

_____ . "The Gospel According to Luke." *The Jerome Biblical Commentary.* See Brown, et al. pp.115–64 (NT).

_____ . *"Rebuilding with Hope: A Commentary on the Books of Haggai and Zechariah.* International Theological Commentary. Grand Rapids, Mich.: Eerdmans, 1988.

Tigay, Jeffrey. *You Shall Have No Other Gods: Israelite Religion in the Light of Hebrew Inscriptions.* Atlanta: Scholars Press, 1986.

Tillich, Paul. *The Courage to Be.* New Haven, Conn.: Yale University Press, 1952.

van der Toorn, Karel, Bob Becking, and Peter W. van der Horst, eds. *Dictionary of Deities and Demons in the Bible.* Rev. ed. Leiden: Brill, 1999.

Vanderkam, James C. *The Dead Sea Scrolls Today.* Grand Rapids, Mich.: Eerdmans, 1994.

Walls, Neal H. *The Goddess Anat in Ugaritic Myth.* Atlanta: Scholars Press, 1992.

Watson, Duane. "Gehenna." *Anchor Bible Dictionary* 2. Pp 926–28.

Wellhausen, Julius. *Prolegomena to the History of Ancient Israel.* Gloucester, Mass.: Peter Smith, 1973.

Westermann, Claus. *Isaiah 40–66: A Commentary.* Philadelphia: Westminster Press, 1969.

———. *Prophetic Oracles of Salvation in the Old Testament.* Louisville, Ky.: Westminster John Knox Press, 1999.

Whybray, R. N. *Isaiah 40–66.* New Century Bible Commentary. Grand Rapids, Mich.: Eerdmans, 1975.

Wilson, A. N. *Paul: The Mind of the Apostle.* New York: W. W. Norton & Co., 1997.

Woods, William. *The History of the Devil.* New York: G. P. Putnam's Sons, 1973.

Wright, N. T. *Romans and the Theology of Paul.* Minneapolis: Fortress Press, 1995.

Wyatt, Nicholas. "Asherah." *Dictionaries of Deities and Demons in the Bible.* See van der Toorn, et al. pp. 99–105.

Von Wyrick, Stephen. "Gehenna." *Eerdmans Dictionary of the Bible.* Grand Rapids, Mich.: Eerdmans, 2000. p. 489.

Xella, P. "Haby." *Dictionary of Deities and Demons in the Bible,* see van der Toorn, et al. p. 377.

Electronic Resources

Adams, Joe. "Temple of Set." *The Religious Movements Homepage Project.* December 8, 2000. http://religiousmovements.lib.virginia.edu/nrms/satanism/tempset.html.

Avesta.org. "The Gathas (Hymns) of Zarathushtra." 15 September 2003. <>.

Bauldauf, Emily. "Studies Show Scary Movies Drive Audience to Euphoria." The Exponent Online. 25 October 2001. 26 April 2003. <>.

Jastrow, Morris, et al. "Avenger of Blood." Jewish Encyclopedia.com. 22 August 2003. <http://jewishencyclopedia.com/view_page.jsp?artid=2162&letter=A&pid=1>

Matthews, Jodi. "Devil Alive and well in U.S. Polls." Daily Ethics.com. 23 April 2003. <>.

Robinson, Jennifer. "The Devil and the Demographic Details." The Gallup Organization. 25 February 2003. 27 July 2004. <http://www.gallup.com/content/login.aspx?ci=7858>.

Smith, Anthony E. "Angra Mainyu." Encyclopedia Mythica. 20 August 2003. <>.

index

recommended reading

Alighieri, Dante. *The Divine Comedy: Inferno.* Translated by Mark Musa. New York: Penguin Books, 2002.

Bamberger, Bernard J. *Fallen Angels.* Philadelphia: Jewish Publication Society of America, 1952.

Carus, Paul. *The History of the Devil and the Idea of Evil.* New York: Gramercy Books, 1996.

Day, Peggy L. *An Adversary in Heaven: "Satan" in the Hebrew Bible.* Atlanta: Scholars Press, 1988.

Forsyth, Neil. *The Old Enemy: Satan and the Combat Myth.* Princeton, N.J.: Princeton University Press, 1987.

Klüger, Rivkah Schärf. *Satan in the Old Testament.* Evanston, Ill.: Northwestern University Press, 1967.

Levenson, Jon D. *Creation and the Persistence of Evil: The Jewish Drama of Divine Omnipotence.* San Francisco: Harper & Row, 1988.

Milton, John. *Paradise Lost.* Edited by Stephen Orgel and Jonathan Goldberg. New York: Oxford University Press, 2004.

Nagel, Myra B. *Deliver Us from Evil: What the Bible Says about Satan.* Cleveland: United Church Press, 1999.

Pagels, Elaine. *The Origin of Satan.* New York: Vintage Books, 1996.

Russell, Jeffrey Burton. *The Devil: Perceptions of Evil from Antiquity to Primitive Christianity.* Ithaca, N.Y.: Cornell University Press, 1977.

————. *Satan: The Early Christian Tradition.* Ithaca, N.Y.: Cornell University Press, 1981.

————. *Lucifer: The Devil in the Middle Ages.* Ithaca, N.Y.: Cornell University Press, 1984.

————. *Mephistopheles: The Devil in the Modern World.* Ithaca, N.Y.: Cornell University Press, 1986.

————. *The Prince of Darkness: Radical Evil and the Power of Good in History.* Ithaca, N.Y.: Cornell University Press, 1988.

Woods, William. *The History of the Devil.* New York: G. P. Putnam's Sons, 1973.